"An excellent volume. Lucid, clear and accessible, it makes semiotic theory relevant to a new audience." – Patricia Ybarra, *Associate Professor of Theatre Arts and Performance Studies, Brown University, USA*

In this wide-ranging study, Ric Knowles demonstrates how the examination and practice of theatre is enhanced by an expanded semiotic approach. Moving from the history and theory of performance analysis to its practical application and paying particular attention to cross-cultural applications, he examines not what a particular piece of theatre means, but how meaning is produced in the process of creating, viewing and analysing theatre.

How Theatre Means presents contemporary case studies and explores intersections between a wide range of theories and methods. Clear and accessible, this book brings a key analytical methodology to life for students, practitioners and scholars.

Ric Knowles is Professor of Theatre Studies at the University of Guelph, Canada, and Editor of *Theatre Journal*. He is the award-winning author and editor of numerous books, including *Theatre & Interculturalism* and *Reading the Material Theatre*.

How Theatre Means

Ric Knowles

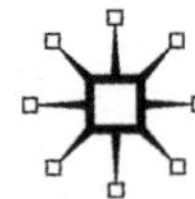

First published 2014 by
PALGRAVE MACMILLAN

Palgrave Macmillan in the UK is an imprint of Macmillan Publishers Limited, registered in England, company number 785998, of Houndmills, Basingstoke, Hampshire RG21 6XS.

Palgrave Macmillan in the US is a division of St Martin's Press LLC, 175 Fifth Avenue, New York, NY 10010.

Palgrave Macmillan is the global academic imprint of the above companies and has companies and representatives throughout the world.

Palgrave® and Macmillan® are registered trademarks in the United States, the United Kingdom, Europe and other countries

ISBN: 978–0–230–23235–8 hardback
ISBN: 978–0–230–23236–5 paperback

This book is printed on paper suitable for recycling and made from fully managed and sustained forest sources. Logging, pulping and manufacturing processes are expected to conform to the environmental regulations of the country of origin.

A catalogue record for this book is available from the British Library.

A catalog record for this book is available from the Library of Congress.

Printed in China

To Christine

Contents

List of Figures

Acknowledgements

As always, it takes a village to raise a book. My own particular village consists of more people than I can name, even in the volume's Works Cited. And I have doubtless been unconsciously influenced by many that I cannot name. But my most immediate intellectual and theatrical village includes members of the Toronto theatre community, the Chocolate Woman Collective, the Canadian Association for Theatre Research, the American Society for Theatre Research, and the Association for Theatre in Higher Education. More particular thanks are due to my colleague and friend Harry Lane for help with the Ibsen, to DD Kugler, Yvette Nolan, and Brian Quirt for saying it's ok to treat the dramaturgy of devised theatre as script analysis, and to Monique Mojica for her help in my efforts to explicate *Chocolate Woman Dreams the Milky Way* and her intellectual and artistic collaboration and friendship lo these many years.

There are several people to thank for help securing (and in some instances, in spite of their best efforts, failing to secure) images and permissions for their use. These include: Maiko Yamamoto of Theatre Replacement, Sylvie Isabelle of Ex Machina, Freddie Ashley of Actor's Express, Ali Molloy of Tarragon Theatre, Joe Stackell of Mabou Mines, Hawa Mire (for d'bi young anitafrika), Louise Jokisch (for Yves Jacques), Christina Kosmoglou of the Onassis Cultural Centre, Gia Nahmans of the Chocolate Woman Collective, Narelle Sissons, Jane Baldwin, Lucinda Morrison of the National Theatre of Great Britain, Yvette Nolan, Isaac Thomas, Falen Johnson, Murray Lynch, Ryan Hartigan, and especially, heroically, Jessica Riley.

The section of Chapter 3 on "Postcolonial and Intercultural Performance" follows closely, in its outline and some of its detail, parts of my 2010 Palgrave volume *Theatre & Interculturalism*, and is reprinted with permission. I am also grateful to Cambridge University Press for permission to reprint the chart on page 19 from my 2004 book, *Reading the Material Theatre*.

Research for *How Theatre Means* was generously supported by the Social Sciences and Humanities Research Council of Canada, and the final preparation of the manuscript was completed while I was a Research Fellow at the International Research Centre "Interweaving Performance Cultures" at the Freie Universität, Berlin. I am grateful to Erika Fischer-Lichte, Christel Weiler, and the staff and students at the Centre for their unfailing support.

Thanks also go to my dedicated research assistants David Lee, Nicholas Murphy, Karen Chung, and especially Jessica Riley, who also read and commented on parts of the manuscript, to the anonymous readers for Palgrave Macmillan, whose suggestions were extremely generative and helped to make this a better book, and to my editor at Palgrave Macmillan, Jenni Burnell, who along with Lucinda Knight, Felicity Noble, Vidhya Jayaprakash, copy editors and indexers were patient, enthusiastic, and supportive.

Chiefly, and always, thanks to my best reader and partner Christine Bold, to whom this book is dedicated in spite of her impatience with semiotics. She read and commented on the manuscript, discussed its contents, strategies, and structures with me at various stages, and saved me from much awkwardness and embarrassment.

Preface

This book is intended for students of theatre from undergraduates to senior scholars and theatre practitioners. It is intended at once to review and survey theories and practices of meaning production in the theatre, to extend those theories and practices into new realms and new ways of thinking, and to offer practical applications of the approach to script analysis, devising, and performance analysis. While trying to introduce complex concepts in language that is as clear and direct as is possible without being reductive, the book also makes a concerted effort to quote from, cite, and refer readers to original thinkers within their historical context rather than relying on secondary or decontextualized summations, and the Works Cited entries are intended to direct readers to the original authors of the ideas under discussion.

The two-part structure of the book is intended not to reify the binary and boundaries of theory and practice, but to encourage the practitioners and producers of theatre and of scholarship to see themselves reflected in one another, to recognize their interdependence, and increasingly to move to inhabit the same bodies. I also hope that both will recognize the value of theory for their own scholarly and theatrical practice, as well as the value of the fundamental dictum that theory must always be practiced, and practice theorized. I encourage readers, then, neither to head straight to Part II, skipping the first part as "too cold" (too theoretical), nor to stop at the end of Part I, dismissing the rest as "too hot" (too applied). I hope that readers will find the two parts into which this book is divided mutually supportive, their interrelationship "just right."

Introduction

Introduction: "How Theatre Means"

As I write this introduction, I am in rehearsal in Toronto for a new play, *Chocolate Woman Dreams the Milky Way*, a devised piece by Guna and Rappahannock playwright/performer Monique Mojica and the Chocolate Woman Collective. The creative team comes from Toronto, New York, Panama City, Guna Yala, Illinois, Montreal, and a few smaller centres in Ontario. There are several languages in the room – Spanish, English, and *Dule Gaya* (the language of the Indigenous people of Guna Yala, an autonomous territory on coastal Panama), plus snatches of French, Cree, and Anishinabe – and no one person speaks more than two of them. The theatrical and cultural codes at play are even more complex, as we try to weave together a new play based on dramaturgical principles derived from Guna women's textile arts and on theatrical languages based on Guna pictographs, all deeply informed by Guna cosmology and epistemology (ways of knowing). How do we create this play? How will audiences read it? The project of this book is to ask how such theatre, or any other theatre, produces its meanings.

How does theatre mean? What kind of question is that? In a Euro-American context it is common to be concerned with matters of interpretation and explanation (hermeneutics and exegesis). It is common, that is, to ask, interpret, and explicate *what* something means. But for students, researchers, and practitioners of theatre in the 21st century, a question that precedes these has to do with the *means* of meaning production, and this question is a semiotic one. Semiotics is concerned not with *what* a particular work means, but with *how* meaning is produced in the process of creating, viewing, analysing, and recording a piece of theatre. It is concerned with the *languages* of the theatre and the ways in which theatrical signification and communication occur. These languages are many, multiple, and intersecting. They include written and spoken languages, but they also include the complex languages of sound, music, gesture, design, and visual communication, all working in consort or in tension with one another, and they increasingly include the languages of a vast array of global "cultural texts," as Juri Lotman calls "any carrier of integral ('textual') meaning including ceremonies, works of art, as well as 'genres' such as 'prayer,' 'law,' 'novel,' etc." ("Theses" 6).

To mean is not the only thing that theatre does – it also entertains, and moves – but it is one of the most important things. This is so because one of theatre's primary functions is to serve as a live forum for the negotiation of values within and between cultures. It is a place where communication happens, and for students of the theatre from the elementary to the most advanced level, to understand how this communication and these negotiations occur – how meanings are encoded and decoded – is essential.

Encoding and decoding are neither simple nor stable. Meaning is not something inherent in a play script or theatrical production, nor is it something that is simply expressed by autonomous (independent) individuals – playwrights, directors, designers, and actors – and understood by autonomous audience members. The meaning of a particular work is neither constant nor universal. Like those who produce and interpret it, a work of theatre is subject to different historical and cultural forces. It is produced *by* cultures, and it is *productive* of culture. As meanings come into being, they change cultures, however subtly, and they change the ways in which future meanings can be produced and read.

Meaning, then, is best understood as a process, something that is provisionally produced by communities, technologies, and cultures engaged in various kinds of social, economic, technological, and pedagogical relationships with one another – including relationships between theatre artists, between audience members, and between the audience and the stage. One of the implications of this is that meaning is less a product for consumption than something that is always *in* production through processes of negotiation across many different codes. And those negotiations can often consist of struggles over who controls the codes.

Over history stories of conquest, colonialism, imperialism, and globalization are in large parts stories of struggle over meaning, as one cultural system seeks to dominate, control, and fix meaning, representing other meaning systems as imprecise, ignorant, primitive, weird, superstitious – or just "other." Indeed, representation – one thing (a word, an image) standing in for another – is at the heart of meaning production: we come to particular understandings of the world by representing it to ourselves and others through words, images, and stories in ways that are necessarily selective, imprecise, and partial, in both senses of the word (incomplete and biased). And we come to recognize things *through* their familiar representations: we learn from representations, including theatrical ones, both what exists (what is worthy of representation, of being noticed), and what to expect of it, what its essential features are.

But all representations are misrepresentations; if they weren't they would be the thing itself, and would be unnecessary. Representations are useful only insofar as they *do* substitute for the "real thing"; that is, they are useful only insofar as they are misrepresentations. That is the work they do. Even what are thought of as realistic or "life-like" representations select, direct focus, draw attention to, or emerge from a particular position or viewpoint, depending on their purpose: the representation of a tree in a forest industry manual will differ from one in an environmentalist text, a landscape painting, or a seed catalogue. A landscape as represented in a geological survey looks very different from the same landscape in a road map; neither coincides in any meaningful way with a photograph of the same landscape, and photographs of the scene from different points of view will be equally inscrutable to one another. Some representations are only recognizable as such by specialists – people who are well versed in a specific language – as when a chemical formula represents a substance that is more familiarly and more frequently represented by a simple word or image: "Table salt" is usually only represented as "NaCl" for chemists, for whom the formula is uniquely useful. But one would never know from the formulaic representation that table salt is white, granular, or helpful in enhancing the flavour of all sorts of food.

Similarly, all recognitions are misrecognitions: when we see a drawing and recognize it as, for example, a tree – (what does it mean to say of a piece of paper with marks on it, "that's a tree"?) – we are giving assent to the depiction in pencil on paper of some general elements of "treeness" standing in for the real thing. (The fact that the paper the sketch is drawn on is actually made from trees plays no part in what we are recognizing, unless of course we work in the pulp and paper industry and are making a special point.) Without such misrecognition communication could not happen.

Accepting or assenting to such misrecognitions always risks operating in the realms of cliché and stereotype, risks participating in a representational economy that values some aspects of what is represented over others, and risks universalizing certain traits. Indeed, we risk policing the "appropriate," "normal," or valued characteristics of elements of the world and of humanity each time we say of a representation, "yes, I recognize that." Even so simple a representation as a stick figure asserts that a "normal" human being has four limbs, as we "recognize" this as a key part of what makes humans human. But *do* all humans have four limbs? A stick figure with a skirt and long hair makes a similar case for what "normal" women look like and what differentiates them from a fall-back standard for humanity that is thereby constructed as male, short-haired, and skirtless.

But trees and humans are not represented in the same ways in all cultures. The representation of a tree in one culture may be totally unrecognizable as such to someone from another. This adds an extra and essential wrinkle to questions of representation, and therefore of meaning production. In cultures north of the tree line, trees may not be the normal objects of representation at all, any more than lions or platypuses are. For all intents and purposes they do not exist. And many cultures have no way of representing their own unique "ethnicity": they are, in their own languages, people, or humans, *tout court*, and when other peoples emerge into representation in those cultures, they do so as something else, something marked as "other." Euro-American attempts in postmodern and postdramatic theory and practice to move *away* from representational ways of making meaning, moreover, come at precisely the time when peoples from historically "othered" cultures are beginning to seize control of their own representation, in theatre and elsewhere, and this is a problem. At a moment in history in which encounters across cultures (and therefore across meaning systems) are increasingly quotidian and increasingly complex, particularly in the large urban centres where theatre most often takes place, it is increasingly urgent to come to a better understanding of how communication happens across difference, and how representation normalizes, "others," or "disappears" its objects.

It is the purpose of this book to provide a brief history and summary of the study of meaning production in the theatre, to map some ways in which the application of a semiotic approach can be useful in both the study and production of theatre and performance, and to consider the value of such an approach to the production and study of theatrical work across social, cultural, and historical difference. The three chapters that constitute Part I foreground theory. Chapter 1 introduces the basic concepts and histories of semiotics as the study of meaning production generally, focusing primarily on the contributions of Swiss linguist Ferdinand de Saussure (1857–1913) and American logician and structural linguist Charles Sanders Peirce (1839–1914). Key to Saussure's work is his account of the sign as the basic unit of communication, its relationship to the "sign system" within which it gets its meaning, and the relationship of sign systems to the social and cultural contexts that control that meaning. His work has major implications for the ways in which texts and cultural texts speak to one another, the ways in which different sign systems are established and controlled, and what interests they serve. Saussure's understanding of languages as sign systems became the foundation for a paradigm shift in fields ranging from anthropology through psychoanalysis and historiography to literary studies that became known as Structuralism. His understanding of sign systems as at once arbitrary and structured around relations rather than absolutes subsequently fuelled a movement in architecture, art, philosophy, and literary studies that came to be known as poststructuralism.

Sharing with Saussure a concern with the nature of signs and insights about their relationality, Charles Peirce is important here largely for his focus on the *interpretation*, rather than simply the production, of signs. He also significantly moved the discussion of meaning production beyond spoken language, the almost exclusive focus of his Swiss contemporary, towards a study of different types of signs in which the relationships between signifier and signified, sign and referent are not always or exclusively arbitrary, and in which the signifier is not always verbal. Peirce allows us to begin to focus on meaning production by audiences, specifically in theatre, and to begin to map out the relationships between the different types of sign that he identifies – particularly the icon, index, and symbol – and different types of theatrical representation in which those signs might most effectively be used.

The second chapter focuses exclusively on the semiotics of drama and theatre, providing a brief history from important early explorations by the Prague School semioticians in the 1930s, through 1980s "scientism," to the present state of the field. The focus here is on laying the groundwork for more applied analysis in later chapters by clarifying key concepts such as those of estrangement, foregrounding, and showing, the *mise en scène* and the performance text, key methods such as actantial analysis, and key issues such as performativity, the role of time, space, spectating, and the impact of theatrical and cultural context on meaning making. This chapter draws examples from specific plays and contemporary productions in order to demonstrate the ways in which conditions of production, conditions of reception, and "the performance itself" function in constantly shifting ways as the intersecting technologies of theatrical meaning making.

Chapter 3 concludes Part I by examining current and proposed future uses of a semiotic approach in intersection with other methods, including feminist, materialist, ethnographic, anthropological, phenomenological, intercultural, and postcolonial. A particular focus is on the benefits and drawbacks of the semiotic approach for the purposes of intercultural analysis, where performances operate at the intersection of cultures that can themselves be understood as sign systems, and most particularly in the performance of contemporary multicultural societies that are understood to be complex ecologies operating at the intersection of such systems.

Along with a resistance to a purely Structuralist or narrowly scientistic approach to a semiotics of performance comes a pragmatism that lives at once with postmodern uncertainties, multicultural complexities, and the sheer messiness of theatrical production, where on-set signs can reveal their materiality by crashing down like badly built flats, and the copulation of signs can issue in real-life pregnancies. This chapter grounds its generalizations in local theatrical practices, demonstrating, for example, the ways in which "things" get roped into serving as "signs" without surrendering – or indeed, while enhancing – the *frisson* of their phenomenological *thingness*, which precedes or exceeds meaning, representation, and interpretation, and which produces powerful emotional affects. And it probes the ways in which materialist and ethnographic semiotics – "sociosemiotics" – can usefully complicate traditional monocultural communication models and introduce ways of positioning the spectator/critic in relation to the theatrical work without assuming structuralist mastery or scientific objectivity.

Part II turns from (mainly) theory to practice, both theatrical and scholarly. Chapter 4 serves as a guide to the application of a semiotic approach to the analysis of scripts and, in the case of devised theatre, performance plans, programs, "scenarios," and resources. It considers the script or scenario, not as a blueprint for performance, an object of interpretation, or a reservoir of meaning to be realized on stage, but as an element of production that participates on relatively equal terms with the many other ingredients that combine in the creation of a performance. The chapter begins with a discussion of analytical method and reading practices, works through ways of identifying the primary modes of meaning-making employed in a given script or performance scenario, and considers what theatrical sign systems might resonate with them. Is character primary? Action? Narrative? Imagery? Rhythm? Gesture? What kinds of signs are employed, and what sign systems do they evoke? What cultural contexts do they emerge from or refer to, and what belief systems do they invoke? Are these systems working in mutually reinforcing or productively conflicting ways? In what ways can directors, dramaturges, actors, designers, theatre historians, scholars, and critics read the same scripts and differently practice what Michael Sidnell has recently called the "semiotic arts of theatre" (Sidnell)? The chapter incorporates two provisional case studies by drawing examples from a translation of Ibsen's classic, *A Doll House*, and from the new "intercultural" devised performance with which I began, *Chocolate Woman Dreams the Milky Way*.

While Chapter 4 begins with a script or scenario and ends with a performance or a scholarly analysis, the fifth chapter begins with the performance "itself" and considers how it might be understood. This chapter focuses on the purposes and limitations of "reading" a performance. In doing so it takes into account the ephemeral nature of performance that, unlike most other art forms, won't sit still for analysis. It therefore considers Marco de Marinis's understanding of the construction of "the performance text" as a "theoretical object" (*The Semiotics of Performance* 2), one that stands in for the performance as the object of analysis, replacing a fleeting *event* with a more stable textual *object*. For directors, dramaturges, designers, and actors, "reading" a performance can involve the ongoing reflective analysis of their own work as part of the creation and rehearsal process, its purpose being to evaluate and modify the work-in-progress or to move on to produce further work. "Reading" a performance might also involve theatre practitioners using semiotic analysis as a way of understanding the work of other artists in order to enrich their own. For scholars such analysis involves, among other things, asking how live performance can be translated into archives and histories, and how the reading process shapes future attempts to recuperate or extend the cultural work done by a given performance or body of work.

In each case the intention is to model ways in which a performance can be read by focusing, again, on primary modes of communication used in the performance "itself," the signs employed and the sign systems evoked, and the nature of their intersection. This chapter distinguishes between a "purely" semiotic approach that assumes, as Jiři Veltruský does ("Man" 84), that everything on stage is a sign (and by implication nothing else), and other approaches (such as the phenomenological) that remind us that objects or actions can and do exceed their sign value, and it considers the application, in consort with a semiotic approach, of other theories and methods appropriate to a specific performance analysis.

The chapter moves through issues of representation and recognition, considers the onstage "world" of the play, and focuses on the semiotics of reception in order to help readers understand the active role of live audiences in the production (not just the interpretation) of meaning. This involves, for example, looking at the ways in which a production that tours changes meaning in the different contexts in which it is received. The chapter returns to *A Doll House* and *Chocolate Woman Dreams the Milky Way*, focusing this time on the plays in production.

The purpose of *How Theatre Means*, then, is threefold: to introduce, summarize, and critique the history and current state of semiotics as a means of understanding meaning production in the theatre; to build upon the semiotic method as currently understood by putting it into conversation with other modes of theatrical analysis and extending its reach into a renewed interculturalism; and to describe and model some applied uses of this expanded semiotic method for both scholars and practitioners of "the semiotic arts of theatre."

Part One
Theory

From practice to theory

There are times in every rehearsal process when a shadow falls between the conception and the act. This often happens as a result of the conversion of a sublime idea into the messy materiality of its realization. And it doesn't just happen when a director's or designer's ideas are too big for her budget and a fully imagined three-dimensional scene setting is "realized," for example, as a cheap painted flat. It often happens, for example, in meetings between a director and a designer, when, after a considerable period of amiable and animated exchange of objects, materials, film clips, snippets of music, sketches, stories, books, ideas, images, and impressions, one looks at the other, or at a (hopefully) preliminary sketch and says (or thinks): "That isn't it at all. That's not what I meant at all."

It happens between designers and technicians, too, when a costume designer sees at a first fitting how her evanescent sketch with its sample bit of silk has been translated into the awkwardness of stitches, patches, and patterns that seemed lovely at sample-size, draped gracelessly over an actor's body that is fleshier or less flexible than first imagined (or than was visible in the photographs); when a set or props designer confronts the realities of what is locally available for purchase or construction; or when a lighting designer discovers that an actor's surprisingly dark skin tones defeat visibility and legibility at the broodingly murky levels originally intended (and that boosting levels destroys the artfully crafted "reveal" designed to follow).

It happens to dramaturges whose structural analyses and helpful insights are met with looks of blank incomprehension by writers or directors who prefer to operate through instinct and impulse, or who simply don't understand the vocabularies of dramaturgical analysis.

It happens all the time working with actors, who are a special case, each of whom has her own ways and paces of working, communicating, and understanding direction. Many directors give up and simply tell their actors what to do, which is not usually very productive – unless perhaps the director is Robert Wilson and/or the show requires automatons.

It happens, perhaps most frequently and most poignantly, when a director at a preview performance sees the show through the audience's eyes for the first time and thinks: "That isn't it at all. That's not what I meant at all."

It happens on every occasion in which theatre artists read reviews, critical accounts, or scholarly analyses of work to which they have contributed and fail to recognize themselves, their intentions, or the show in which they took part; and, conversely, every time journalists, critics, or scholars greet with disbelief, disappointment, incredulity, or indifference information in interviews, panel discussions, or talkbacks about what the theatre artists involved in a production actually thought they were doing.

And finally it happens time after time when audience members, reviewers, and scholars fail to read the codes in performances emerging from cultures and identity positions other than their own, and dismiss those performances as amateurish, awkward, inscrutable, or inferior.

These scenarios raise compelling questions about communication within the theatre and between the theatre and its audiences, and they, or scenarios like them, have prompted a considerable amount of theorization over the last hundred years and more about "how theatre means." Are there languages of the stage that, if clearly articulated and explicated, might facilitate more precise communication among its practitioners and between them and its audiences? Are there specific vocabularies that might bridge the gaps between conceptualization and realization? Between production and reception? Between performance cultures and disciplines? Are there ways of thinking and talking about what theatre does that might help to avoid the kinds of miscommunication that these too-familiar scenarios represent? Is there a body of theatre and performance theory that might help?

I believe that there is. Part I of this book surveys some of the considerable scholarship that has been devoted to theories of theatrical communication and representation, and tries to advance the cause by probing ways in which the languages of the stage might be clarified and refined. This includes asking difficult questions having to do with how we talk about the nature of theatre (what makes something theatrical); the performativity of theatre (what theatre does); the value of theatre; the characteristic elements that distinguish theatre from and relate it to narrative, poetry, music, visual art, sculpture, story-telling, performance art, ritual, and other types of performance; its diverse frames, forms, and structures; and the role within it of various and sundry modes of communication such as character, role, language, story, plot, action, imitation, inflection, gesture, movement, shape, pattern, rhythm, pitch, and tempo. These are large and small theoretical questions that are worth pursuing on their own, but that are far from just or purely theoretical. What follows in Part I takes them up analytically and theoretically; Part II will consider some of their applications.

1 Meaning

The study of the generation and circulation of meaning in societies, including, here, theatre, is called semiotics (or semiology). Initially a branch of linguistics, semiotics in its modern form was founded independently around the turn of the 20th century by the American Charles Sanders Peirce (1839–1914) and the Swiss Ferdinand de Saussure (1857–1913), though both were building upon a tradition that goes back to antiquity (see Jakobson). The work of Saussure, in particular, became the basis for a major paradigm shift in the humanities and social sciences known as Structuralism. Structuralism involves considering the world as made up, not of independently existing or pre-existing objects that are perceived and identified clearly and separately, but of relationships that are established within an overarching structure. For the structuralist, the nature of every object or element in the world derives from and can only be perceived in relation to the larger system, or structure, in which it participates. The nature of things rests not in the things themselves or any sort of clearly delimited essence peculiar to them, but in their perceived relationships to (and difference from) other things – in broad strokes, sweet versus sour, black versus white, tragedy versus comedy, but in more nuanced examples the fine divisions along the *continuum* of taste, along the colour spectrum or along a spectrum that includes tragicomedy, or satire. Blue is only blue insofar as it is not green (or cyan, or turquoise, or any number of hues in between that may only be given a name and considered significant in the context of lighting gels or paint chip samples), or on the other hand insofar as it is not violet, purple, or red. Structures are at any given moment complete and coherent within themselves, they refer to nothing outside of themselves, and they are governed by principles intrinsic to them and to which they and all of their constituent parts conform. Crucially, they are held in place by convention – a kind of social agreement, negotiated or coerced. Structuralists study the abstract but totalizing structures that give shape and meaning to the world.

Saussure and his legacy

One such structure is spoken language, the object of Saussure's study and the model for structuralists such as psychoanalyst Jacques Lacan (1901–81) and anthropologist Claude Lévi-Strauss (1908–2009), who argued, respectively, that human psyches and human cultures are structured like languages. For Saussure and those who came after him, language may best be understood as a tool through which humans perceive things; that is, it is not a tool used to describe a world that pre-exists that description, but a tool through which to *constitute* that world. For Saussure, then, a word is not a label for something that exists independently of how it is named; rather our understanding of what exists in the world is a product of mental concepts that are themselves the products of the languages we speak. Some cognitive studies scholars and others dispute the semiotic claim for the precedence of language (McConachie, *Engaging*; McConachie and Hart, *Performance*), but for Saussure, unarticulated thought is "simply a vague, shapeless mass" (Saussure 110), while sound, too, is "an equally featureless plane" (110), an undifferentiated continuum of noise. Think of a baby, whose gaze does not fix on anything or distinguish one thing from another, and who makes sounds that seem otherworldly, ranging freely over the sound spectrum in ways adults are not capable of and society does not reward with understanding. Or think, again, of the colour spectrum, a certain range along which society has determined to label "blue."

What language performs, according to Saussure, is a set of differentiations, or "articulations," as Saussure calls them in his posthumously published lectures, *Course in General Linguistics* (111). Language divides each of the two continuums, concepts and sounds, and matches them with or articulates them against one another in ways that allow thought to be made precise. "Articulation," he argues, "may refer to the division of the chain of speech into syllables, or to the division of the chain of meanings into meaningful units" (10). Language – "a system of distinct signs corresponding to distinct ideas" (10) – acts "as an intermediary between thought and sound, in such a way that the combination of both necessarily produces a mutually complementary delimitation of units" (110).

The location at which idea and sound come together – the basic unit of communication – is the sign. The linguistic sign consists of two inseparable but theoretically distinguishable parts (like the two sides of a sheet of paper), and Saussure calls these co-dependent parts the *signifier* and *signified*. The *signifier* has material existence in the world; the *signified* is purely conceptual. In the case of spoken language, Saussure's primary concern, the signifier is sound, the signified the idea or concept that is conjured in the mind by that sound or combination of sounds. When we speak the signifier "cat" the idea of a cat (the signified) is conjured in the mind. But the sign has no absolute or independent value, and the relationship between the sign and signifier (the sound "cat" and the mental image of a cat) is arbitrary.

The sign has meaning only in relation to the *sign system* (in Saussure's case, the spoken language) of which it is part, and that system is one of differences. As Saussure argues, "a linguistic entity is not defined until it is *delimited*, i.e. separated from whatever there may be on either side of it in a sequence of sounds" (102, emphasis in original). The signifier "cat" is only significant, for example, insofar as it is not, and is distinguishable (by one consonant or one vowel) from, "cap," "bat," "cut," or "rat." Meanwhile, the signified, the mental image of a cat, is significant only insofar as it is not, but is distinguishable from, that of a dog, horse, rat, or any other thing. *"In the language itself,"* Saussure argues, *"there are only differences.* [...] The language includes neither ideas nor sounds existing prior to the linguistic system, but only conceptual and phonetic differences arising out of that system" (118, emphasis in original).

Saussure makes an issue of the distinction between differences that a language or society deems to be significant and those that are disregarded, as when, in French, the different pronunciations of the letter "r" – uvular consonant (a guttural sound made at the back of the throat), apical trill (made by the tip of the tongue against the roof of the mouth), or even Germanic "*ch*" – are disregarded in everyday speech as insignificant, while in German the difference between "*r*" and "*ch*" is crucially important (117). And it is clear beyond Saussure's examples that different accents, different pronunciations, are only deemed to be significant when the important differences that a specific linguistic community recognizes are obscured. Different speakers of English may pronounce the "*th*" in "the," "with," or "through" in different ways, but it is only when and if "through" becomes confused with "true," for example, that this difficulty inhibits communication. (These differences might, however, also function as a signifier of class or cultural difference, an issue having to do with the policing, in the theatre and the world, of "proper" accents and "correct" pronunciations. "This" and "dis" might have the same meaning, but might signify different social and cultural positionings in their speakers.) In most western languages, differences in pitch usually have no significance at all, except for emphasis, while in most Asian languages, while the pitches themselves have no absolute value, the relationships among pitches employed in a single utterance have determining importance.

On the side of the signified, the world is also divided by languages into differences that a specific linguistic community has arbitrarily decided are significant, a determination that shifts over time but has major material consequences for the lived reality of people in the world. An example of this is racial designation: A person is only Caucasian in the contemporary world, for example, insofar as she is not Asian or African; another is only Japanese insofar as she is not Chinese, or is Chinese insofar as she is not from Hong Kong, Taiwan – or perhaps even Tibet. A century ago in the United States Irish and Jewish immigrants were considered to be people of colour; now they are "white." And today many people who are considered to be "white" in their homelands in the Middle East become "people of colour" when they emigrate to Europe or North America.

This issue of *significant* differences is crucial to theatre, where "linguistic" conventions can be established over the course of a single performance, in which audiences can come to understand when, why, and how differences – and connections – actually *make* any difference. In Robert Lepage's international hit *The Far Side of the Moon*, a panel with a circular window, depending on the context by which it is framed, shifts between representing a womb, the window in a laundromat washing machine, and the portal in a spacecraft. A rope emanating from it shifts between representing an umbilical cord and the life support line for an astronaut's spacewalk (Figure 1.1).

Audiences seem to have no difficulty "reading" these signs, and indeed take considerable delight in perceiving the unlikely connections when one signifier evokes unexpectedly different signifieds, functioning as visual puns. Audiences know that the onstage cord – the signifier – "is" neither umbilical nor life support, but the idea of each is alternatively conjured in the mind. In Canadian playwright James Reaney's signature play, *Sticks and Stones*, a pair of sticks serves variously to represent barriers or links between people – fences or stiles. The sticks represent weapons when raised and pointed, a fiddle when crossed horizontally and bowed, a crucifix when crossed vertically. In

Figure 1.1 **Yves Jaques in Ex Machina's 2012 production of Robert Lepage's *The Far Side of the Moon***
Source: Photo by Despina Spyrou ©Despina Spyrou/Onassis Cultural Centre-Athens.

each case, the semiosis is established and agreed upon economically, provisionally, and clearly through the simple expedient of evoking a comprehensible set of differential relationships. This is a theatrical microcosm of how Saussure claims that all linguistic systems function. In shows deriving from cultures other than that of a dominant audience, or in shows before audiences from many cultures, however, more work may have to be done establishing conventions through which understanding is achieved. In African American playwright Susan-Lori Parks's *America Play*, or *Top Dog, Underdog*, most American audiences and many others understand that a tall top hat and beard signify Abraham Lincoln, even when they are worn by a Black man, which nevertheless registers a disruption of the seamlessness of the semiosis and the "naturalness" of the representation (Figure 1.2). In *Chocolate Woman Dreams the Milky Way*, however, the four central women from Guna cosmology who shape the action have to introduce themselves and their significance to any but a Guna audience.

What gives the individual sign its value is its participation in the larger structure – the language, the *sign system* – within which it derives its meaning. Crucially, Saussure insists that the *meaning* and the *value* of a sign are distinct things. Meaning, he argues, is simply the mental counterpart of a pattern or sequence of sounds, assigned arbitrarily to those sounds by convention: "cat" *means* the concept of a particular kind of four-legged furry mammal. Value, on the other hand, always involves the invocation of something dissimilar for which the sign can be exchanged, and of something similar to which it can be compared. The value of a unit of currency, for example, is determined at once by a dissimilar item for which it can be exchanged (a ten dollar bill can be exchanged for a bottle of wine), *and* by a similar item, a unit of currency of a different denomination, to which it can be compared (a ten dollar bill is worth two fives). Within a simple sign system, a flashing light on the back of a car can be exchanged for something dissimilar – the idea of turning left – and compared to

Figure 1.2 Gary Yates in the 2001 Actor's Express, Atlanta production of Suzan-Lori Parks's *The America Play*, dir. Weir Harman

Source: Photo by Michelle Hollberg, courtesy Freddie Ashley.

something similar – the light on the right-hand side of the same car that is not flashing. Similarly, in a more complex sign system such as a language, a word can be substituted (or *exchanged*) for something entirely dissimilar – "cat" for the mental image of a particular type of four-legged furry mammal – and *compared* to something similar – another word that is to a greater or lesser degree similar, such as "cap" or "bat" – and these two relationships are how we determine its value in the linguistic marketplace.

In the theatre, an actor is most often "exchanged" for a character within the dramatic fiction and "compared" to another actor playing a different character. Understanding this signifying relationship is generally taken for granted – actors play roles – but it can become particularly crucial in productions (of such plays as Plautus's *Menaechmi* or Shakespeare's *Comedy of Errors* or *Twelfth Night*) that deal with mistaken identities or twins, or even in those, common in contemporary theatre, that employ doubling (in which a single actor plays multiple roles). Each of the performers in *Chocolate Woman Dreams the Milky* plays (is exchanged for) four roles, but unlike the doubling in naturalistic theatre, this *comparison* between these roles is based on similarity rather than difference: the audience comes to see the different roles as aspects of parallel, mutually informing stories.

A sign system, however, can only function *synchronically*; it is complete and stable only at one fixed moment in time. Just as the exchange or purchasing value of a dollar changes over time (diachronically), so too does the value of a sign, though in neither case is any individual user of the system able to implement such changes. Not only is the value of a sign stable only in a synchronic present, it is stable only insofar as its community assents to, enacts, and evokes the system through each utterance that participates in that system. "The language is never complete in any single individual," Saussure argues, "but exists perfectly only in the collectivity"; in fact, he argues, it consists of a "social bond" among its speakers

(13) – an issue that is of vital importance to marginalized or threatened cultures.

It is also important to note that a sign *system*, as such, has no material existence in the "real" world. It never comes into existence anywhere in its entirety but is implicit in, and evoked by, each individual utterance (which, only a fragment in itself, nevertheless does have material reality as sound). Saussure privileges the sign system as a whole and calls it the *langue*; the individual utterance he refers to as *parole*, comparing *langue* to a musical work, *parole* to different performances of that work in a way that has obvious application to theatre (Saussure 18). In theatre, if an individual "utterance," or "*parole*" is understood to be a complete onstage moment, or indeed a whole theatrical production, it can invoke a range or complex intersection of languages ("*langues*") – what French philosopher Roland Barthes (1915–80) calls "*a density of signs*" ("Literature" 262, emphasis in original), each of which – spoken language, gesture, costume, lighting, and so on – invokes a different sign system (*langue*), and all of which *taken together* constitute the language of the stage.

But it is one of Saussure's most important and most enabling (if controversial) contributions to observe, as already noted, that "the process which selects one particular sound-sequence to correspond to one particular idea is entirely arbitrary" (111), and therefore "*the linguistic sign is arbitrary*" (67, emphasis in original). What holds the sign in place, Saussure asserts, is no absolute or logical connection among its parts; in fact, "it exists only in virtue of a kind of contract agreed between the members of a community" (14). The English-speaking community somehow agrees that "cat," rather than "chat," or "grmfp," will conjure in the mind the idea of a particular type of furry mammal, or more ominously that "Asian" or "Indian" will conjure in the mind certain racialized characteristics and behaviours.

Saussure doesn't fully tease out the implications of this meaning-through-consensus, though he does observe that, "from the point of view of the linguistic community, the [sign] is imposed rather than freely chosen" (71), and his brief discussion of the ways in which "colonization [...] transports a language into new environments" (21) hints at the power dynamics that come into play around the control of meaning, particularly across economically or militarily unequal cultures. For if signification is fundamentally arbitrary and there is no "natural" connection between signifier and signified, sign and referent, then it is subject to manipulation. This raises key questions about *who controls the semiosis*, and in what or whose interests meanings are established, stabilized, and maintained. Indeed, each time a single utterance, or *parole*, evokes a larger *langue*, it is bringing into play what Roland Barthes calls "myth," or what his compatriot and contemporary philosopher Michel Foucault (1926–84) calls "discourse." And, crucially, languages, myths, and discourses are inevitably ideologically coded; that is, they carry with them specific ways of thinking about the world that they naturalize, or take for granted, and they enforce certain possible meanings or modes of understanding to the exclusion of others.

In his early structuralist work, and in particular his 1957 book, *Mythologies*, Barthes began with "a feeling of impatience at the sight of the 'naturalness' with which newspapers, art, and common sense constantly dress up a reality which, even though it is the one we live in, is undoubtedly determined by history [...]. I wanted to track down, in the decorative display of *what-goes-without-saying*, the ideological abuse which [...] is hidden there" (11, emphasis in original). Barthes built directly upon Saussurian semiotics to investigate "myth" – by which he means any "system of communication," including "photography, cinema, reporting, sport, shows, publicity," and presumably theatre (109, 110) – as "*a second order semiological system*" (114, emphasis in original). Myth constitutes a second order system because it "is made of material that has already been worked on" (that is, already has sign value), and because it encodes not-so-innocent "messages" with its (apparently transparent) meanings through the building of a "semiological chain" (110, 114). Each link in such a chain consists of a signifier and a signified constituting a sign, the totality of which becomes the signifier in the chain's next link. Each part of a mythical signifying system evokes what Barthes calls "a global sign, the final term of a first semiological chain" (114). In a famous example he demonstrates this (implied) final term as ideological. Barthes describes the cover photograph of a magazine in which a young Black man in a French army uniform is pictured, eyes uplifted, saluting the French tricolour:

> All this is the *meaning* of the picture. But [...] I see very well what it signifies to me: that France is a great Empire, that all her sons, without any colour discrimination, faithfully serve under her flag, and that there is no better answer to the detractors of an alleged colonialism than the zeal shown by this young Negro [sic] in serving his so-called oppressors. I am therefore again faced with a greater semiological system: there is a signifier, itself already formed with a previous system (*a black soldier is giving the French salute*); there is a signified (it is here a purposeful mixture of Frenchness and militariness); finally, there is a presence of the signified through the signifier. (116, emphasis in original)

To provide an example from the theatre, in a production of a Shakespearean history play a simple piece of stage furniture such as an ordinary desk chair can function as the first item in a semiological chain that moves from signifier (the chair) to signified (a chair within the stage fiction) through to the idea of a throne, then to that of royalty, then to that of the divine right of kings, and "finally" (the global sign) to an entire myth, or "message" that naturalizes social stratification and hierarchy.

Foucault's "discourse" echoes Barthes' "myth" insofar as it refers to a communications system, or system of signs, but

Foucault's term is used to refer more specifically to a set of *enoncés* (statements, units of knowledge) strung together that regulate or delimit what it is possible to say about a certain subject. In *The Order of Things* (1966) and its successor, *The Archaeology of Knowledge* (1969), Foucault treats certain patterns of *enoncés* as networks of underdetermined, or not verifiably appropriate choices that are made, not necessarily consciously, to exclude, control, gain status, or reinforce particular social institutions, and thereby to serve particular interests through the circulation of "power/knowledge" in society (*Discipline and Punish,* 1975). Examples of discourses, or "discursive formations," might include legal or medical discourses, or the discourses of cultural theory, which can feel closed to non-specialists, which uphold the privileges of specific institutions, govern what can be uttered when and where, and serve as sites in which power and knowledge (or more accurately "power/knowledge") circulate. A familiar theatrical example might be the often arcane discourse of theatrical lighting, with its leikos and fresnels, gobbos and gels, which can often feel to outsiders like an exclusive preserve, one peppered with industry brand names that directly serve the interests of specific dominant manufacturers – and, at a later stage in the semiological chain, the capitalist system. This specialized discourse also serves to obscure the ideological underpinnings of the sign systems through which stage lighting communicates, allowing its effects to be produced as if by magic.

The implications of Saussure's semiotics in conjunction with its extension into Barthes' myth and Foucault's discourse are enormous. In his essay on "The Mirror Stage," for example, structuralist psychoanalyst Jacques Lacan, building on Saussure, argues that human subjectivity (identity) is shaped by entry into language (or the symbolic order, which he also calls "the law of the father") to which the individual is henceforth "subjected." This happens at the moment of recognition of the other (the mother and the self as other) that he calls the "mirror stage." When the infant encounters the self as other at the mirror stage of psychological development, according to Lacan, he [sic] encounters "identity" or selfness alienated through language (what does it mean to look in a mirror and say, "*that* (out there) 'is' *me*"? What does it mean to say "I" (to represent the self in language)? What does it mean to say "I am a boy"? "I am Indian"? "I am an Afro-German woman with a disability"? What does it mean to enter into language as a site of difference and differentiation? And this moment, in which the child is able, as in Saussure, to *articulate* the self, the mother, and the other as distinct from the pre-Oedipal abstract mass of sheer *being*, recurs and is reinforced throughout life as a kind of biblical fall from the innocence of unity with undifferentiated being, that is nevertheless also an entry into knowledge and power. Insofar as the theatre functions as a site at which human subjectivity is constituted and explored, and as a place where desire is played out through actors/others, the stage can often function as a Lacanian mirror. Through processes such as empathy, the audience can witness the self played out in discourse as other and can both experience and come to an understanding of the pleasures, powers, and alienations effected by their existence as human subjects.

Not surprisingly, Lacan's semiotic approach to the human psyche has opened up the opportunity for a great deal of productive psychoanalytical criticism of theatrical meaning-making, and much of this work has been feminist. A 2002 article published by Anne Marie Rekdal in *Scandinavian Studies* serves as an example. Rekdal examines Ibsen's *A Doll House* through a Lacanian lens, arguing that its heroine, Nora, is torn between the *jouissance* of transgressing the law of the father and her entrapment within that law. Rekdal argues that what Nora undergoes in the play is a "subjective-existential crisis" (152) that leads to a rebellion against that law, and that represents Ibsen's positing, in her departure from the family home and abandonment of her husband and children, of "an alternative ethical system to the Oedipal and patriarchal" (178). Significantly, this rebellion is achieved, not by way of language or the symbolic order – represented in the play by the threatening letter that is visibly and ominously in the mailbox – but through Nora's dancing of the famous wordless and wild *tarantella* at the heart of the play.

The limitations of a Lacanian approach are perhaps most apparent in work that derives from non-patriarchal cultures, where entry into language is less about entry into "the law of the father," or into "power/knowledge," and less about alienation from a pre-linguistic fullness of being, than it is about entrance into a cosmology dominated, as most of the world's Indigenous cultures are, by *relations* with the world and by an awareness of the interconnectedness of all things. When Dule Girl returns to Guna Yala at the end of *Chocolate Woman Dreams the Milky Way*, at which time her face is painted with the signs of Guna womanhood, she enters a sense of oneness with creation and culture. Hers is a coming of age that is characterized by fullness rather than alienation.

In his major work, *Structural Anthropology,* Claude Lévi-Strauss contends that cultures too, like the psyche for Lacan, are structured like languages. The early chapters of the first volume of *Structural Anthropology* wrestle with the relationship between linguistics and anthropology in the constitution of a systematic and totalizing structuralist "human sciences." There Lévi-Strauss focuses on the revolutionary role that structural linguistics has played for the social sciences and offers it as a model for anthropology to follow. He argues that kinship, food, political ideology, ritual, cooking, and other practices are partial expressions of a larger cultural structure, language, or myth that is never made explicit or conscious and has no concrete existence as a whole, but is evoked by these practices that derive their meaning only in relation to it. And it is these unconscious foundations, he argues, rather than empirical observation of specific practices, that are the proper object of study for anthropologists.

Lévi-Strauss's closest engagement with Saussure comes in a later chapter in the same volume, "The Structural Study of Myth." The chapter begins with Saussure's distinction between *langue* and *parole,* which Lévi-Strauss extends, like Barthes, to a third term, "myth," but unlike Barthes' myth, that of Lévi-Strauss is understood as "mythical stories," stories that Lévi-Strauss says are at once the unique, surprising, and unexpected (in their detail) foundational stories of specific cultures and yet similar (in their structures) across cultures around the world (208). He explains that similarity by considering myth to *be* language (*langue*) – "functioning on an especially high level where meaning succeeds practically at 'taking off' from the linguistic ground [*parole*] on which it keeps on rolling" (210). He offers as an example a structuralist analysis of the story of Oedipus, which he claims with notable western ethnocentrism "is well known to everyone" (213), which is of course foundational for the psychoanalytic theories of both Freud and Lacan, and which, in Sophocles' *Oedipus Rex*, served as the model for Aristotle's *Poetics*, the foundational text for the western study of dramatic literature. Lévi-Strauss's choice of case study was far from random, then, or innocent.

Both Lacan and Lévi-Strauss have rightly come under attack from various quarters for their universalizing and masculinist tendencies, but if their arguments have any validity – and their significant influence suggests that they do, even if it is not a totalizing one – then the languages, myths, and discourses that are entered into by western subjects at the Lacanian "mirror stage" contribute significantly and determinately to the constitution of who "we" are, both as individuals and as societies. When we study meaning production through language, then, we are studying, at a fundamental and formative level, "who 'we' are."

Later the structuralist certainties and totalities assumed by Saussure, Lacan, Lévi-Strauss, the early Barthes, and to a lesser extent Foucault (though he denied that he was a structuralist) would be "deconstructed" by the poststructuralists, including Barthes himself at a later stage, but especially by French philosopher Jacques Derrida (1930–2004), who focused on the always deferred nature of signification, when each sign in what Barthes had called a semiological chain becomes the next signifier, and so on *ad infinitum*. Derrida coined the term "differance" (or in French, *différance*), the replacement of "e" by "a" playing on the fact that the French verb "*différer*" can mean both "to defer" and "to differ." "Differance" thereby captures at once the inevitable *deferral* of meanings that are carved out through *difference* ("differance defers-differs" [*Of Grammatology* 66]), while also playing with the fact that, spoken, the spelling change from "e" to "a" *makes no difference*: it can't be heard (Derrida, "Différance"). Derrida argued that there is, in fact, no global or "transcendental" signifier or signified that begins or completes the chain of signification, originates or confirms (or controls) final meaning: "in language," he argues, echoing Saussure, "there are only differences" ("Différance" 11). But this enabling deconstruction of global certainties was already implicit, as Derrida himself argues in his critique of Saussure in *Of Grammatology* (27–73), in Saussure's assertion of the fundamentally arbitrary (or as Derrida says "unmotivated") nature of the signifier/signified relationship and the reliance of signification on linguistic and conceptual differentiations.

In the theatre, an early, pre-Derridean application of this argument might be understood to emerge from the theory and practice of the German playwright Bertolt Brecht (1898–1956), whose socialist politics led him to develop an aesthetic that resisted the representation of historical inevitability (such as "fate") and encoded the possibility of social change. Brecht's concept of the "not…but" was developed as part of an acting method for his "epic theatre." It involved staging, not historical inevitability, but historicized (that is, historically and culturally contextualized) *choice*:

> When [an actor] appears on stage, besides what he actually is doing he will in all essential points discover, specify, imply what he is not doing; that is to say he will act in such

> a way that the alternative emerges as clearly as possible [...]. Whatever he doesn't do must be contained and conserved in what he does. In this way every sentence and every gesture signifies a decision; the character remains under observation and is tested. The technical term for this procedure is "fixing the 'not...but'." (Brecht 137)

In epic theatre the audience is always made aware, through an actor's *demonstrating* rather than *inhabiting* a role, of the character's options: every onstage action is shadowed by what Derrida would call the "traces" of the choices not taken, and the significations not pursued. Brecht's theatre is a rich testing ground for semiotic analysis, since his so-called "defamiliarization" techniques crucially involve denaturalizing the signifier-signified relationship. If each signifier bears the traces of another signifier, as Elin Diamond has pointed out, this "wreaks havoc on identity [...]; if an identity is always different from itself it can no longer *be* an identity" (48). What Brecht's staging of the "not...but" performs is a potentially radical critique of representations of identity grounded in such apparently stable things as gender, sexuality, nation, culture, and race. Indeed, it potentially undermines any understanding of human subjectivity (selfhood that is formed, at least in part, by those things to which one is "subject") as unified, self-contained, or autonomous (independent, able to make choices freely). If the self is understood to be a subject rather than an identity (with its implications of oneness), it is possible to afford it agency (as when the "I" is the grammatical subject of a sentence), while also recognizing that it is constituted socially by a heterogeneous mix of influences – prominent among which are the historically and culturally specific myths and discourses in which the self participates and to which it has been "subjected" and is now "subject."

It is this potential to destabilize unified representations of identity that has made a semiotic approach central to feminists, postcolonialists, and cultural materialists who are centrally concerned with uncovering the ideological encoding of gender, race, and class, respectively, within dominant systems of representation, including those of the stage. When a theatre audience gives consent to a representation – when we accept that the figure onstage with long hair, wearing a skirt and makeup, and behaving coyly "is" a woman – it is what the French Marxist philosopher Louis Althusser (1918–90) calls "hailed," or "interpellated" into an ideological system ("Ideology" 170–7), in this case what cultural anthropologist Gayle Rubin (1949–) calls "the sex/gender system" that identifies certain prescribed behaviours as inherently or naturally feminine (34–41). Theatrical representations of race in figures such as the stage Irishman, the "noble savage," "squaw" or "Indian Princess," or in the grotesqueries of blackface minstrelsy, have been particularly egregious in their interpellation of audiences into racist regimes, as audiences learn to "recognize" characteristics and behaviours represented as "natural" to certain peoples. Politically alternative theatre has needed consistently to develop and deploy techniques such as Brechtian defamiliarization (*verfremdung*) in order to destabilize rather than reify such representations, and to find ways of staging identities as multiple, fluid, and subject to a multiplicity of divergent myths and discourses. Helen Gilbert has discussed, for example, the ways in which Indigenous playwrights Daniel David Moses (Delaware, from Canada) and Wesley Enoch (Murri, from Australia) have used "whiteface" Indigenous minstrelsy in their plays to destabilize the fixity of race while affirming the complex and positive identities of Aboriginal peoples (Gilbert).

The enabling heterogeneity of the mix of discourses that constitute human subjectivity has been labelled "dialogism" by the Russian linguist and literary critic Mikhail Bakhtin (1895–1975), whose engagement with Saussure's linguistics in the 1920 book *Marxism and the Philosophy of Language* (a work of disputed authorship often attributed to his Soviet colleague and collaborator V.N. Volosinov, 1895–1936), launched a lifelong study of "utterances" (roughly, Saussure's *paroles*). Bakhtin shifted Saussure's focus from the "universalist" structure – the *langue* – to the unique phenomenon, the utterance (*parole*), which is *made* unique by its social and historical context. Utterances, then, are not simply linguistic but also *social* phenomena "constructed between two socially organized persons" at the moment in which they are heard or read (Volosinov 85). According to Bahktin's "sociolinguistics," all utterances, which can range from a single sound or gesture to a full-length novel, are made up of a polyphony of languages – what Bakhtin calls "heteroglossia." These languages are drawn from a variety of "speech genres" – social, professional, and cultural communication systems (see Bahktin, *Speech Genres*).

Bakhtin's speech genres are like Foucault's discourses, but for Bakhtin they coexist within a single utterance, potentially denaturalizing one another and disrupting claims to monologic authority or totalizing expression. Some utterances, of course, are more dialogic than others: the epic, for example, is monologic for Bakhtin, aspiring to be the final (theological) Word (Derrida's transcendental signified); but the novel, and in particular the "polyphonic novel" of Dostoevsky and the "carnivalesque" of Rabelais, exemplifies the dialogic text, which consists of "a plurality of independent and unmerged voices and consciousnesses, a genuine polyphony of fully valid voices" (*Rabelais; Problems* 6). Ironically, given its basis in dialogue, Bakhtin did not find the fundamentally naturalistic drama of his day particularly dialogic (though he celebrated the dialogism of the carnivalesque medieval theatre), because he felt that it was "almost always constructed out of represented, objectified discourses" (*Problems* 188). He saw in drama an attempt to bring together in dialogue, but *not* to merge, voices that were in themselves monologic, and were therefore "alien to genuine polyphony" (*Problems* 34): "Dramatic dialogue is determined by a collision between individuals who exist within the limits of a single unitary language" (*Dialogic* 405).

But Bakhtin was citing the drama of a very particular moment and kind, and many others have found the concept of dialogism useful in the semiotic analysis of theatre, particularly of contemporary theatre that eschews naturalistic closures, employs doubling, direct address, or "dialogic monologue" (Knowles and Harvie) or eschews "footlights," which Bakhtin interprets as anything which "separates the aesthetic event from lived life" (*Art* 217). Helene Keyssar, for example, critiquing Bakhtin's exclusion of drama from the realm of true polyphony, assembles a list of dialogic plays that range from *Woyzeck* through *Ubu Roi*, Beckett, and Brecht, to contemporary African American and feminist plays (95). She puts the concept of dialogism to productive feminist use in her analysis of Wendy Wasserstein's 1988 play *The Heidi Chronicles* and María Irene Fornés's 1977 *Fefu and Her Friends* (95–104). In 2010, Kwok-kan Tam applied Bakhtinian dialogism productively to explicate even so traditionally monologic a play as Ibsen's *A Doll House*, shifting the grounds of dialogism from a strictly linguistic to a psychological orientation, and reading the central character Nora's transformation as a transition over the course of the play "from a monologic self to a dialogic self" (83).

But perhaps the most productive and influential application of Bahktin's theories of dialogism and the carnivalesque has come about through their reworking in the hands of the poststructuralist Bulgarian-French philosopher, psychoanalyst, literary critic, novelist, and feminist Julia Kristeva (1941–). In a 1966 essay, "Word, Dialogue and the Novel" Kristeva coined the concept of "intertextuality" out of an attempt to merge Saussure's semiotics with Bakhtin's dialogism, defining it elsewhere as the "transposition of one (or several) sign-system(s) into another" (*Revolution* 59–60). For Kristeva, citing Socratic dialogue, meaning itself "is a product of a dialogical relationship among speakers" ("Word" 81), and "any text is constructed as a mosaic of quotations" ("Word" 66). It is this intertexuality, Kristeva argues, that is the politically productive component of discourse. It is the dialogic elements of language that "destroy man's epic and tragic unity [Kristeva is *not* using the universal masculine here] as well as his belief in identity and causality; they indicate that he has lost his totality and no longer coincides with himself" ("Word" 83). "The carnival challenges God, authority, and social law;" indeed, "insofar as it is dialogical," Kristeva argues, "it is rebellious" ("Word" 79).

Although, like Bahktin, Kristeva focuses her analysis on Menippean (carnivalesque) discourse and the polyphonic novel, she also cites Antonin Artaud's theatre of cruelty, and refers to dialogic intertextuality as "spectacle, but without a stage" ("Word" 78), as "dramatization" ("Word" 79). "All poetic [that is, intertextual] discourse is dramatization," she argues, where different voices contend as conflicting, unmerged dramatic postulates – as theatre – and thereby "relativize each other" ("Word" 78). Kristeva later abandoned the term "intertextuality" because she felt it had too often been understood in the "banal sense of 'study of sources'," replacing it with "transposition" (*Revolution* 60), but the term has proven to be extraordinarily productive. Scholars have explored scenic intertextuality between *commedia dell arte* and Theatre of the Oppressed (Heritage), intertexuality in contemporary Lithuanian theatre (Staniškytė), in musical theatre, in Latin American theatre, in early modern theatre, in vaudeville, in multi-ethnic and Indigenous theatre (Maufort and Figuera) – the list is endless. But theatre might best be seen as *fundamentally* intertexual, a site at which the various discourses that constitute its "cybernetic machine" (Barthes, "Literature" 261) come together and productively "relativize" each other.

Charles Peirce: sign, object, and interpretant; icon, index, and symbol

While Saussure's work grew out of the discipline of linguistics and is contained in the slim volume, *Course in General*

Linguistics, consisting of edited lecture notes taken by his students and published after his death, Charles Sanders Peirce produced a daunting body of work, much of it published only posthumously, and only a portion of it assembled by Harvard University Press in the eight-volume maze that is the *Collected Papers*, by Indiana University Press in the chronologically-arranged two-volume *The Essential Peirce*, and also by IUP in the so-far eight-volume (of a projected thirty) *Writings of Charles Sanders Peirce*. Peirce's discussion of "semeiotic" is not developed in isolation, but accrues alongside, and is fundamental to, his theories of logic, mathematics, and philosophical pragmatics. His writings on semiotics, some of them gathered together in the 1991 University of North Carolina Press volume, *Peirce on Signs*, evolved over the course of his life, and in this work he provided literally dozens of different definitions of the sign.

But what is central and consistent is that, while for Saussure the sign was a dyad (made up of two parts, the signifier and signified), for Peirce, the sign was a relation – a "sign relation" – that is *tri*adic, consisting of three essential parts: the sign, the object, and the interpretant. What Peirce calls the "sign," or *representamen*, is defined not by its essence but by its function: to represent, or *stand for* something – to be interpreted. The "object" is what is represented in the sign, what the sign stands for, or the subject matter of the sign relation (having to do with all three parts), and this is what is "value added" to Saussure's dyad. The object can be anything that is thinkable. The interpretant, finally, is the meaning of the sign – similar to Saussure's "signified": an idea or effect as it is interpreted, usefully insisting, as Saussure does not, on the *act* of interpretation. To summarize and simplify, the sign stands *for* the object *to* the interpretant; or, in perhaps Peirce's simplest articulation, "a sign is an object which stands for another to some mind" ("On the Nature of Signs" 141).

One of the significances of Peirce's tripartite sign relation is the emphasis it places on the act of interpretation (which for him consisted, and was constitutive, of thought). For Peirce a sign exists in order to be interpreted; if it is not interpreted, it is not a sign. But the *interpretant* is not the same as the *interpreter*. As Roman Jakobson points out, the interpreter is "the receiver and decoder of a message"; the interpretant is *part* of the sign, "the key which the receiver uses to understand the message," (442), or in Peirce's words, "all that is explicit in the sign itself, apart from its context and circumstances of utterance" (*Collected Papers*, 5 325).

The implications of this distinction are important, in part because it suggests that all signification involves an act of translation of signs into other signs and so on (like Barthes's semiological chain), and in part because it foregrounds the "context and circumstances of utterance" in the real, material world. And for Peirce, unlike Saussure, the "real world" – what Peirce calls "some external permanency [...] something upon which our thinking has no effect" ("Fixation" 120) – exists independently of semiosis. Indeed, even if its characteristics depend upon systems of signs and representations, for Peirce the external world – the referent, or that to which the sign relation in its totality ultimately (or eventually) refers – is determinate of the truth value of the representation, the "final [vs. 'dynamic'] interpretant" (*Semiotic and Significs* 111) against which it can be measured or tested by a community (see Fischer 120–34). Finally, the "circumstances of utterance" for Peirce include prior (or "collateral") knowledge of the sign relation's object (its subject matter), without which the sign could not be interpreted ("Pragmatism" 409). This focus on reception of the sign is one element in Peirce's thinking that makes his work significant for the study and practice of theatre, where "real-world" testing and the prior experience of audiences are crucial to communication. It is particularly crucial in the case of intercultural performance where "the density of signs" Barthes refers to occurs not only across the languages of the stage but also across cultural differences that play themselves out experientially in real, material ways.

Peirce's understanding of what might serve as a sign extends far beyond spoken or written language. Indeed, as Jakobson says, his "semiotic edifice encloses the whole multiplicity of significative phenomena, whether a knock on the door, a footprint, a spontaneous cry, a painting, a musical score, a conversation, a silent meditation, a piece of writing, a syllogism, an algebraic equation, a geometric diagram, a weather vane, or a simple bookmark" (442). And he discusses each of these things and more, at length. He does not discuss theatre, but the expansiveness of his semiotic lends itself to the analysis of a form that includes so many elements, so many different ways of signifying, such semiotic richness. His classification of signs, in fact, contains elements that are almost uniquely valuable to theatre studies.

Peirce assembled a staggeringly complex classificatory system consisting of "ten main trichotomies" ("Excerpts" 483–91), what one of his editors calls "the most advanced theory of signs ever fashioned" (Houser xxx), but for theatre practitioners and scholars his identification of three *types* of sign is particularly useful:

> There are three kinds of signs. Firstly, there are *likenesses*, or icons; which serve to convey ideas of the things they represent simply by imitating them. Secondly, there are *indications*, or indices, which show something about things, on account of their being physically connected with them. Such is a guidepost, which points down the road to be taken, or a relative pronoun which is placed just after the name of the thing intended to be denoted, or a vocative exclamation, as "Hi! There," which acts upon the nerves of the person addressed and focuses his [sic] attention. Thirdly, there are *symbols*, or general signs, which have become associated with their meanings by usage. Such are most words, and phrases, and speeches, and books, and libraries. ("What is a Sign" 5, emphasis in original; see also "One, Two, Three" and "Sign")

It will be clear that only one of these, the symbol, fits with Saussure's statement that all signs are arbitrary, the result of convention. Insofar as Saussure was concerned primarily with spoken language (and even there qualified his assertion somewhat late in the *Course*), the linguist and the logician are in agreement about this.

Peirce's classification of one type of signification as *iconic* has frequently been considered especially useful for the analysis of theatre, where the likenesses between the actor and the character she plays, between the furniture on stage and the furniture it represents within the fiction of the play, and so on, make the theatrical medium uniquely iconic. And indeed the stage, particularly the naturalistic stage, has frequently taken this iconicity to extremes, when real rabbits frolicked in the forest of Arden in 19th-century productions of *As You Like It*, or when Christine in Strindberg's *Miss Julie* cooks real food on a real stove in real time. And there is no doubt that particularly powerful effects can be achieved when an onstage sign and its real-life referent approach identity, though it is also a truism that the use of the "real" onstage – as in the case of children, dogs, working clocks, or fire – can serve to fracture rather than reinforce the illusion, particularly in naturalistic work.

But not all theatrical representation is iconic, a mode that is most suited to naturalism or realism, where verisimilitude is key, and where what is re-presented has already happened: Peirce argues that the icon "has such being as belongs to past experience" (qtd in Jakobson 427). Indeed, Bertolt Brecht developed a method of acting for his epic theatre that is fundamentally *indexical*, in which the actor was encouraged to "show" or demonstrate rather than strive to "become" the character she is playing, in effect pointing indexically to key characteristics without aspiring to iconic similarity (Brecht 136–40). Because, as Peirce argues, the index "has the being of present experience" (Jakobson 427), it is particularly conducive to political theatre and to situations in which the "action" takes place in the minds and bodily receptors of the audience. Other experimental forms such as expressionist, symbolist, absurd, poststructuralist, postmodernist, or what Hans-Thies Lehmann calls "postdramatic theatre" (theatre that attempts to rely neither on representation of the external world nor on the developmental structuring of time) are likely to draw upon the *symbolic*, where the arbitrariness of sign-referent relationships can be productively exploited and the taken-for-grantedness of too easy recognitions undermined. For this type of experimentation, the symbolic mode is essential, for as Peirce argues, "the value of a symbol is that it serves to make thought and conduct rational and enables us to predict the future" (Jakobson 427) – or at the very least, to make audiences sit less comfortably in their seats and certainties.

Peirce was clear that any sign could, and almost always does, have characteristics of more than one of his three types (the iconic, the indexical, and the symbolic). This is certainly true in the theatre, where a degree of iconicity seems to be required in order for there to be recognition and for communication to take place, but where signs also frequently point indexically to extra-diegetic space and time (outside of the represented action), and where spoken or other symbolic language is generally used. Peirce himself points to the importance of icons, and to a lesser extent indices, for intercultural communication (what he calls "intercommunication"), where the shared conventions that are necessary for symbolic signs, such as most spoken or written language, may not exist ("What" 6). (This may be why theatrical productions designed for international touring tend not to rely heavily on spoken text.) But it is clear that directors, designers, and actors in the contemporary theatre need to develop some consciousness of the types of sign that are used in their productions. If a work is to be political, an overreliance on iconicity may tend to reify rather than disrupt dominant representational regimes, whereas the use of indexical signs might help to promote political awareness and historical consciousness by alienating ideological taken-for-granteds. An existentialist worldview, however, one invested in deep psychological drives, or one dominated by postmodern uncertainties, might be best communicated through the use of the symbolic, where meaning is already inherently arbitrary.

This chapter has focused on the foundations, implications, and legacy of the modern study of meaning production, with suggestions for its application to the study and practice of theatre. In the next chapter the focus will be on the history and practice of semiotics as it has developed in specific application to drama and theatre.

2 Theatre

Prague school contributions

Theatre's *"density of signs"* makes it an ideal subject for semiotic analysis (Barthes, "Literature" 262, emphasis in original). But semiotic theory and analysis as applied specifically to drama and theatre only began to develop in Europe fifteen years after the posthumous publication of Saussure's *Course*, with the appearance in 1931 of Otakar Zich's *Estetika dramatického umění: teoretická dramaturgie* (*Aesthetics of the Art of Drama*) and Jan Mukařovský's "Tentativo di analisi del fenomeno delll'attore" ("An Attempted Structural Analysis of the Phenomenon of the Actor"). These publications were foundational for the work on drama and theatre of the Prague School Structuralists throughout the 1930s and 40s, which was continuous with the literary poetics of the earlier so-called Russian Formalists, with whom they shared membership. The Prague School introduced to theatre and performance studies and into theatrical practice a number of key concepts that have continuing importance, including such basic devices as foregrounding (*aktualisace*) and showing (*ostension*), extending into many of the central concerns of theatrical practice.

Two of the key contributions of the Prague School derived directly from Russian Formalist Viktor Shklovsky's 1925 concept of *"ostranenie,"* variously translated as "making strange," "estrangement," or "defamiliarization," – a concept that is directly relevant to Brecht's later *verfremdungseffekt*, or "defamiliarization" effect (see Chapter 1). For Shklovsky, one of the key functions of art was to make ordinary, taken-for-granted elements of life visible again by making them "strange," "seeing things out of their usual context" (9) or removing them from the sphere of "automized perception" (6), and thereby seeing them "as if for the first time" (6).

As applied to drama and theatre by Prague School theoreticians this making strange emerges as *aktualisace* (foregrounding), and *ostension* (showing). *Aktualisace* can simply involve the drawing of some element of a production to the audience's attention, foregrounding it as what in later chapters I call a show's primary mode of communication. For Prague School member Jiří Veltruský (1919–94), "the figure at the peak" of the theatre's communication system is the (lead) actor ("Man" 85) – though as his compatriot Jindřich Honzl (1893–1953) argued, this hierarchy is not the same for all historical periods, or crucially, I would add, all cultures, in some of which the community rather than the individual is at the centre. But *aktualisace* also involves an element of denaturalization. Fellow Prague School theorist Bohuslav Havránek (1893–1978) distinguishes between automization and foregrounding (*aktualisace*). In the former he finds an element of the taken-for-granted, where the means of expression does not draw attention to itself and the relationship between signifier and signified is taken as given; in the latter he points to devices that present themselves in ways that are "uncommon," unusual, or striking – serving more than the simple purpose of direct communication (9–10). Havránek is discussing poetic language, but as Keir Elam reminds us, "foregrounding is essentially a spatial metaphor" (*Semiotics* 16), and in spite of efforts by some experimental directors to the contrary, it is difficult to imagine it *not* happening in the theatre. Directors routinely wrestle with control of focus (what the audience is looking at), designers construct frames and perspectives using colour, shape and light to catch and direct the audience's eye, and actors routinely upstage one another (foregrounding themselves), or try to avoid doing so. Indeed, the simple act of placing in theatrical space something that is not normally seen there – mud, running water, fire, a falling leaf – can allow it to be seen afresh because it is out of context. Similarly, words, artefacts, or performance forms, when taken out of their accustomed cultural contexts, can be seen differently, as if in quotation marks.

Herta Schmid, following Ivo Osolsobě (1928–2012), traces the concept of *ostension* back to St. Augustine, and she regards it as "one of the fundamentals of the art of theatre" (68). Simply put, ostension is showing. It is the act, for example, of demonstrating or explaining what something is, not through description, definition, or telling, but through the act of putting forward (ostending) a concrete example of the thing being indicated. Elam uses the examples of a child who asks "what's a pebble?" being shown one picked up from the beach, and of a person who orders a beer by showing an empty bottle to the server (*Semiotics* 26). He calls ostension "the most 'primitive' form of signification," and cites Umberto Eco's argument that it is "the most basic instance of performance" (Elam, *Semiotics* 26; Eco "Semiotics" 110). In a sense this is because the act of showing is what distinguishes theatre and performance from other arts and communication systems. In fact performance *consists* of ostending actors, objects, and actions through the use of indices (see Chapter 1), foregrounding (*aktualisace*), or pointing (*deixis* – gestures, or words such as pronouns or names – I, you, here, there, this, that – that are in themselves semantically empty but derive their meaning from the place in which they're used or the persons using them). But of course ostension is also necessarily selective. As Marco De Marinis points out, "the act of ostension always makes some of the concrete traits pertinent at the expense of others" (*Semiotics* 88), and it is this selective act of ostension that constitutes the artfulness of theatre as well as its potential to distort. In performance, moreover, things are at once ostended as the things "themselves" *and* as signs, insofar as they stand in for other things in their class (a chair on stage for a chair within the fiction, an actor for a character, and so on). This doubleness is part of the richness of performance that was emphasized by the Prague School but often forgotten by later drama and theatre semioticians.

As I have indicated, Jan Mukařovský (1891–1975) might be regarded as one of the founders of the semiotics of drama and theatre, but in his so-called "anti-semiotic turn" (Schmid 73–9), in apparent contradiction to the dictum that everything on stage is a sign, he declared that the work of art was simultaneously *a sign and a thing,* in constant tension, depending on whether its sign-ness or its thingness was ostended (Mukařovský, "Intentionality"). Mukařovský was writing about the work of art as an aesthetic object, but he was not alone in recognizing the simultaneous phenomenal and signifying qualities of things in the theatre. Indeed, his Prague-School colleague Petr Bogatyrev (1893–1971) applies this insight, not just to the overall artwork, but to the doubleness of costumes and other objects on stage, which function as "both material object [clothing] and sign [of period, social class, occasion, and so on]" ("Costume" 13). In fact, he argues, "cases where costume is only a sign are quite rare" (14).

When ostended, things can become signs, but in doing so, they nevertheless retain their "thingness," which exceeds their sign value as "non-semiotic surplus," in the words of Herta Schmid (78). Later scholars have made much of this thingness, including phenomenologists of the theatre such as Bert States, who uses the examples of functioning clocks, fire, running water, children, and animals as things that "do not always or entirely surrender their objective nature to the sign/image function" (*Great Reckonings* 29). They insist on (also) being what they are. But States treats among such "things" virtually everything that makes up theatre, including, for example, the sound of an actor speaking her or his lines, sound that, he argues, "is not consumed in its sense" (*Great Reckonings* 26). This insight has become the basis for an antisemiotic turn in theatre studies since the 1990s that manifests itself in approaches through phenomenology, affect theory, and most recently, cognitive studies, where scholars such as Bruce McConachie argue that some of the basic insights of semiotics are "empirically incorrect"

(*Engaging* 212). I will take these approaches up more fully in Chapter 3.

Beyond such fundamental concepts as foregrounding and ostension, the Prague school introduced and extended its semiotic analysis to a long list of theatrical topics, ranging from Chinese Theatre (Brušák), Greek theatre (Honzl, "Hierarchy"), and folk theatre (Bogatyrev, "Semiotics," "Forms"); to dramatic text (Veltruský, "Dramatic"), dialogue (Veltruský, "Basic," *Drama*), plot (Veltruský, *Drama*), costume (Bogatyrev, "Costume"), sets and props (Honzl "Dynamics"; Veltruský, "Man"), directing (Honzl, "Pohyb"), acting (Honzl, "Herecká"; Veltruský, "Man"), delivery (Burián, "Příspěvek"), mime and gesture (Mukařovský, "Tentativo"); and many other aspects of theatrical production. Much of this work, as Veronika Ambros has argued persuasively, was forged within a "laboratory" context in Prague in the 1930s, where semiotic analysis and theatrical experimentation were very much linked. Indeed Honzl and Burián, cited above as theoreticians, were also leading avant-garde directors, Bogatyrev's work on folk theatre was transformed to the stage, and Burián's productions in turn inspired one of Mukařovský's key essays (Ambros 46). This practical approach to a field of study that is often criticized in its later incarnations for engaging in theory for its own sake – "we theorized too much," as one of its leading theorists has lamented (De Toro 112) – is a key reason why a return to Prague School insights is important, especially for theatre practitioners. Indeed, it might serve as a model for a future "semiotic pragmatics," as Michael Sidnell terms it in calling for a new theatrical praxis that he calls "semiotic arts of theatre" (11). Chapters 4 and 5 of this book are intended in part to respond to this call.

Beyond Prague

The work of the Prague school was cut short, first by the Communist takeover of Czechoslovakia in 1948, and again by the Soviet invasion ending the so-called Prague Spring in 1968 (as the Russian Formalists' work had earlier been foreshortened by the Russian revolution and the Soviet ban on formalism). They had accomplished much, and their work continued to be influential as many of them individually, along with other scholars, built upon their foundations. What they didn't do was attempt to develop the kind of formal taxonomies of theatrical signs that constituted the work of so many semiologists of drama and theatre in the 1970s, 80s, and 90s, beginning with Tadeuz Kowzan's generative 1968 contribution, "The Sign in the Theater."

Kowzan's taxonomy is relatively basic, and involves thirteen intersecting theatrical sign systems, mostly centring on the actor. These include word, tone, mime, gesture, movement, make-up, hair style, costume, properties, settings, lighting, music, and sound effects, each classified as temporal or spatial, auditive or visual, associated with the actor or outside of the actor, and also classified as spoken text, bodily expression, the actor's appearance, the appearance of the stage, or "inarticulate" (non-verbal) sounds. Subsequent mappings expanded upon Kowzan's in various ways, including taking reception and offstage contexts into account, and distinguishing between different types of codification, such as Keir Elam's "theatrical," "cultural" and "dramatic" codes and subcodes, which he maps across twelve categories (*Semiotics* 51–6). But attempts to apply these taxonomical exercises to the practical analysis of theatrical performances or dramatic texts, such as Elam's 18-column, 21-page "dramatological score" of the first 79 lines of *Hamlet* (*Semiotics* 168–89), have proven to be virtually inscrutable, and certainly useless for practitioners. As Fernand de Toro has recently argued, "this segmentation," this attempt "to establish clear, controllable, classifiable, and stable units [...] rapidly proved inadequate, particularly when the attempt was to determine the minimal units of communication," and particularly when it was "carried out independently of its cultural and social context" (110). Such classificatory systems, moreover, are also easily aligned with a kind of subjugating power/knowledge that subtends colonialism, imperialism, and other forms of domination (Foucault, *Power/Knowledge*). They were met, for the most part, with scorn by theatre artists, particularly in the English-speaking world.

Much of this later work did nevertheless also produce and develop concepts and approaches that have been extremely useful in performance analysis, in particular by moving writing about the theatre beyond sophisticated gossip, pop-psychology, and literary impressionism to something much more precise, and by shifting the vocabulary of some rehearsal halls, at least, in similar ways. Chief among these concepts and approaches have been tools for the analysis of "character"; of language; of story, plot, and action; of time; of space; of *mise en scène*; and of performance text. Each of these is worth considering on its own.

Character

"Character" is a problematic word for scholars of theatre and performance – and perhaps not problematic enough for many practitioners – largely because of the baggage it carries from the Euro-American tradition as it exists outside of the theatre. Indeed, one of the central, though not often articulated, reasons for the division between theatre and performance in recent years has had to do with an attempt on the part of the latter to escape the idea that actors play, and people have, consistent, individual, and coherent "characters" in the dominant understandings of the term as they emerge from 19th-century European psychology, fiction, and morality (in which people "*have* [good or bad] character," or are understood to be "people of character") – understandings that have been reified in the dominant Hollywood film tradition and in television drama. One of the major contributions of a structuralist approach to the study of theatre and performance has been to move it beyond the kinds of character analysis that has often, in academic and journalistic criticism, in rehearsal halls, and in secondary school assignments, resembled the amateur psychoanalysis or ethical assessment of fictional figures as if they were "real people."

Such understandings have often seemed foreign, quaint, or naïve to scholars and practitioners from outside of the western tradition. Within the European context a different approach to character in theatre began with the Russian formalist Vladimir Propp (1895–1970), the French philosopher Étienne Souriau (1892–1979), and the Lithuanian A.J. Greimas (1917–92) of the Paris School of Semiotics. Propp did not study theatre as such, but his 1928 book, *Morphology of the Folktale*, undertook the structural analysis of Russian folktales according to the "act spheres" (he identifies seven) of their "dramatis personae." Souriau, in his 1959 book *Les Deux Cent Mille Situations Dramatique* (The 200,000 Dramatic Situations), identifies six similar "functions." Building on Propp's work, Greimas in his 1966 book *Structural Semantics* proposed an "*actantial*" model that associates "acteurs" with particular narrative actions or forces, rather than with psychological motivations or objectives. Importantly, for Greimas "acteurs" included not only characters, but also animals, things, the weather, or even abstractions, any of which can exert pressure on the action. The most thorough application to drama and theatre of the actantial model has been carried out by Anne Ubersfeld, in her 1978 three-volume book *Lire le théâtre* (the first volume of which was translated in 1999 as *Reading Theatre*).

The actantial model is, as Ubersfeld concedes, "incontestably a summary approach" (62). It can occasionally seem rigid, taxonomic, and prescriptive, and it tends to inscribe oppositional binaries between subject and object, sender and receiver, hero and villain, helper and opponent, and so on. In all of these ways the model betrays a certain Eurocentrism. It also tends to betray its roots in the analysis of narrative, adapting somewhat awkwardly to the stage. Nevertheless, the model usefully articulates the fundamental principle that character, as Ubersfeld puts it, is "the locus of *functions* and no longer [...] a substance-copy of a human being" (72, emphasis in original), and as such it is useful for understanding theatrical forms beyond those of western naturalism with its emphasis on delving the depths of human nature and motivation. In the actantial model performers, human and otherwise, *do* things rather than *have* characteristics and motivations. Following this, I consider the stage to be populated with what I think of as "dramatic postulates" – "what-if" propositions, rather than simply characters, and this way of thinking can be extremely helpful for those engaged in theatrical devising, which often involves free-ranging exploration and privileges sites, images, props, and actions over character and story.

Each dramatic postulate exerts a range of magnetic attractions and repulsions within what Martin Esslin calls "the field of drama," and each exerts its own narrative and performative force. The analysis of a fundamentally naturalistic play or performance might involve considering, for example, what forces Nora in *A Doll House* brings into play among many others within the fictional world of the representation, rather than why she behaves the way she does according to the psychological analysis of cause-and-effect motivations that are often based on "back stories" invented by actors or critics. In "postdramatic" plays such as Heiner Müller's *Hamletmachine* (Figure 2.1) where the actors speak stage directions and the relationship between actor and text is uncertain – or indeed in any play that focuses on the materiality of text, or in which the script resists attributing lines to individual speakers (as in the landscape plays of Gertrude Stein, or in Sarah Kane's *4.48 Psychosis)* – actantial analysis is rewarded with clear understandings of the forces at play that constitute the performance's complex orchestration of tension, suspension, complication, and release, but that elude traditional character-based analysis. But actantial analysis can fruitfully be applied to many plays outside of the character-driven western naturalist tradition, plays such as *Chocolate Woman Dreams the*

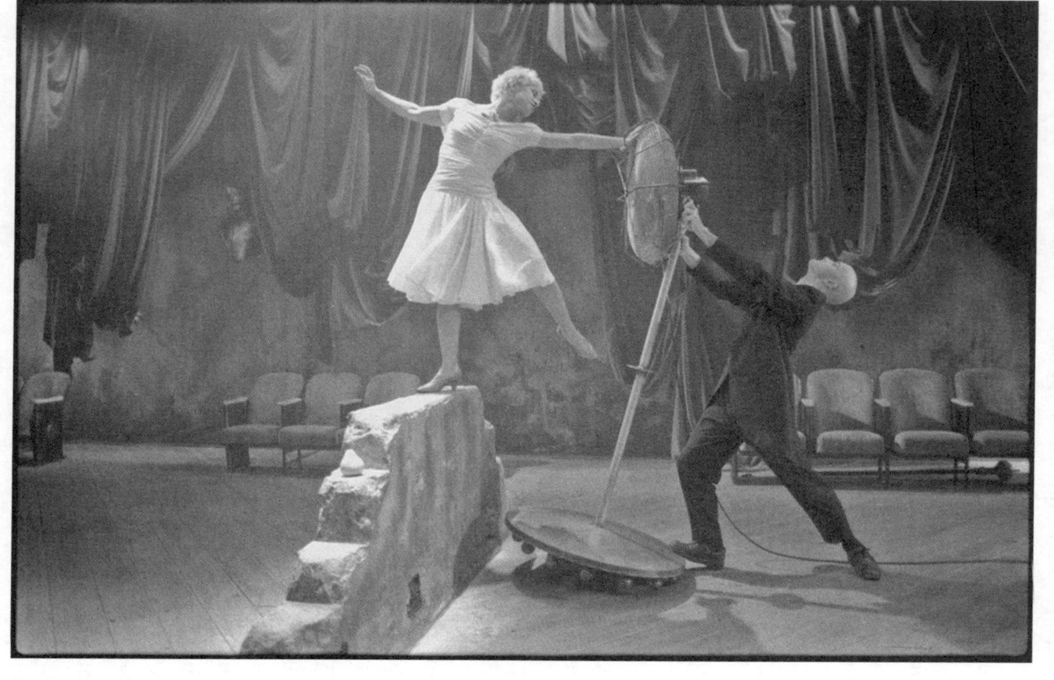

Figure 2.1 **Johanne Madore and Rodrigue Proteau in the 1987 Carbone 14 production of Heiner Müller's *Hamletmachine* in Montreal, dir. Gilles Maheu**

Source: Photo by Yves Dubé.

Milky Way, where the central performer is acted upon by four female figures from Guna cosmology, each embodying forces that bring her safely home, but none requiring psychological justification.

Language

The "actantial" approach to the analysis of character and other "*acteurs*" is complemented by what has become known as the "performative" turn in the semiotics of drama and theatre (see Elam, *Semiotics* 142–53, "Much Ado"; De Marinis *Semiotics* 150–7), which draws on the work of John Searle and J.L Austin to consider language on the stage less as simply *descriptive* or *declarative* than as *performative*, less as simply *representing* an action than as *performing* one. Instances of speech as action occur whenever an utterance promises, threatens, warns, commits, constitutes, denies, declares, offers, offends, accuses, appoints, affirms, sentences, marries, baptizes, and so on. But virtually every utterance can be understood to have some element or degree of performative force insofar as all utterances have elements of *assertion* or *persuasion*. Outside of western technologies of representation, speech, and in particular prayer and invocation, has always been understood to have powerful, even potentially dangerous performative qualities, especially when it invokes or implicates ancestral or spiritual worlds.

Neither Austin nor Searle was talking about theatre; in fact Austin explicitly indicates that a speech act will be "in a peculiar way hollow if said by an actor on a stage" (Austin 22), because actors are not authorized to perform the acts, do not "really mean" what they say. But it is clear that *within* the fictional world each act of speaking *does* something: it changes the relationship between the characters, between the characters and the action. When these speech acts are taken together to form a play's dialogue, they can be understood to *constitute* the dramatic action: they move things forward.

And as De Marinis notes, onstage dialogue also "acts" on the audience outside of the world of the fiction, or as Austin puts it, "produce[s] certain consequential effects upon the feelings, thoughts, and actions of the audience" (De Marinis *Semiotics* 56; Austin 101). Indeed, Luigi Pirandello has called dramatic dialogue "spoken action," and for the makers of theatre it is always a good idea to consider, not simply what a line of dialogue or a unit of text says or tells us, but also what it *does*. But speech acts are not all that constitute a play's action.

Story, plot, and action

Story, plot, and action are what actants (human or otherwise) enact, the force fields within which "dramatic postulates" function. For the purposes of this book, story (also known as *fabula*) is understood as a raw chronological sequencing of events, action as what *happens* or what is *done* (usually involving change), and plot as how it's all put together. Most semiotic analyses of drama and theatre, emerging on the one hand from linguistics and on the other from narratology (the study of narrative), focus to a considerable extent on the story that is "told" at the expense of the actions that are performed, and because they also emerge from Structuralism they focus on plot as the organization of the story. They focus on what Elaine Aston and George Savona call "the transformation of story into plot" (10). Much of this work, beginning with Veltruský's observation that the formal divisions of units of action into acts and scenes is "a matter of convention" (*Drama* 82), consists of analyses of such conventions (the three-act structure, the five-act structure, the "French scene" – in which a new scene begins whenever a character enters or exits the stage).

Some of this work takes on a distinctly prescriptive feel, as theorists try to determine how to construct a "good play." Work that focuses on action tends to define it by way of intentionality. Summarizing the philosophical theory of action,

Keir Elam describes the conditions necessary for the performance of an action as follows: "there is a being, conscious of his [sic] doings, who intentionally brings about a change of some kind, to some end, in a given context" – and, Elam adds, to a given purpose (*Semiotics* 109). This is a peculiarly teleological (end-driven) understanding of what constitutes action, and it is useful primarily for theatrical works that concern themselves with cause-and-effect sequences involving the representation of successful or failed human projects. It works far less well for postmodern, poststructuralist, postdramatic, or devised work-in-progress, or for culturally specific or intercultural performances such as *Chocolate Woman Dreams the Milky Way* that are neither mimetic nor linear.

It may be useful, however, to consider the structuring of theatre and performance as something that, unique to the arts, happens in both time and space, as is suggested by the naming of the two units into which plays are traditionally divided: *acts* (which happen over time) and *scenes* (which occupy space). Structure is something that is crafted by playwrights, directors, and dramaturges (who are explicitly charged with focusing on structure in new play development), and it serves directly to shape the impact and meaning of a performance. Performances don't simply "have" a structure, but are crafted in space and time by practicing artists and audiences, and they are an essential part of meaning production, reinforcing or undermining conscious thematics.

Time

Theatre and performance "take place" in time; that is, they employ temporal sequencing and duration to communicate with an audience that comes together with the performers for a specific period in what is generally known as "real time." Within that duration – proverbially "the two hours traffic of the stage" – the timing of the dramatic action can be organized in whatever way is purposeful, communicating through sequencing, duration, tempo, rhythm, and so on. While stories begin with an initiating event and move consecutively through to an end, plots often rearrange chronology, beginning, perhaps, *in medias res* (in the middle of things), or even at the end, perhaps including flashbacks, or skipping over periods in which "nothing happens" – and some plots indeed organize actions that do not constitute stories in any recognizable sense.

Many plays from *Oedipus Rex* to *A Doll House* turn on the revelation of actions that precede those depicted on the stage. Arthur Schnitzler's 1897 play *La Ronde* uses a kind of relay structure, in which one character only from each scene carries on into the next, temporal "development" imitating the round dance after which the play is named. *Same Time Next Year,* by Bernard Slade, involves two characters, married to others, meeting once a year for twenty-four years for an affair, the "action" of the play primarily involving their discussion of what happens between their meetings. One recent award-winning Canadian play, Colleen Murphy's *The December Man,* begins at the end and moves chronologically backward to the story's beginning. African American Ntozake Shange's *for coloured girls who have considered suicide/ when the rainbow is enuf* has no single story or central character and no clear indicators of temporality; rather it lyrically orchestrates the bodies of seven Black women dressed in different colours who begin in isolation, fragmentation, and distress and move toward community, ultimately assembling the rainbow of the play's title.

Each of these and many other structures shape and are shaped by what the plays or performances are setting out to do, and what meanings they are attempting to convey. In the case of *Oedipus,* the focus is on consequences; in the case of *A Doll House,* on realizations; and in the case of *The December Man* (which deals with the so-called "Montreal massacre," in which thirteen engineering students and one staff member were murdered because they were women) – or virtually any work that begins with the end of the story – the focus is not on "what happens next?" but on "why did this happen?" or even "how could this possibly have happened?" And in the case of *for coloured girls* the focus is on assembling a community of minoritized women within something that might be understood as mythical time: non-linear, non-historical, cyclical (Eliade, *Myth of Reality*; *Myth of the Eternal*).

Semioticians have found various ways of discussing and analysing temporality in the theatre that are useful for artists orchestrating performances and scholars and artists analysing them. Elam identifies four "temporal levels" in the theatre, not including "actual performance time" (the time of the encounter between the audience and the performers): *discourse time*, the fictional "now" of the action and enunciation – the "present" in which speech happens; *plot time*, the order in which events are shown or reported; *chronological time*, the order in which the events reported would have occurred; and *historical time*, the historical period from which the events are drawn, which is moved forward to constitute the "now" of the fiction (Elam *Semiotics* 105–7). These distinctions are analytically useful, particularly in clarifying the dramatic present (discourse time) as the moment in which performative *action* happens and discoveries and transformations occur. They are perhaps particularly useful for practitioners, who need to discover ways of marking, clarifying, and distinguishing different temporal registers and to be sensitive to the temporal, durational, and transformational experience of audiences.

While Elam brackets off "actual performance time," Anne Ubersfeld identifies this as one of theatre's "two distinct temporalities," arguing that it is the relationship between "the time it takes for a performance to be completed" and "the time pertaining to the represented action" that constitutes "*theatrical time*" (126). This formulation is useful in distinguishing between theatre (in which the represented action is almost inevitably already completed in the past, to be re-enacted on stage in the present) and performance (which aspires to happen fully in the present). It is also analytically useful for its acknowledgement of the rhythms of the work, and for its focus on audience experience in the moment of reception and the audience's role in constructing meaning in "real time."

One of the difficulties about time for semioticians is that, while it can be represented (through verbal indicators, the presence of clocks and sundials and so on), time *itself* is non-representational: "time is, by its very nature, outside mimesis," as Ubersfeld says (134). Time in the theatre often tends to function as an organizational principle (much in the way it does in music through tempos, time signatures, and structural divisions into bars, phrases, movements, and so on), and as such, in addition to the sheer phenomenological effect of its immediate rhythms and durations (as in the "slow-motion" work of an artist such as Robert Wilson), it can employ structural principles derived from such things as the rhythms of nature in a 24-hour or annual cycle in much the way that ceremonies, rituals, and communities structure themselves. Literary structuralists such as Northrop Frye and C.L. Barber have made much of such patterns in individual works by artists such as Shakespeare and in the structuring of dramatic genres and entire canons. Indeed, in his *Anatomy of Criticism* Frye categorizes the entire literary and dramatic canon in four seasonal parts: the mythos of spring (comedy), the mythos of summer (romance), the mythos of autumn (tragedy) and the mythos of winter (irony, or satire) (163–239). This cyclical (vs progressive) understanding of time is similar to that of many of the Indigenous peoples of the world, for whom past and future only exist as functions of an ongoing and eternal present, and for whom specific narratives are not unique, but serve as instances of larger, ongoing cultural stories.

Space

Stories are not the only things that structure and are structured by performances, which are primarily constituted by *action(s)*. Indeed, a performance can take place, as in much performance art and postdramatic theatre, without a story, except insofar as audiences themselves often construct stories out of what they see. But performance cannot occur without some form of action, and actions quite literally "take place" – they occur in space as well as time. As many performance artists and theorists have argued, action is not merely mimetic (as in Aristotle's definition of tragedy as "the imitation of an action" (12)), nor is it merely representational, in the semiotic sense in which a signifier represents a signified, or a sign stands in for a "real world" referent. There are times, or ways of seeing, in which an action is best considered phenomenologically, as something to which human consciousness, at least initially, responds directly, viscerally, and unreflectively without the intermediary of meaning or interpretation. Nevertheless, actions feed meaning systems, and however they are intended, they tend ultimately to be "understood," or "read" by audiences as meaningful.

Theatrical action is also relational, in that it carves out spaces between performers and between spectators and performers, and these spatial relationships are charged with meaning. Proximity or distance and the movement through space are central to meaning-making in the theatre, as are the vertical and horizontal axes of the spaces of performance and reception, the arrangement of actors and audiences into groups, the arrangement of the auditorium, the stage, and the performers in ways that direct the audience's gaze. "Blocking" in the theatre (the arrangement and movement of actors in space) is used to produce tension, reveal relationships of power, relative status, distance, or intimacy as actors group themselves together, stand apart, invade one another's personal space, or organize themselves in dynamic or static, comfortable or tense relationships to one another, the set, and the furnishings. When Hamlet typically stands downstage right, silent and dressed in black in Act 1, scene 2 of Shakespeare's play as the colourfully-dressed court upstage left celebrates his mother's wedding, we know all we need to know about his situation long before he speaks his line, "oh that this too, too sullied flesh would melt" (I.2.129). When Krogstad quietly invades the Helmer's comfortable middle-class home in the second act of *A Doll House*, the threat he wields is palpable. When Stanley Kowalski typically invades the personal space of his sister-in-law, Blanche Dubois, early in Tennessee Williams' *A Streetcar Named Desire*, the atmosphere immediately becomes charged.

Theatre and performance semiotics has much to learn from proxemics, a term coined by social anthropologist Edward T. Hall in 1963 to refer to the study of spatial (or territorial) relationships. Audiences can read a great deal about the relationships between characters, their level of interpersonal comfort or intimacy, their relative and shifting status (see Johnstone), their degrees of power or authority, by the ways, including posture, gesture, and movement, in which they occupy space. This includes, analytically, paying attention to different cultural codings of spatial relationships, and expanding the spectrum of what Hall identifies as intimate (touching, embracing), personal (close friends, family), social (acquaintances) and public space – this last presumably including the public address of the theatre and the most frequent relationship between the audience and the stage. But not always. Attending a mega-musical involving crashing chandeliers or landing helicopters – or attending one of Max Reinhardt's outdoor spectacles or those at Berlin's 3500-seat Grosses Schauspielhaus ("the theatre of the five thousand") in the 1920s (see Styan) – involves a very particular kind of spectatorship. It is an experience of a very different kind from, for example, the intimate cross-cultural one of sitting knee-to-knee as solo audience at *BIOBOXES: Artifacting Human Experience* (Figure 2.2), a production by Vancouver's Theatre Replacement in which the stage sits on the shoulders of solo actors from different cultures, and individual audience members successively visiting the six "box stages" decide which language they would like to listen

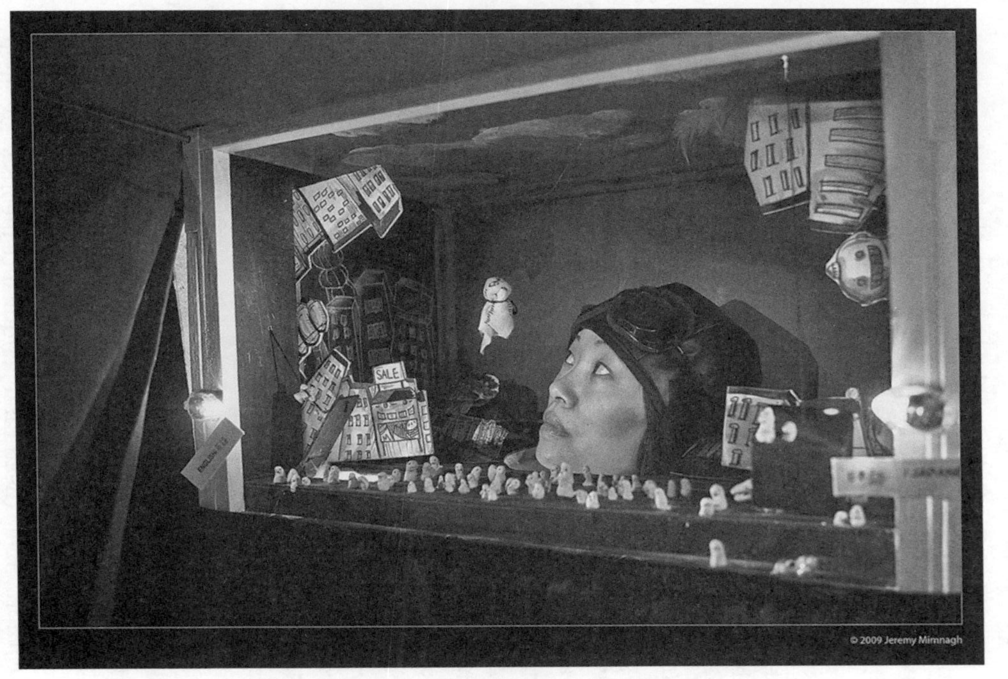

Figure 2.2 Cindy Mochizuki in Theatre Replacement's *BIOBOXES: Artifacting Human Experience*, dir. James Long and Maiko Bae Yamamoto
Source: Photo by Jeremy Mimnagh.

in (the actors change languages at the flick of a switch) and worry about where to position their hands or whether their breath is fresh (see Kim).

Spatial relationships apply to more than interpersonal and intercultural relationships between and among bodies in space. They also have to do with the spatial arrangement of things. In addition to the functions of stage objects identified by Ubersfeld – to serve both as concrete presences and as "figures," iconic, indexical, and metaphorical (122–4) – Andrew Sofer points to their movement and use in space. These, he argues, are what define them as props (as opposed to set pieces and furnishings, whose semiotic significance is largely static, at least within scenes). In *The Stage Life of Props* Sofer's case studies include the Eucharist wafer in the medieval theatre, the bloody handkerchief on the Elizabethan stage, the skull in Jacobean theatre, the fan in Restoration and early-18th-century comedy, and the gun on the modern stage. In each case, the prop is understood as a "mobile physical object" (20). Props are not just *things* (though their thingness has its own uses); they are also, like bodies, spatial and temporal *signifiers*, whose movement through space and time is tracked by audiences and productive of meaning. As Sofer argues, "a prop is an object that goes on a journey; hence props trace spatial trajectories and create temporal narratives as they track through a given performance," and these are "dimensions that allow the object to mean in performance" (2).

In recent years there has been what Elinor Fuchs and Una Chaudhuri call a "spatial turn" (2) in theatre studies. Theatre scholars have drawn on the insights of cultural and other geographers' discussion of space not as something given, empty, or "absolute," but as a set of social relationships that is *produced*. Some theatre and performance theorists have used these new geographical understandings of space and place to find ways of analysing work that resists classical readings rooted in mimetic narrative. Dean Wilcox, for example, in a 2003 essay on "Ambient Space," develops an approach that brings together the work on space and place of geographer Yi-Fu Tuan (place is space endowed with value) with that of philosopher Edward Casey (space becomes place when it is inhabited) in order to examine 20th-century modernist and postmodernist performances from John Cage to the Bauhaus to Samuel Beckett to Richard Foreman, where space is less important for its representational than its organizational qualities – and this is still more true of site-specific performances in which the place of performance "presents itself" (Lehmann 152), and can be considered a co-creator of the action. Other theatre scholars consider "social space," in Henri Lefebvre's three-part classification, to consist of spatial *practice* (competencies in traversing and negotiating space within a particular social formation), *representations of space* (built environments – including theatres – that spatialize social order and social power), and *representational spaces* (oppositional or "underground" codings of space, including those of art) (Lefebvre 33).

Explicating these classifications, theatre historian Michal Kobialka has usefully identified *spatial practice* as "perceived," *representations of space* as "conceived," and *representational spaces* as "lived" (559). Lefebvre's concept of representational spaces resonates with what anthropologist and performance studies progenitor Victor Turner (1920–83) had earlier called the "liminoid" (in-between) spaces where art, play, and performance can generate social change, and with what Michel Foucault called "heterotopic" space (*Order* xv–xxiv; "Of Other Spaces"), glossed by Kevin Hetherington as "spaces of alternate [social] ordering" (viii). None of these conceptualizations is expressly semiotic in approach, but each addresses issues of meaning production and social change, including those having to do with how sign systems and therefore meaning change over time.

Some of the most important work by theatre scholars grappling with "places of performance" (Carlson, *Places*), and the spaces that performance constitutes, has had considerable significance for the understanding of the production of meaning since the 1990s. Marvin Carlson kick-started a minor industry when he published *Places of Performance: The Semiotics of Theatre Architecture* in 1989, primarily because he "read" (semiotically), not only the architecture of theatre buildings, as his subtitle suggests, but also the location of performance within cities and even, in his opening chapter, "the city [itself] as theatre" (14–37). This work has been followed by extensive studies of the ways in which cities perform, and are performed by, their occupants and visitors alike (see Garner, "Urban"; Hopkins, Orr, and Solga), or the ways in which "city stages" are shaped by material conditions best understood through the lenses of political economy, urban planning, and physical or quantitative as well as cultural geography (see McKinnie).

Carlson is perhaps at his most compelling in his discussion of the medieval city as contestable urban space for the staging of religious, civic, and royal power (14–21). And it is also the study of medieval theatre that has produced one of the most generative conceptualizations of stage space to date: Robert Weimann's distinction between the *locus* and *platea*, introduced in his 1978 book, *Shakespeare and the Popular Tradition in Theatre*, and developed further in *Author's Pen and Actor's Voice*, two decades later.

Weimann finds on medieval and early modern stages a productive tension between, on the one hand, *loci* – specific representational (or mimetic) spaces that participate in the play's *fabula* and are occupied by the play's characters; and, on the other hand, *platea* – non-representational, unlocalized public space that is occupied and shared by the actors and the audience, is contestable, and is very much part of the non-mimetic moment of performance. In the medieval and early modern theatre the *loci* were assigned to the powerful, but the *platea* was the subversive space of devils, clowns, fools, and ordinary folk, who ran among or enjoyed special relationships with audiences (particularly the so-called "groundlings," who enjoyed the audience spaces closest to them). The *platea* was often the forestage, where intimacies and alliances between the actors and the tradespersons, apprentices, and *hoi poloi* were shared.

Weimann's schema has implications throughout the history of theatre, and it kicks in whenever direct address, the breaking of the so-called fourth wall, or other metatheatrical devices are employed. Tom in Tennessee Williams's classic *The Glass Menagerie* moves from *platea* to *locus* as he shifts from narrating to representing his family and his younger self. The "Stage Manager" in Thornton Wilder's *Our Town* occupies a shifting *platea* as he metatheatrically introduces, characterizes, and reflects upon the play's various characters in their respective *loci* in the fictional town of Grover's Corners. But always in the theatre there is the tension between the "then" of the represented story and the "now" of its representation, between the story and the storytelling, between narrative and performance, and this tension is the interpretative space where meaning is negotiated.

Weimann's analysis of staging practices resonates intriguingly with Michel de Certeau's distinction in *The Practice of Everyday Life* between place – the fixed *loci* from which the powerful deploy *strategy*, and space – the shifting grounds (*platea*) upon which the marginalized, colonized, or otherwise disempowered, exercise *tactics* (guerrilla-style) in response (xix–xx, 34–39). De Certeau introduces these distinctions in the same book in which his famous chapter "Walking in the City" appears, a key essay "poised between poetry and semiotics" (During 151) in which he discusses the ways in which ordinary folk negotiate their individual, agential, and tactical routes at ground level through a city planned in the abstract – strategically – as if from above. Performance studies scholarship has productively taken on the combined challenges of Weimann and de Certeau. D.J. Hopkins begins his 2000 book, *City/Stage/Globe* the same way de Certeau opens "Walking in the City," with the view from the twin towers of the former World Trade Centre in Manhattan, from which the city planners' grids were clearly legible. He proceeds to demonstrate how such a reading of the city "from above" as representational (and therefore semiotic) space emerged in the early modern period, replacing the street-level, tactical experience of the medieval city as performed and contestable public space.

An interest in variously contestable public space drives the work of a number of scholars who have followed Carlson. David Wiles, in his 2003 book, *A Short History of Western Theatre Space*, takes a multifaceted approach to conceptualizing theatrical space that considers power relations inflected in seven types of performance space over time: "sacred space" (temples, cathedrals, altars, and other spaces set apart from the quotidian); "processional space" (through which performance, performers, and participants move); "public space" (squares, piazzas, marketplaces, and hubs); "sympotic space" (banquet halls, cafés, bars, and music halls where the performance is not the only thing consumed); "the cosmic circle" (theatrical spaces that at once reflect Platonist metaphysics and the ancient "circle of society"); "the cave" (or "cube," into which the individual spectator peers at shadows and reflections as through a fourth wall); and finally "the empty space" (that holy grail of modernist practitioners, the myth that any space can be one of sheer, ahistorical potentiality).

Postcolonialist theatre scholar Joanne Tompkins, in her 2006 book, *Unsettling Space*, treats the contestability of theatrical space quite differently, though she, too, deals with power relations, including those between settler/invader and Aboriginal populations whose enactments encode different understandings of space. Tompkins considers what Una Chaudhuri calls modern theatre's "geopathology": "the double-edged problem of place and place as a problem" (Chaudhuri, *Staging Place* 53), analysing spatiality (particularly spatial instability) as a productive tool of *un*settlement in postcolonial settler/invader societies, in Tompkins' case Australia. "When space, place, and landscape are staged in stark geopathological terms, they look back to history, but they also contribute to the development of a different future" (163).

The book-length study that explicitly employs a semiotic approach and has significantly shaped subsequent scholarship on theatrical space, including my own (Knowles, *Reading* 66–91), is Gay McAuley's 1999 *Space in Performance: Making Meaning in the Theatre*. McAuley opens her book with an epigraph – "the theatre is space" – from Anne Ubersfeld, whose semiotic work influences her study profoundly, and she structures her book around a development from Ubersfeld's and fellow semiotician Patrice Pavis's taxonomies of spatial function in the theatre (Ubersfeld 94–125; Pavis, *Dictionary* 344–5). Indeed McAuley's introductory taxonomy – considering the "social reality," "the physical/fictional relationship," "location and fiction," "textual space," and "thematic space" (25) – is characteristic of the many taxonomies of 1980s and 90s theatre semiotics. What McAuley does with these in application, however, is a revelation.

In discussing physical space McAuley pays close analytical attention not only to the usual suspects – the theatre building, the stage (which she calls "presentational space"), and the audience-stage relationship – but also to "audience space," including such things as stairways and corridors, cloakrooms, bars and restaurants, and box office, as well as "practitioner space" backstage and, most notably, rehearsal halls, which may be off-site but which are where a production takes its shape and takes on much of its meaning. These rooms leave indelible traces and need to be considered carefully by practitioners, historians, and theorists alike. Subsequent chapters consider with equal nuance the placement and movement of bodies in performance; the relationship between space and the ways in which acts and scenes are structured, mapped, and scored by directors, dramaturges, and actors; the tracking, use, shifting meanings, and spatial semiotics of props, real and unreal, present or absent, used or misused in rehearsal and in performance; the spatial dimensions of language and text, including their physical "placement" in performance; and the spectatorial experience of space by people who "go" to the theatre, where they engage in complex ways with the processes of looking and exchanging looks across the varying distances between themselves as well as between themselves and the actors.

Discussing Ubersfeld, McAuley argues in her introduction for an understanding of "dramatic space" as something that involves "the dramatic geography of the action as a whole and is indeed a means of conceptualizing the whole action or narrative content of the play" (19). Spatial arrangement, taken together with that other organizing principle discussed above, temporal sequencing, as combined means of "conceptualizing the whole action," leads to another key concept in the semiotic analysis of theatre and performance: what has come to be known as the *mise-en-scène*.

Mise en scène

Patrice Pavis, who has perhaps contributed more than anyone else to a theorization of the concept, defines the *mise-en-scène* as "the bringing together or confrontation, in a given space and time, of different signifying systems, for an audience" ("From Text" 86). If plot is the purview of the playwright, deviser, and dramaturge, *mise-en-scène* is usually understood to be that of the director, in collaboration with the entire creative team and, ultimately, with audiences. The concept of the *mise-en-scène* emerged only after the emergence of the director (in French, "*metteur-en-scène*") as an independent artist or *auteur* in the late 19th century in Europe. But as Pavis says, "though the director has not always existed, there has always been a *mise-en-scène*" (*Languages* 137). And although Pavis rightly points out that the concept of the *mise-en-scène* emerged from and is "localized in" the west (*Analyzing* 303), the term is capacious enough to be applicable to organizing principles behind a broad range of theatre and performance practices emerging from most cultures and intercultures.

Mise-en-scène does not refer to the staging "of" a dramatic text or scenario, the "realizing" of a such a text's potential, or (in semiotic terms) the translation of textual signs into the signs of performance. Nor is the *mise-en-scène* something that is always explicitly articulated; it is best understood as a process rather than a blueprint for a final product. It is "a signifying *activity* founded in meaning-making by inter-relating heterogeneous elements," sign systems that employ different codes (*Languages* 137, emphasis added). Pavis uses the examples of dramatic text, which is based in a linguistic system that is fundamentally symbolic (in Peirce's sense) and therefore arbitrary, as opposed to performance, which is primarily iconic, based on a resemblance between a sign and its referent. "Speaking semiologically," he says, "linguistic arbitrariness and stage iconicity cannot be reconciled or mutually cancelled out" (*Languages* 143.) They can, however, be brought together dialectically, either in a kind of synthesis or in productive tension, and this is the function of the *mise-en-scène* and in practice the role of the director. This assemblage, moreover, extends beyond the broad categories of text and performance to the languages of movement and gesture, vocal expression, set, light, and costume design, sound and music, some of which are spatial, some temporal, some spatio-temporal, but all of which employ distinctive coding systems brought together polyphonically on the stage. There is, of course, always a different weighing of these modes of communication, each *mise-en-scène* foregrounding, highlighting, blending, contrasting, and harmonizing elements differently, and it is these differences on which semiotic analyses of performance need to focus for scholars and practitioners alike.

One of the great advantages of the concept of the *mise-en-scène* is its abandoning of the hopeless search for a basic unit of stage communication, the elusive integrated sign, in favour of something Pavis elsewhere calls an "integrated semiology" (*Analyzing* 323). A focus on the *mise-en-scène* also has the potential to reverse the trend I have described in theatre semiotics in the 1970s and 80s towards increasing segmentation. Rather than dismantling, fragmenting, or segmenting a performance, Pavis argues, "the spectator needs to perceive and thus describe the totality, or at least an ensemble, of systems that are themselves already structured and organized, that is, what is understood nowadays by the term *mise-en-scène*" (*Analyzing* 8).

Performance text

If *mise-en-scène* is a structural system that functions as the glue that holds the various sign-systems at work in a performance together, the performance text – another key, if more contentious concept – is what is read by audiences and analysts. The performance text is quite distinct from the dramatic text (the literary artefact that often gets confused with "the play"), or from the script (which is one of the many contributors to, or traces of, the performance), in that it concerns itself with all aspects of performance even when there are no words involved, but "textualizes" them in order that they can be "read." Pavis argues that "the performance text is the mise-en-scène considered not as an empirical object, but as an abstract system, an organized ensemble of signs" (*Analyzing* 8–9). He usefully refers to "the *writing* of the performance text *by* the *mise en scène*" (*Languages* 158, emphasis added).

If Pavis has been the key figure in the theorization of the *mise-en-scène,* Marco de Marinis, in 1982 (translated into English in 1993), has most explicitly and controversially theorized the performance text. In a project that begins by "abandon[ing] the search for the definition of a language of theater" (*Semiotics* 2), de Marinis turns away from the *mise-en-scène* toward the construction of the performance text, understood as a more capacious entity. For de Marinis, the performance text is distinct not only from the dramatic text, but also from the theatrical performance. The latter, he argues, "involves theater as a material object, the phenomenal field that is immediately available to perception" (48). The theatrical performance, that is, is the event that the audience encounters and to which it immediately (phenomenologically) responds. "Performance text," according to de Marinis, "refers instead to a *theoretical object* [...], the theoretical model of an aspect [the textual aspect] of the observable performance phenomenon" (48, emphasis in original). The performance text, for de Marinis, is "an explanatory principle" constructed through the process of analysis rather than merely the pre-existing object of such analysis, and it *constitutes* all of the various elements of performance *as textual* (though De Marinis is careful to indicate that "reading" a performance as text "does not exhaust all aspects of theater" (1)). Like the *mise-en-scène,* the performance text is "characterized by a double heterogeneity, in its expressive media as well as its codes" (61) by "'ephemeral' presence, lack of persistence, [...] multiplicity of codes, multidimensionality" and its organization into a coherent entity that de Marinis calls "the textual structure of performance" (83) (which might be understood as the equivalent, on the reception side, of the *mise-en-scène*).

De Marinis's formulation has been criticized by Michael Sidnell for dematerializing the performance text as merely a mental construction and thereby contributing to the mounting frustration with semiotics in the 1990s and beyond, particularly among practitioners (Sidnell 16). But the move has its advantages in acknowledging pragmatically that, because of the ephemerality of performance and the multiplicity of positions and conditions of its reception, analysis can rarely consider the theatrical performance "itself." Indeed, most writing about theatre deals with reconstructions of various kinds, at worst analysing the writer's own notes and memories, at best the material remains of productions housed in archives or recorded on film and video. As a "theoretical object," however, the performance text systematizes the processes of reconstruction and analysis while also taking full account of the role of the spectator in the production of meaning.

Audiences and spectatorship

The final chapter of de Marinis's *The Semiotics of Performance* is devoted to "The Spectator's Task" (158–88) in decoding the performance text. Reception, as decoding, has always been at least implicit in the semiotic analysis of drama and theatre, but the turn from considering the spectator as simply "the target of theatrical manipulation," in de Marinis's words, to considering her as "the coproducer of the performance, the active creator of its meanings" (158) – apart from the key contributions of Brecht as both practitioner and theorist – emerges only in the 1980s and 90s.

As a Marxist, Brecht was primarily interested in the role of theatre in the activation of audiences for the purposes of producing social change. Brecht critiqued the soporific role that he felt had been assigned to audiences in the dramatic or illusionistic theatre since Aristotle. His "epic theatre," in both theory and practice, was dedicated to developing an interactive relationship between the audience and the stage, positioning characters, actors, and audiences within history, eschewing universalist discourses and presenting the possibility of change. Through devices such as the defamiliarization effect (*verfremdungseffekt*, Brecht 192), the "not-but" (25, discussed in Chapter 1), historicization (190), and the gestus (86, 198, a moment at which the social attitudes encoded in the *mise-en-scène* crystalize and become visible), epic theatre aims to activate spectators' awareness and assessment of social and discursive ideologies that inform the production. Brecht's plays are full of "gestic" moments, the most frequently cited being Mother Courage's silent scream at her own complicit role in the loss of her son in *Mother Courage and Her Children*, figuring at once her anguish and her need for survival while projecting the social cause of both: war makes people act in contemptible ways. But there are gestic moments throughout the history of theatre, ranging from the moment in Shakespeare's *Richard II* when the crown "freezes" briefly between Richard and Bolingbroke before it passes to the usurper; to the arrival of the corpse of the central character's son, Olunde, in Nigerian playwright Wole Soyinka's *Death and the King's Horseman,* at which point the relationship between the spiritual and quotidian, traditional and contemporary worlds of the play tragically crystalize; to nodal points in the most naturalistic of plays. Even in the paradigmatic realist drama, Strindberg's *Miss Julie,* the servant Jean's cleaning of the Count's boots – especially when he cleans them using his own spit, as in Mike Figgis's 1999 film version of the play – functions as a gestic moment *par excellence,* crystalizing class relations and their impact on and implications for individuals. Each of these and other such moments demands a response, an interpretation that is actively engaged, not simply with character, but with the social significance of the action. As Susan Bennett argues, Brecht called for the production and reception of theatre as "a co-operative venture," producing Louis Althusser's "new spectator, an actor who starts where the performance ends" (Bennett 30; Althusser, *For Marx* 151).

Writing in 1982 and virtually reintroducing the study of reception in the theatre, De Marinis brings together approaches to reception from literary theory, and proposes the idea of a "Model Spectator" (*Semiotics* 166; see also De Marinis, "Dramaturgy"), based on Umberto Eco's "model reader" ("The Role" 7), one who is inscribed in, implied by, and indeed instituted in the performance text, whose encyclopaedic knowledge creates the conditions for "*complete communication* [to] be fulfilled" (167, emphasis in original). Acknowledging the difference between a hypothetical Model Spectator and a "real" one, de Marinis proceeds to examine various kinds and degrees of "theatrical competence" (171) that shape reception as well as production. De Marinis defines theatrical competence as "the *sum total of knowledge, rules, and skills that account for the ability to produce performance texts as well as the ability to understand them*" (171, emphasis in original). Fundamental examples of such competencies include understanding, in a proscenium arrangement, the convention that within the fictional world of a naturalist performance there is an invisible "fourth wall" between the stage and the audience, or in theatres of various styles and periods understanding that asides cannot be overheard by other characters on the stage or that soliloquies provide windows into the unspoken thoughts of the characters who deliver them.

The relevance of a spectator's competence extends beyond the basic and crucial familiarity with and capacity to "read" the theatrical codes and conventions that constitute performance *as* performance in any given culture or period. Such competencies also involve what Keir Elam (drawing on Julia Kristeva, see Chapter 1) calls the "intertextual" (Elam, *Semiotics* 83): the capacity to recognize and understand the traces of other voices, discourses, texts, cultural texts, and performances necessarily embedded in the text, scenery, acting, directorial style, and so on, as well as the capacity to respond to broader extra-textual cultural references. Theatrical examples include the knowledge of the generic and stylistic conventions of tragedy, comedy, kabuki, or Kathakali. Still more complex examples of more specialized knowledge include the capacity to recognize intertextual references and citations of previous work (recognizing, for example, the cast and action of Shakespeare's *Hamlet* in Tom Stoppard's *Rosencrantz and Guildenstern Are Dead*) or even knowledge of the *corpus* of work by specific writers and directors without which a given production might be simply baffling or annoying (understanding the role, for example, of the strings that inexplicably crisscross the stage and auditorium in the work of experimental American director Richard Foreman).

The more experience the spectator has, and the more deeply she is embedded in or closely aligned with the production's theatrical and cultural codes, the closer she approaches de Marinis's conception of model spectatorship, but also the more likely she is to be bored – a negotiation of which practitioners need to be particularly and constantly aware. As Elam notes, part of the pleasure of spectatorship, when it does not simply involve the passive consumption of familiar theatrical comfort food, is in learning the codes, including assisting in the establishment, however provisionally, of new ones (*Semiotics* 85). And as Elaine Aston and George Savona point out, "the history of any period of theatre involves the history of the education of the spectator in particular habits of spectatorship" (160). This interplay between the familiar and the new or different has driven the constant search for theatrical innovation throughout theatre history, and has also been at the root of healthy and unhealthy intercultural experiments. On the other hand, rarely has new work from outside dominant cultural traditions failed to be met with incredulity on the part of some spectators or reviewers who felt themselves to be disenfranchised: "that was all well and good, but how am I supposed to *understand* it?"

Three of the most generative concepts in reception studies, borrowed from the reader response theories of Wolfgang Iser, Stanley Fish, and Hans Robert Jauss, respectively, have been that of textual "blanks," or "gaps," that of the "interpretative community," and especially that of the spectator's "horizon of expectations." Each of these has been applied to the theatre by Marvin Carlson and Susan Bennett, most extensively by the latter in her now standard study, *Theatre Audiences: A Theory of Production and Reception.* Iser posits the idea that a text controls successful reading, but does so through the use of gaps, or blanks, which draw the reader in and allow her to contribute imaginatively to the completion of the work (Iser, *The Act* 168–9). Anne Ubersfeld uses the same word – "gaps" – to describe openings in the dramatic text that are filled in performance (29), but it might be more useful to consider gaps left within performances themselves. Bennett points to intermissions as examples, but perhaps the use of offstage spaces or even sounds is more generative. Whenever an actor exits through an onstage doorway to enter an offstage world that is left to the audience's imaginations, spectators are asked to fill in gaps, to imagine for themselves what the offstage kitchen, bedroom, backyard, or town might look and feel like. Action, too, frequently takes place offstage and is the more powerful for being left to the audience's imagination. Powerful examples of this are the sound of the door slamming that concludes *A Doll House*, the gunshot heard "*from within*" at the end of *Hedda Gabler* (Ibsen 777), or the climactic actions of Greek tragedies as reported by messengers.

Iser labelled his gap-filling reader *The Implied Reader*, which clarifies the degree to which he felt the text controls the reader's performance. The concept is not unrelated to Eco's Model Reader, or to Stanley Fish's concept of the "interpretative community," which, however, looks less to textual mechanisms that contain and constrain readerly meaning production than to socially defined communities, "made up of those who share interpretative strategies not for reading (in the conventional sense) but for writing texts, for constituting their properties and assigning their intentions" (Fish 171). For Fish, reading strategies *precede* texts, indeed *constitute* (or "write") them, and are primarily socially conditioned. As Bennett suggests, however (43), Fish is remarkably unconcerned with most of the identity characteristics that one might associate with communities: class, politics, gender, sexuality, ethnicity, race, or ability. Indeed, Fish's categories of linguistic and literary competence and semantic knowledge risk (re)inscribing hierarchies of interpretation within the academy or among other specialized readers, in spite of his apparently liberatory agenda.

What might it mean to consider theatre audiences as "interpretative communities"? Theatre audiences, after all, might be understood more readily to share theatrical and cultural competence than the readers of books, given that they gather to view a performance, for possibly similar reasons, at the same place and time, preconditioned, perhaps, by similar local knowledges. Audiences for the premiere of Métis playwright Marie Clements's *The Unnatural and Accidental Women*, for example, assembled at Vancouver's Firehall Theatre, just blocks from where the femicides that are the play's subject took place, knowing that the murderer had recently been released on parole. This specialized local knowledge might valuably be understood to constitute those audiences as interpretative communities of a very particular kind.

On the other hand, what would it mean to consider audiences, particularly in the culturally heterogeneous cities of the 21st century, as intersections of *different* interpretative communities, experiencing as much "psychic polyphony" (Carlson, *Theatre Semiotics* 95) because of their diverse reading strategies as they do because of the "heterogeneity of expressive media" interacting on the stage? As Dennis Kennedy says, "audiences are pluralistic [...], gender, class, ethnicity, sexuality, education, health and age all condition reception" (188).

Insofar as the audience for a specific performance *can* be understood to constitute a relatively stable interpretative community, it is perhaps because it has been constituted *as* an audience to share a range of "horizons of expectations," as Jauss calls them. Jauss considers three factors that create such expectations: genre, intertextuality, and "the opposition between fiction and reality" (Jauss 25). Each of these obtains in the reception of theatrical works, where the last has particular resonance given iconicity (resemblance between signifier and signified, sign and referent) as theatre's dominant signifying mode.

There are many crucial ways in which horizons of expectation for performances, and therefore audience responses, can be shaped, both consciously and unconsciously. These include, in addition to those cited by Jauss: the theatre's or theatre company's history, mandate, and target audience; the reputation and profile of the artists; publicity and review discourse, posters, programs, and advertising; the façade, architecture, and front-of-house spaces, facilities, and amenities of the performance space; ticket pricing and procedures; audience-stage relationships; the auditorium and seating arrangements; the neighbourhood in which the space is located; access and modes of transportation; and the historical and cultural moment of reception, including recent events, local, national and international politics, popular culture, and the prevailing *Weltanschauung* (world view). An audience attending the Comédie-Française – "the theatre of Molière," France's centuries-old state theatre in the 18th century Salle Richelieu in Paris's first arrondissement, and the Parisian home of French classical theatre – comes with significantly different expectations from one attending a production by the lesbian troupe Split Britches at the WOW café, a woman's performance venue four floors above street level in New York's Lower East Side. Each spectator arrives prepared to "read" the production through particular lenses, and to produce significantly different meanings.

A show advertised as a "laugh riot," featuring the star of a popular television sit-com and presented at a comedy club with a well-stocked and comfortable lobby bar or even table service, has a good chance of meeting its target audience. But Marvin Carlson retells the cautionary tale of a notable production that failed to meet the expectations it had generated. The American premiere of Samuel Beckett's existentialist/absurdist classic, *Waiting for Godot*, at the 1956 reopening of the Coconut Grove Playhouse, a former movie theatre in Miami, was billed as "The Laugh Sensation of Two Continents" (qtd in Carlson, *Theatre Semiotics* 21). It featured well-known comic actors Bert Lahr and Tom Ewell (recent stars of *Harvey* and *The Seven-Year Itch*, respectively). The audience left in droves. Most productions fall between these poles, as theatres attempt to push the boundaries of audience expectation, while audiences hope to be surprised and challenged within the limits of their own comfort zones. And some audiences are more tractable than others: opera audiences are notoriously recalcitrant; off-off

Broadway tends to attract a more iconoclastic crowd. Targeted community audiences for culturally specific work often afford it a level of understanding that more general or mainstream audiences don't.

In recent years, since the publication of the first edition of Bennett's *Theatre Audiences*, scholars have tended to write less about audiences and more about spectators and spectatorship (though Helen Freshwater's 2009 *Theatre & Audience* is an exception to the rule). I suspect that this is partly because "the audience" refers to a collectivity, while "the spectator" connotes something more individualistic and atomized, indicative of a more fractured or pluralistic (or postmodern) understanding of reception. It may also be the case that, since the English language publication of Guy Debord's *The Society of the Spectacle* and Jean Baudrillard's *Simulacra and Simulation*, both in 1994, scholars have been preoccupied by spectatorship as a defining and all-pervasive feature of contemporary life not limited to the staging of shows or performances. Finally, since the ascendancy of performance studies in the academy and the advent of globalization and global touring in "the entertainment industries" (one thinks, for example, of the work of Robert Lepage, Yukio Ninagawa, and Robert Wilson), there has been much less emphasis on text, or indeed on representation, in semiotic and other studies of theatre and performance. It is true that de Marinis's translator chose to discuss "the model *spectator*" ("spettatore" in Italian can be translated as spectator, audience member, witness, or onlooker), but de Marinis is clearly talking about the *reader* of a "performance text." Scholars such as Dennis Kennedy in his 2009 book *The Spectator and the Spectacle* and influential French philosopher Jacques Rancière in *The Emancipated Spectator*, first published in French in 2008 and translated into English in 2009, have concerned themselves with spectatorship as an independent and primary activity rather than a secondary, parasitic, or even interpretative one that is dictated or controlled by the spectacle itself. Rancière's "emancipated spectator" is an active, individual subject, not the member of an audience-as-community; his project is to "challenge the opposition between viewing and acting": "viewing," he argues, "is also an action" (13), and "being a spectator is not some passive condition that we should transform into activity. It is our normal situation" (17). Ultimately, this version of spectatorship is concerned with the limits of (semiotic) representation itself: for Rancière, sometimes a spectacle is just a spectacle.

3 Disseminations

In 2008 Yana Meerzon edited a special issue of the journal *Semiotica* that set out "to reevaluate the relevance and the possibilities of semiotic approaches to performance and drama analysis, theatre criticism and performance studies today" (1). In her invitation to contributors, she asked them to consider, as a starting point, Keir Elam's "'Post'-Script" to his 2002 second edition of *The Semiotics of Drama and Theatre*, in which Elam noted that, while semiotics – "in its structuralist guise" (194) – "has long lost its cultural pre-eminence" (193), it nevertheless subtends many of the theoretical approaches that appear to have superseded it. Elam finds in many of these approaches what he calls "a closet semiotics" (195), and traces the afterlife of semiotics in work that is haunted by the semiotic approach, but dare not, as it were, speak its name.

Elam focuses his "post-script" around various "posts," including the post-structuralist, organized into four categories: reactions to the semiotic approach (in the British press and British and American professional theatre, largely negative); institutionalizations (in guides, dictionaries, and academic institutions); extensions (in late-coming translations and new publications, notably feminist ones); and disseminations, which he refers to as "the 'post'-semiotic diaspora of the sign" (215).

It is this last category that I wish to pursue here in a way that Elam doesn't, considering what I think of as "critical intersections" between semiotics and other practices, many of which claim to have superseded it but which, as Sylvija Jestrović argues, with Elam, are "grounded in a suppressed semiotic approach" (Jestrović 95). I have addressed many of the critiques of semiotics and continuities between semiotics and one branch of poststructuralist thought, deconstruction, in Chapter 1 – and indeed, as time passes the continuities seem increasingly prominent, to the degree that the two are now frequently lumped together: "Semiotics," as Janelle Reinelt summarizes it, "provides a means of articulating the production of meaning-in-performance, while deconstruction provides purpose or motive (the dismantling of usually operative logics of interpretation" ("Introduction" 113). Other disseminations and intersections can usefully be divided into two types, which Reinelt refers to as "libidinal investments" and "materiality" ("Performance" 8), and which I call the *phenomenological* (including theories of affect and cognition) and the *materialist* (including feminist, new historicist, cultural materialist, postcolonialist, and intercultural).

Phenomenology and its doubles

Phenomenology itself (understood as the study of the direct encounter of human consciousness with the phenomenal world or, in theatre studies, with what's on stage) has sometimes been seen as the anti-representational polar opposite of semiotics, but the two approaches now tend to be seen as complementary, "different aspects that often occur simultaneously in the process of creation and reception necessitating a combined methodological approach" (Jestrović 95). As we've seen in Chapter 2, above, this observation is not entirely new; indeed, Jan Mukařovský of the Prague School semioticians resisted the view that everything ostended to the view of the audience was totally subsumed in its sign value, and in more recent years theatre phenomenologist Bert States interrupted the rush to semiotic analysis to make the same point. According to States, "The problem with semiotics is that in addressing theater as a system of codes it necessarily dissects the perceptual impression theater makes on the spectator. [...] When the critic posits a division in the art image, he [sic] may be saying something about language, but he is no longer talking about art, or at least about the affective power of art" (*Great Reckonings* 7). It is "the affective power" of art that I address in this section.

The phenomenology of theatre is partly about the "showness" of the show (and the "thingness" of the things in it), and partly about the perception of the spectator and her direct, purportedly unmediated encounter with it – though this lack of mediation is a theoretical ideal rather than a practical possibility. Initially at least it is less about meaning than about the experience of a human subject encountering its object. As such, phenomenology can be understood to claim *precedence*, insofar as it claims, or tries, to account for that encounter as it happens (as if) for the first time. As Patrice Pavis argues, while this encounter with "thingness" – the body-to-body encounter of the audience with the performance's materiality – should be sustained as long as possible in order to allow the "libidinal" aesthetic experience to be fully absorbed and the consciousness to be "impressed" by that materiality (*Analyzing* 19), that same materiality, together with its "eventness," inevitably "evaporates into an immaterial signified" (18). When Nora frenetically rehearses the tarantella in the second act of Ibsen's *A Doll House*, the spectator may initially be startled into seeing the character, and the dance, afresh, as if for the first time, in a way that seems to exceed interpretation. Eventually, however, the experience dwindles into meaning (or what Nicholas Ridout calls "the grave that is semiotics" (104)), though it is manifestly read differently by each of the characters on stage and by the audience. What is clear is that phenomenology and semiology, in the first instance, agree about the materiality of the signifier.

As a critical or analytical approach, Bert O. States has described phenomenology as an *attitude* ("the phenomenological attitude") that is fundamentally personal, accepting, impressionist, and *mimetic* – even tautological. As an *attitude*, then, it is distinct from what Fernando de Toro calls "semiotic *thinking*" (123, emphasis added), which is fundamentally social, analytical, and translational, abstracting (and therefore distancing) meaning from experience and translating it into the terms of another discourse. As such – as attitude versus thought – the two approaches may be understood to be less hostile than complementary, or even to be sequential technologies for describing the theatrical event, in which (as Pavis suggests) encounter precedes analysis. As Joseph Roach says, "working together [phenomenology and semiotics] provide a kind of binocular vision: phenomenology sees the stage as direct experience ('everything is nothing but itself'); semiotics sees it as wholly significative ('everything is something else')" (354).

What phenomenology brings to semiotics is a combination of immediacy, an awareness of actors and audience members as perceiving bodies (see Garner, *Bodied Spaces* 49), and a valuing of the thingness of things on stage (including bodies), that in taking on their roles as signs are always nevertheless capable of exceeding their sign value. The physiological thrill of the immediate phenomenological encounter of perceiving bodies has provided the impetus for an "affective turn" in theatre and performance as in other studies (Clough). Erin Hurley distinguishes among three types of "feeling" in the theatre: affect ("immediate," "uncontrollable," "skin-level" "muscular and/or glandular responses" (13)); emotion ("an act of interpretation of bodily responses" (19)); and mood ("background states that raise or lower our susceptibility to emotional stimuli" (21, quoting Evans 68)). *Affect* is the thrill that rushes through the body when, in Hurley's example, the high-wire artist at Cirque du Soleil's 2007 show *KOOZÄ* appears to slip and (almost!) fall ("our hearts race, our pupils dilate, and goose pimples rise" (Hurley 12)). (This affect, unfortunately, is now heightened in the wake of actual accidents at Cirque shows in Las Vegas in June and November of 2013 that caused the death of one performer and the hospitalization of another.) *Mood* is the feeling produced by any anticipatory drum rolls, silences, or dramatic light cues that may prepare us for the moment. *Emotion* is the identification of our physiological responses as having added up to excitement, or fear.

These concepts are useful in themselves as tools for understanding how audiences respond physically and (then) emotionally to action in the theatre; they are also extremely useful in understanding the *structuring* of the theatrical event through inciting and releasing tension, elongating and compressing time, and shaping the sequencing of events through successive affective states. Hurley also provides some important conceptual tools that serve to address the analysis of feeling in the theatre, chiefly the idea of "feeling labour" ("theatre's solicitation, management, and display of feelings" (4)) and "feeling technologies" ("mechanisms that do something with feeling" (28)).

Clearly affect, in Hurley's sense, is closest to the immediacy that phenomenology most values and that most sets it apart from semiotics. Emotion, however, inflects the semiotic in interesting ways, partly because it is explicitly interpretative ("I reacted like that because I care about this"), and partly because, like meanings, emotions are relational (20). "Emotion" Hurley argues, "takes us out of ourselves by taking subjective experiences and inserting them into a social context of meaning and relation" (21). Hurley's technologies of feeling – language, plot, scenography, acting, character – are also the (complementary) technologies of meaning production. At its best, affect theory can bring to semiotics the capacity to mediate between the intensely personal and the social, and can motivate the study of meaning by demonstrating that, and perhaps why, it matters to us.

Hurley spends a significant portion of her short book worrying away at a subject that underpins her enterprise but about which she is clearly ambivalent and which is unacknowledged in the book's index: the relationship between affect theory and cognitive science (though the index does list *neuro*science, an important distinction that I suspect is the source of her ambivalence). "Cognitive Science" is a field and an administrative unit in the academy dominated by philosophers and psychologists that is sometimes regarded with scepticism by neuro- and other "hard" scientists. This is also an area that the contributors to Meerzon's special Theatre and Drama issue of *Semiotica* advocate putting into conversation with a newly interdisciplinary semiotics, and again, it has links to phenomenology, with which, "with its emphasis on empathic and emotional engagement" it has much in common (McConachie and Hart 6). Michael Sidnell cites Neal Bruss on the material, organic, "bio-semiotic" origins of psychoanalytic theory (Sidnell 28; Bruss) and applies these to role playing in theatre practice. Semiotics also has a once and future branch in medical diagnosis and an on-going life in biological science, as the wide influence of the work of biosemiotician Jakob von Uexküll would suggest, and as an important recent book on semiotic biology edited by Claus Emmeche and Kalevi Kull and subtitled "Life is the Action of Signs" demonstrates. Its introduction acknowledges "the relatedness of linguistic (Saussurean) semiotics and biological structuralism" (Kull, Emmeche, and Hoffmeyer 8), and its contributors draw heavily on Peircean semiotics throughout.

This semiotic turn in the biological sciences would seem to call into question the claims by some proponents of the cognitive turn in theatre studies that science somehow disproves the errors of semiotics (and with it poststructuralism) as "unscientific" (McConachie, *Theatre* 57), failing to pass the test of "empirical falsifiability" (McConachie, "Falsifiable"). According to some, cognitive science has "proven" that meaning *precedes* language in the individual brain rather than being constituted by and through language, and that therefore direct, psychophysical connections can be made between the bodies of performers and those of spectators, unmediated by conditioning or social context. Claims are also made that cognitive science has proven false Saussure's dictum that the relationship between the material signifier and signified as mental image is arbitrary, though I would suggest that all it has demonstrated is iconicity: some signs resemble their referents. And indeed theatre semiotician Eli Rozik has drawn significantly on the discoveries of cognitive neuroscience around "metaphoric thinking" and the brain's capacity to think imagistically as ways of exploring the workings of stage iconicity (Rozik, *Metaphoric* 3–4 and *passim*).

In the excesses of its still early days, some proponents of a cognitive science approach to theatre studies seem to replicate the excessive claims of the early days of semiotics itself, which Saussure initially proposed as a "science *which studies the role of signs as part of social life*" (Saussure 15, emphasis in original), offering an objective correction to the "errors" of earlier linguistic studies (4). At its worst, this scholarship promotes caricatures of a semiotics which purportedly "direct[s] scholars to narrow spectatorial activity to the reading of signs on stage," activity it "unscientifically" assumes to be "primarily engaged in trying to understand the symbolic meanings of a theatrical performance" (McConachie *Theatre* 57).

Semiotics, except perhaps in some imagined purist form, makes no such assumptions. But at its best, and when it's not proselytizing – and its antisemiotic moment seems fortunately to have passed – a cognitive science approach has contributed to an expanded agenda for semiotic analysis and its understanding of "the making of meaning" (McConachie and Hart 6). What Rozik proposes in his reconsideration of iconicity in the *Semiotica* special issue is iconicity's redefinition in terms of "imagistic thinking" ("Homogeneous" 188). This is entirely compatible with and informed by the insights of cognitive science concerning brain imaging. It is compatible, in particular, with cognitive scientist Gerald Edelman's and cognitive philosopher Mark Johnson's understandings of embodied and non-representational mental "concepts" (McConachie, *Engaging*; Edelman and Tononi 104; Johnson 157). If States is right in his reading of neurobiologist Jean-Pierre Changeaux that art, including the arts of the theatre, can be understood to give concrete material existence to the brain's imagings, then the brain's production of "mental objects" can be understood and studied as a primary source (rather than a simple receiver or processor) of theatrical representations: signs (States *Pleasure* 20, cited in Hurley 31–2). As Shakespeare's Theseus has it in *A Midsummer Night's Dream,* "as imagination bodies forth/ The forms of things unknown, the poet's pen/Turns them into shapes, and gives to aery nothing/A local habitation and a name" (V.1.14–17). The study of *how* the imagination "bodies forth/The forms of things unknown" can only support the semiotic study of how those forms-become-shapes produce theatrical meaning.

The application of cognitive science to theatre studies has been overwhelmingly dominated by theatre scholars' response to the celebrated discovery by Vittorio Gallese in 1996 of "mirror neurons" in macaque monkeys (see Gallese et al.; Gallese) and the subsequent confirmation that such neurons also exist in humans. What Gallese and his partners demonstrated was that the observation of others engaged in a purposeful activity triggers the same response in the brain of observers as it would if they were themselves engaged in that activity. This physical (neuronal) participation in observed activity has been understood to corroborate and increase our understanding of what has been a key concept in theatre studies for centuries: empathy (or empathic identification – the capacity "to sense the emotions and read the intentions of another" (McConachie, *Theatre* 16)). And like emotion, empathy is essential to our engagement with those theatrical signs known as characters, and is perhaps one of the things that keeps us sufficiently engaged to (want to) read the signs. Indeed, it's unclear – and the experiment has not been undertaken in controlled conditions – whether an empathic response to a dramatic character relies on the spectator's prior reading of them *as* characters engaged in "purposeful activity" that is fictional (or is purposeful for the fictional character in a different way than it is for the actor who performs the activities with the purpose of representing characters).

Empathy is, moreover, a problematic concept, in the theatre as elsewhere, particularly because of its potential to "eat" its other, appropriating and ultimately negating the other's experience by making it one's own. Dominick LaCapra warns against "unchecked identification, vicarious experience, and surrogate victimhood" (40), while Sarah Ahmed characterizes empathy as "a 'wish feeling,' in which subjects 'feel' something other than what another feels in the very moment of imagining they could feel what another feels" (30). Bryoni Trezise parses Ahmed's argument as "intimating that at the heart of empathy there exists an important, but often overlooked, discordance between an intention to enact it and the actuality of performing it." "Perhaps," she suggests, "empathy might always already be diverting itself from its own central cause" (216). Finally, both Ahmed and Susan Leigh Foster relate empathy to the cultural production of "the stranger" as "other," both historically and in the contemporary context of globalization and multiculturalism. Ahmed argues that "emotions may involve 'being moved' for some precisely by fixing others as 'having' certain characteristics. The circulation of objects of emotion involves the transformation of others into objects of feeling," and thereby objectifies them (11). Affect, then, is potentially complicit with representation in the cultural production of the (stereotyped) "other." When audiences for over forty years empathized with "Indian" characters in plays such as John Augustus Stone's 1829 *Metamora: The Last of the Wampanoags*, as noble remnants of an inevitably dying race, they were no closer to understanding, and they did actual Native Americans no favours.

Another concept emerging from the cognitive approach to theatre studies is that of "conceptual blending," which is understood to be the basis of role playing and therefore, again, central to the operations of the theatre. As applied to theatre, conceptual blending refers to the double consciousness of spectators who are able to keep in mind (as it were) the simultaneous, sequential, or oscillating, but always variable perception of an "actor/character" rather than simply to suspend their disbelief in the fictional representation. Bruce McConachie cites as an example a spectator watching Marlon Brando play Stanley Kowalksi in *A Streetcar Named Desire* and being more aware of Brando the actor than of Tennessee Williams's fictional character; however, when the same spectator sees an unknown actor in the role, the character may come to the forefront of her perception (*Engaging* 44). This is a useful corrective to a simplified semiotic approach that engages with representation as one dimensional: "Brando" in performance is always an actor *and* a signifier of multiple resonances (his previous roles, his public persona), arguably even a "brand" in the marketing sense.

Perhaps the most important contribution of the application of cognitive science to theatre studies is the confirmation (the idea is not new) that "the mind is embodied" (McConachie, *Theatre* 1), that the visceral, kinaesthetic responses of the embodied subject are among the primary technologies of meaning production. Semiotics understood as the study of the production of meaning in the theatre can certainly benefit from the reminder that meaning, thought, and cognition are muscular, visceral, and (emotionally) engaged, not simply the provenance of detached, "slit-eyed analysts" (Berger 159). But Susan Leigh Foster argues in *Choreographing Empathy*, a book that is heavily influenced by cognitive studies' discovery of mirror neurons and its conclusions about empathetic responses, this does not mean that meanings are not socially produced or are not produced differently in different cultures and different historical periods (126–73).

Phenomenology, affect theory, and cognitive science, then, can make significant contributions to semiotics by reminding performance analysts that meaning is the multifaceted product of thought, emotion, and physiological response working together. But each of these approaches is also susceptible to abuse. What all of these approaches share is the risk of privileging the individual and psychological over the social and historical, while also reifying the idea of a universal human subject. Each, therefore, risks being called upon to serve a reactionary ideology that effaces difference. Even as sophisticated a theorist as States has a tendency to use a universal first-person plural, to ask questions such as "who does not?" and "who has not?," to make statements such as "one has always" ("Phenomenological" 34), and to talk about "*the* [universal human] mind" and "*the* mode of thought and expression the mind *naturally* adopts" ("Phenomenological" 35, emphasis added). This tendency is still more pronounced among less careful proponents of a cognitive approach – less careful, perhaps, because they believe themselves to be proponents of an "objective" and universal science. As a corrective to this universalizing tendency, while semiology is forging its interdisciplinary alliances it needs also to collaborate with a range of materialist approaches that share its interest in representation, but not its idealist roots. It needs, that is, to develop a sociosemiotics.

Sociosemiotics

The section of Elam's "'post'-script" on "disseminations" notes that "the chief accusation of post-structuralist criticism towards semiotics has been that of excessive formalism" (216) and an avoidance of any engagement with ideology – a legacy, no doubt, of its roots in structuralist linguistics. And indeed, semiotics in its earliest incarnations was, and was criticized by poststructuralists for being, a fundamentally idealist discourse. But in discussing these politicized critiques, Elam also argues that the "post" in post-structuralism "took on the meaning of going beyond rather than merely doing away with structuralism" (216), not superseding it, but rather "politicizing and relativizing [...] its objectives" (221). Several of the contributors to Meerzon's special issue of *Semiotica* call for flexible interdisciplinary engagement with post-structuralism in its politicized form in feminism, new historicism, cultural materialism, postmodernism, postcolonialism and politicized interculturalism.

Feminist theory

Marvin Carlson notes the close ties between early feminist work in theatre studies and semiotics, citing as a significant step forward for the latter Sue-Ellen Case's argument in *Feminism and Theatre* that cultural encoding – fundamental to semiotic analysis – consists of "the imprint of ideology upon the sign" (Carlson, "Intercultural" 130; Case 116). He argues elsewhere that for Case, Jill Dolan, and "this new [late 1980s] generation" of semioticians, "semiotics was no longer a study of the elements of theatrical communication based on an assumption of objective and value-free selection of signs by the artist, but rather of the way in which the sign thus selected worked to reinforce the dominant ideology or beliefs of their cultural context" ("Semiotics" 21). As I argued in the Introduction to this book, this is how ideology works through recognition and interpellation: when Nora first enters in a typical production of *A Doll House* with long curly hair, wearing a frilly dress, unpacking the shopping, and responding chirpily to being addressed by her husband as "my little lark twittering out there" ("Yes, it is," she replies, completing the play's first lines of dialogue (125–6)), we "recognize" her as a woman. In doing so we are giving our assent to this as an accurate representation of women, and we are thereby hailed into a sex-gender system that tells us that this is what women are like, this is what women are for.

But "by revealing the dynamics of this process," Carlson continues, feminist "semiotics provided the first step toward the development of alternative practices" (20–1) – alternative practices that extended beyond feminism, gender, and queer studies into cultural studies; performance studies; cultural materialist, new historicist, and postcolonial studies; and indeed into any area concerned with representation, particularly the representation of gendered, sexual, or racialized identities. Among such alternative practices for the representation of gender and sexuality are cross dressing, drag, camp, mimicry, queer parody, transgender performance, and what Jose Muñoz calls "disidentification" (working inside of, while nevertheless critiquing, dominant culture). When the young boy playing the heroine, Rosalind, who has been playing the boy, Ganymede, steps forward at the end of Shakespeare's *As You Like It* and promises, "If I were a woman I'd kiss as many of you as had beards that pleased me" (Epilogue 18–19), we are perhaps less securely grounded in dominant gender ideologies. When a drag queen or king exhibits by sheer virtuosity (or sometimes even by clunkiness) the performative nature of all gender roles, we can become positively unmoored. And even in *A Doll House*, when well into the first act Nora confesses her urge to say "to hell and be damned" (141), the seamless representation of her 19th-century femininity begins to unravel; when she exits at the end of the play, slamming the door, the entire sex-gender edifice is shaken.

Carlson also finds in feminist work, including film theory, sophisticated contributions to the semiotics of spectatorship by way of the psychoanalytical theories of Jacques Lacan, whose theories of self-alienation through entry into the (semiotic) "symbolic order" (or "the law of the father") undergird the productive notion of "the male gaze." Laura Mulvey, in an essay on classic Hollywood cinema that has been widely influential in theatre studies, demonstrates the ways in which such a gaze is constituted as male through narcissism (identification with an active male hero who owns the camera position and drives the action) and fetishism (objectification of a passive female figure in moments of decorative spectacle that interrupt the action). In this analysis the female spectator who wishes to enjoy the show is forced to efface her position as woman and assume that of a male viewer.

The concept of the male gaze has developed over the years into considerations of the orientalist gaze, the colonizing gaze, and the objectifying gaze more generally, each of which similarly demands the adoption of a dominant viewing position. It has also issued in the theory and practice of productively resistant strategies such as "staging the gaze" and "returning the gaze," both phrases that have made it into the titles of more than one book (see Freedman, Bannerji). When in *A Doll House* Nora dances the tarantella as the eroticized object of the gaze of her husband, Doctor Rank, and the audience, that gaze is disrupted, triangulated, and problematized by the entry of Mrs Linde and her simple exclamation, "Ah – !" (175). When performance artist Annie Sprinkle, in the "public cervix announcement" portion of her 1991 performance, *Post-porn Modernist,* invited individual spectators, with the help of a flashlight and a speculum, to examine her cervix as she and the rest of the (paying) audience watched, most found this reversal of the gaze unsettling at best, perhaps because, as Nicholas Ridout suggests, it foregrounded a parallel economic relationship between theatre and prostitution as leisure industries (27–8). At least one participant found it "terrifying" ("Annie").

New historicism and cultural materialism

Elam spends much of the "disseminations" section of his "'Post'-Script" on new historicism, which might be regarded as the American branch of cultural materialist discourse practiced in the UK by Catherine Belsey, Jonathan Dollimore, Alan Sinfield and others (see Brannigan, Ryan, Scott Wilson). The new historicist enterprise of the 1980s and 90s led by literary theorist Stephen Greenblatt, much of it centred on the drama of the early modern period, was committed to reading every expressive act within its historical and social context, to "reading" all documents and artefacts as culturally produced and culturally productive "texts." Like cultural materialism, it privileged the social over the individual and the historical over the universal or transcendent, and it has been widely influential in asserting the ways in which creative practice is necessarily embedded in the culture from which it emerges while also serving to *shape* that culture and potentially to change it. Elam finds in new historicism, and in particular in the work of Greenblatt, "an often undeclared or 'closet' semiotics ... that might benefit from greater theoretical explicitness or (self-)awareness" (Elam, *Semiotics* 218). He criticizes the new historicist project for masking its base in "a general semiotic model, namely the principle of similitude and resemblance" (219), and for its lack of reference to performance, but acknowledges that it brought to semiotics a much needed "opening up to the ideological play of power" (220). That is, it raised the question I asked in Chapter 1: *who controls the semiosis,* and in whose interests?

As we have seen, the semiotic study of theatre and performance also tended to focus in its earliest incarnations on language and the dramatic text, after which it expanded to consider performances themselves, the performance text, and the audience. The final step in this expansion, under the influence of new historicist and cultural materialist discourses, moves to consider meaning systems that extend far beyond the performance "itself" to what Marvin Carlson calls "the entire theatre experience" (*Theatre* xiii). Carlson has undertaken much of this work, notably in his 1989 book, *Places of Performance,* where he considers the semiotics of theatre architecture and its relationship to urban planning, analysing medieval cathedrals, Greek amphitheatres, Italian Renaissance palace and palazzo theatres, façade theatres, and others all in relation to the urban environments from which they derived their meanings. And in each case, from the ways in which "narrow and tortuous" streets resisted triumphant displays of royal power during medieval royal entries (10–11) to the deliberate segregation of social classes in the auditoria of 19th-century Europe (149), Carlson demonstrates that these spaces were sites of ideological struggle.

Susan Bennett has considered what she calls the "threshold" (milieu, façade, box office, and program) and "post-performance" experiences (125–39; 163–5), and again, both are, as she argues, "ideologically coded" (126). Bennett has also probed the relationships between the theatrical event and the larger culture, and between production and reception as social processes (86–106; 106–24). There have also been various sophisticated semiotic analyses of framing devices such as applause and curtain calls. Martin Revermann, for example, considers the curtain call to be a threshold phase, where "two modes of semiotization" coincide and collide (193; see also Ridout 161–8), while Baz Kershaw productively examines applause, including curtain calls, as a sign of the increasing "taming of the audience" ("Oh" 141) and their gradual shift since 1945 from patrons to clients to customers. And there are few theatre goers in the English-speaking world, at least, who haven't at one time or another resented the coercive force of extended orchestrated applause or obligatory standing ovations.

In my 2004 book, *Reading the Material Theatre*, I formulate a "materialist semiotics" that brings the semiotics of drama and theatre together with the cultural materialist analyses of representations and with cultural studies analyses of readers as active and independent users of cultural productions. The shared assumption underlying all of this work is that cultural productions, including theatre and performance, neither *contain* meaning nor uni-dimensionally shape behaviour or belief; rather they *produce* meaning through the discursive work of an interpretative community and through the lived, everyday relationship of people with texts, including performance texts. I schematize the relationship among conditions of production, performance text, and conditions of reception as the political unconscious of a production – the meaning it produces independently of conscious coding – working through the mutually constitutive poles of a meaning-producing triangle:

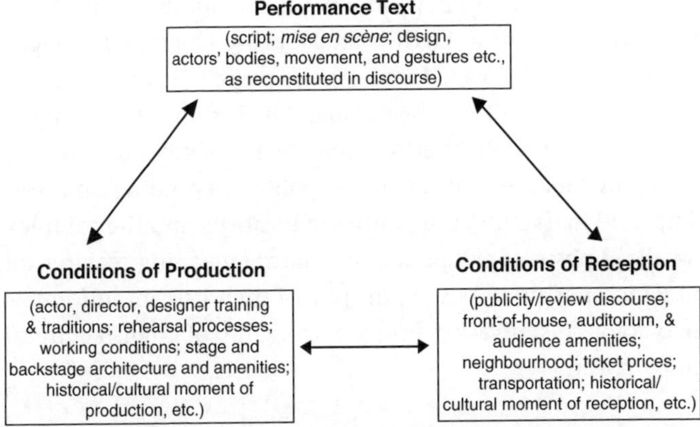

(Knowles, *Reading* 19)

Each pole of the triangle is constituted by multiple ideologically coded systems working in consort or in tension with one another. Meaning in a given performance situation – the social and cultural work done by the performance, its performativity, and its force – is the effect of all of these systems, and each pole of the interpretative triangle, working dynamically and relationally together. The degree to which reception is (pre) determined by theatrically and culturally dominant contexts and mechanisms, and the degree to which resistant meanings are available (or to which meaning systems are open to a free play of signification or contained to predetermined meanings) depends upon the amount of productive tension and slippage within and among the corners. But at the connotative (associative) level each element in each corner of the triangle, and each of the corners taken together, encodes its own "myth," in Barthes's sense, and its own ideologies. It is the bringing of these myths and ideologies together in productive tension that potentially denaturalizes them, makes them visible, and enters them into "intersemiotic" negotiation with one another, and it is crucial for theatre artists to be conscious, not only of what they are trying to encode and communicate, but of the ways in which their meanings are shaped and contained by signifiers that extend beyond what they consciously place on the stage. When the English Shakespeare Company brought its production of *The Henrys* (Shakespeare's *Henry IV parts 1 and 2* and *Henry V*) to "the colonies" in Toronto, for example, its avowedly socialist performance text was sabotaged by the company's failure to attend to the politics of funding, sponsorship, and marketing, the politics of location, and the complex localized postcolonial politics of cultural meaning-making, all of which positioned them, in spite of their best intentions, as neo-colonialist invaders firmly in the camp of English cultural imperialism.

Postcolonial and intercultural performance

Perhaps the most urgent call made by the contributors to Meerzon's special issue of *Semiotica* is for semiotics fully to explore cultural difference. Silvija Jestrović, for example, discusses the ways in which "a well-recognized and established semiotic pattern in one culture becomes the means for negotiating the sign-referent relationship in another" (103) and thereby opens up avenues for exploration involving translation studies, multicultural studies, postcolonial studies, and intercultural theatre studies. In the same volume Marvin Carlson, discussing contemporary theatrical interculturalisms (including cultural studies and postcolonialism), calls this "the road not (yet) taken" in semiotic analysis ("Intercultural" 129). Carlson concludes his contribution to the special issue with an urgent plea that semiotics be allowed "the freedom to explore highly intricate and challenging patterns of signification offered by the modern multicultural work, with its constantly shifting configurations of audience, artists, and cultural context" (141).

We saw at the end of Chapter 2 that philosopher Jacques Rancière has challenged the traditional wisdom that theatre constitutes and consolidates audiences as communities that react as one. Increasingly, especially in large "global cities" (the term was coined by Saskia Sassen) where populations are increasingly diverse, theatres attract non-homogeneous audiences, divergent "interpretative communities" with different reading strategies, different theatrical and cultural competencies, and different horizons of expectations, all assembled in the same space, but not necessarily producing the same meanings. And it has been recognized from the beginnings of semiotics as a discipline that sign systems are culturally specific; indeed semiotics has long had a special interest in performance that crosses cultures. One of the initiators and early leaders of the study of intercultural performance, Patrice Pavis, in his influential 1992 volume *Theatre at the Crossroads of Cultures*, follows anthropologist Clifford Geertz in defining culture *as* (among other things) "a signifying system" (Pavis, *Theatre* 8). Pavis launches his study, not out of any interest in cross-cultural communication as such, but for the purposes of renewing the semiotic method of performance analysis:

> What is at stake [he argues] is the possibility of a universal, precise performance analysis and of an adequate notation system. [...]. Instead of looking for further refinement of western performance analysis, we can institute another approach, the study of intercultural theatre, in the hope that it will produce a new way of understanding theatre practice and will thus contribute to promoting a new methodology of performance analysis. (3–4)

If the stage, with its multiplicity of intersecting sign-systems, is an ideal test case for semiotics, the intercultural city, its stages and audiences, with their multiplicity of intersecting interpretative communities, might equally be considered the perfect test for the semiotics of theatre and performance, and perhaps especially for the semiotics of production and reception. It is interesting that the early systematic theorists of intercultural performance were primarily drawn from the ranks of the semioticians, most notably Pavis and Erika Fischer-Lichte ("Staging"; "Theatre").

I have elsewhere traced the history of theatrical interculturalism and its analysis (Knowles, *Theatre),* tracking in the 20th century two key streams: Brecht and the materialists, and Artaud and the universalists, including Jerzy Grotowski, Eugenio Barba, and Peter Brook. It's a fraught history, mostly dominated by charismatic western men shoring up a decadent western tradition by "discovering," appropriating, and decontextualizing eastern and "Other" performance forms. For Brecht this meant "discovering" what he was looking for: a non-naturalistic model for the *verfremdungseffekt* (defamiliarization effect), which he found in the work of Chinese actor Mei Linfang (91–9). For the universalists it meant mining "oriental," African, or Indigenous peoples' ritual and performance forms for their supposed pre-cultural, "pre-expressive," or primitive universalism: the pure "truths" that precede the supposed contaminations and accidentals of culture. "Man [sic]," Grotowski asserts, "precedes difference" (qtd in Marranca 16).

There are others who have disagreed with the universalists, writers for whom difference is itself significant, and for whom it is not immediately apparent that those ways in which the peoples of the world are perceived (usually by dominant cultures) to be fundamentally the same are more important than the ways in which they are, perhaps also fundamentally, different. In this critical tradition, it is significant that many of those in the latter group – including Rustom Bharucha, Biodun Jeyifo, Gautam Dasgupta, Una Chaudhuri ("Future"), and others – come from non-western cultural traditions. For these critics, to deploy a sign or cultural text outside of its cultural context (or to frame it within a foreign sign system) is necessarily to re-signify it in ways that most often do violence to both the sign and the context. For them an "intercultural" production such as French director Ariane Mnouchkine's "Indian" *Twelfth Night* in 1982 was not the rich, resonant, and sensuous evocation of the east that many western critics felt it to be. Indeed, Bharucha felt that its "self-conscious images of a phantasmagoric 'India'" embodied "the worst indulgences of 'orientalism'": "I did not see 'India' in Mnouchkine's spectacle," he writes; "I saw France" (*Theatre* 244; see also *Politics* and "Sombody's").

Analysis of intercultural work has also followed two streams. The earliest systematic model of intercultural communication in the theatre was devised by Pavis as a tool for the analysis of English director Peter Brook's famously problematic adaptation of the sacred Hindu text, *The Mahabharata*. Pavis's famous "hour-glass" model involved a binary division between the source ("other") and target (western) cultures, reifying the west-and-the-rest binary, but accurately modelling the universalists' practices. Pavis's hourglass inscribed a pattern of distillation of source-culture signs to their apparent (pre-cultural) essences, and a subsequent expansion using the semiosis of the target culture. In this process the cultural and artistic "modelling" of the source culture is "adapted" through theatrical production to the artistic and cultural "modelling" of the target culture in order to achieve "readability" at the point of reception in the west (*Theatre* 185). The result is a watered down and distorted version of the original, one that only benefits the (western) producers and often does violence to the (non-western) source cultures. Pavis's hourglass assumed, moreover, a kind of cultural (and therefore semiotic) homogeneity in each of the participating cultures, as well as in the receiving audience.

Pavis's semiotic model was challenged by a second analytical stream, emerging from postcolonial theory, where the primacy of western reception and dominant-culture "readability" was replaced by a concern for the politics of cross-cultural collaboration, and specifically with power relationships and the question of who benefits from such collaboration. The most direct postcolonialist response to the Pavis model came from Jacqueline Lo and Helen Gilbert, whose 2002 article, "Toward a Topography of Cross-Cultural Theatre Praxis," proposed an alternative model, a kind of horizontal hourglass, which represents intercultural exchange as a two-way flow, with both partners considered as sources, while a target culture, the audience, is positioned along a continuum between them into which both cultures feed. The strength of their model, Lo and Gilbert argue, is that it "locates all intercultural activity within an identifiable socio-political context" – but it does not do so for its audience, the "anticipated" but problematically uncharacterized "target culture" (45).

Pavis's concern was for the health of the semiotic method (echoing Saussure's rather astonishing observations that "colonization... transports a language into new environments, and this brings about changes in the language" (Saussure 21) and that "even savages [sic] grasp territorial divergences in linguistic usage" (189). Postcolonialists are more concerned with the contribution of the sign systems of performance to the act of colonization; they focus on the colonized rather than on the languages themselves. Thus Andrzej Wirth, noting "the flow of exchanges" that characterize contemporary intercultural performance, calls for "another model in which the very notion of source and target is invalidated" (Wirth 284), and Rustom Bharucha proposes and practices "*intra*cultural" explorations within India that dislodge the identification of culture with nation-state and prioritize the "interactivity" of different cultures, including cross-cultural collaboration *between* "othered" cultures. He describes, for example, an adaptation of Nigerian Chinua Achebe's novel, *Things Fall Apart* (an already intercultural phrase borrowed from W. B. Yeats and T. S. Eliot), by a cultural group, Ninasam, in a small Hindu village in southern India, in collaboration with a marginalized Siddhi community who had been transplanted as slaves from Africa by the Arabs, Portuguese, and Dutch (*Theatre* 229–32).

Julie Holledge and Joanne Tompkins, on the other hand, focus their analysis on intercultural work by women from non-dominant groups from around the world, employing a materialist approach that focuses less on aesthetics than politics, using a methodology that brings cultural and performance studies into a methodological mix that complicates semiotics' focus on representation. They trace the cultural exchange of Ibsen's *A Doll House* and Sophocles' *Antigone* through Japan, China, Iran, and Argentina; explore the divergent meanings attributed to Korean and Aboriginal women's ritual performances when staged in urban Australia; address different cultural positionings of public and private space in "returning home" plays from Algeria, South Africa, and Ghana; and analyse the female performing body as the site of intercultural encounter, looking at Japanese women's performance in Australia and at solo women performers from Japan and Québec who combine diverse cultural influences in their work.

Christopher Balme, in his 1999 book *Decolonizing the Stage*, shifts attention to theatrical productions by third- and fourth-world communities, again globally, but Balme's approach is explicitly and systematically semiotic. He focuses on "the process whereby culturally heterogeneous signs and codes are merged together," which he calls "theatrical syncretism" (Balme 1). The concept of syncretism is derived from comparative religion, particularly during the colonial period, and it signifies the process by which elements of two or more religions are merged to produce change. It is related to concepts such as créolization or hybridity as used by postcolonial theorists, including Homi Bhabha in *The Location of Culture*, where he argues that "the interstitial passage between fixed identifications opens up the possibility of a cultural hybridity that entertains difference without an assumed or imposed hierarchy" (4).

Some aspects of the show with which I opened this book fit the bill. Monique Mojica's *Chocolate Woman Dreams the Milky*

Way, about the journey home of a lost "Dule Girl" (a woman of the Guna people of coastal Panama), is framed by the weaving together of: the Haudenosaunee (Iroquois) creation story of Sky Woman falling from the heavens to land on turtle's back and create the earth from a retrieved clump of mud; the story of Alice in Wonderland falling down the rabbit hole, filtered through Jefferson Airplane's 1967 song, "White Rabbit"; the Guna story of Olonadili, youngest of the daughters of the stars, who came to earth and was caught by humans; and the Paul Vance and Lee Pockriss song, "Catch a Falling Star," made famous by Perry Como's 1957 recording. The dramaturgical deep structure of this truly syncretic theatre piece, which I will use as a case study in Part II, is based on the textile arts of the women of Guna Yala and the Guna cosmology that those artforms embody.

Balme is concerned with meaning, and his focus is textual, but his version of semiotics is different from that of Pavis, in that it focuses on cultural texts as carriers of meaning that are fully comprehensible only within the culture that produces and uses them. Most importantly, he is concerned with what happens when, in the hands of Indigenous or colonized artists as in the case of *Chocolate Woman Dreams the Milky Way*, Indigenous performance elements are syncretized with the western theatrical tradition as a response to the western tendency to homogenize, to exclude, and to privilege formal, stylistic, racial, or cultural "purity" (Balme 8).

Because Balme concentrates on work produced by Indigenous peoples within their own cultural context in response to colonization rather than on intercultural work produced for western audiences under the synthesizing control of western directors or playwrights (what Esther Kim Lee calls "hegemonic intercultural theatre" (571)), his book invaluably complicates the linearity of Pavis's analysis. His emphasis on language, ritual, orality, and embodiment also complicates western textuality and raises crucial questions not only about the hierarchies of verbal language in intercultural practice but also about the language of the body, issues of translation, and the negotiation of meaning in performance. In his conclusion, however, Balme acknowledges the fundamentally aesthetic nature of much of his inquiry, which avoids until its final pages the question of the portability of the syncretic theatre he examines and the ways in which local conditions of reception frame the possibilities for cross-cultural exchange.

It is the local conditions of reception that interested Susan Bennett when in 1997 she published a revised edition of *Theatre Audiences* with an added chapter on "Spectatorship Across Culture." In outlining her focus on "issues of spectatorship when the theatrical product does not coincide to a substantial degree with the cultural education and practice of the audience" (166), Bennett cogently observes that "it takes one culturally specific spectator [of a culture different from that of the creators] to make an intercultural performance" (171). "The audience," she argues, "is the material evidence of a target culture and the factor of their horizons of expectations becomes heightened in such conditions" (171). Focusing on work such as African American Anna Deavere Smith's *Fires in the Mirror* and *Twilight Los Angeles* that probe cultural conflict, represent different sides in that conflict, and consciously aim to gather together as audiences "people who would not normally be gathered in the same space," Bennett usefully points to the potential for performance to promote dialogue "precisely on the grounds of that diversity" (179). We might extend her insight to work such as Argentinian Canadian Guillermo Verdecchia's *Fronteras Americanas* that uses untranslated Spanish – "for dose of you who want a translation of dat, come and see me after de show" (41) – consciously to divide its audiences between Spanish speakers and members of "de Saxonian community" (40) in order to produce the felt experience of exclusion and minoritization among members of the dominant culture. "Are you a Group?" asks the grotesque Latino stereotype, Facundo Morales Segundo (aka Wideload McKennah).

> Do you know each other? No, well, some of you know de person next to you but collectively, you are strangers. Estrangers in de night. But perhaps by the end of the evening you will have shared an experience. You will have gone through dis show together and it will have created a common bond among you, a common reference point.
>
> That's the theory anyway. That the theatre is valuable because a bunch of strangers come together and share an experience. But is it true? I mean how can you be sharing an experience when you are all (thankfully) different people? You have different jobs, different sexual orientations, different lives, different histories. You are all watching dis show from a different perspective. [...] (53)

It is this valuing and highlighting of difference, I suggest, that is the appropriate work of intercultural performance. This is what Bennett is referring to when she argues that "[i]f intercultural theatre is to extend its own processes and questions into the fields of meaning produced by the spectators, then the compromises and conciliations, as well as the translations, need to find a language in performance – to draw attention to themselves, as it were, and to find their complexity embedded in the receptive processes that the performance stimulates" (200).

The final chapter of Patrice Pavis's 1996 book, *Analyzing Performance* (translated into English in 2003), turns to "the anthropological approach and intercultural analysis" (271) as a kind of synthesis of the psychological and sociological approaches to theatrical reception that he had proposed in his previous two chapters. Pavis first argues that "if the object of an anthropological analysis of performance must be constantly redefined and broadened in order for its cultural complexity to be grasped, we must rethink the existing methodology for analysis, by adapting a 'Western' semiology ('manufactured' in the West) to non-Western traditions and intercultural production." He then introduces "a new notion: that of ethnoscenology" (288). Pavis fails to acknowledge the problematics of a "we" who "must" do the adapting, is presumably western, and is still in control of the discourse, but he proceeds to outline an approach that privileges "parallel series" of signs over minimal units, "energy" over meaning, the concrete over the abstract, the "autonomy of elements" over "hierarchical arrangements," "partial perspectives" over centralization, "differential density" over homogeneity, and syncretism over purity (290–6). His conclusion calls for an "integrated semiology" (314), one that "requires cultural semiotics to observe how a culture or cultures are inscribed in the object described, and how writing itself imprints its mark on this object" (325).

Jane Turner's analysis of Eugenio Barba's intercultural *Ego Faust*, in Meerzon's issue of *Semiotica*, develops and applies Pavis's "ethnoscenological" or "ethnoscenographic" approach, demonstrating ways in which it can serve as "a challenge to the Eurocentric gaze" (143) on which it nevertheless focuses:

> This ethnoscenographic position incorporates both a semiotic and anthropological approach to analysis that enables the spectator/critic to better acknowledge his or her own cultural baggage as well as avoid the tendency to condense or displace any ambiguous or seemingly discrepant aspects of performance. Both Barba's and Pavis's work feeds an ethnoscenographic position that offers the spectator the opportunity of engaging with the experience of a performance event where he or she is not merely the passive receiver but able to participate in a dialogue with culturally diverse performance practices. (Turner 165)

My own short 2010 book, *Theatre & Interculturalism*, does not assume that audiences for intercultural work will be exclusively western, but argues essentially for a kind of "interculturalism-from-below" that bypasses white brokerage and involves solidarities and collaborations across real, acknowledged, and respected material differences. What is needed, I argue, is a model of scholarship that is humble before the dizzying multiplicities of its intercultural objects of study; that is cognisant of the researcher's own positioning and the process of scholarship, from whatever cultures it emerges, as itself necessarily intercultural performance; and that does its homework in terms of attempting to understand cultural and performance forms *in situ*. Further, what is needed is a model of scholarship that understands the multiple performances of difference, local and global, as *processes*, circulations of energy, in which previously marginalized cultures are seen to work *together* rather than *against*, constructing genuine, rhizomatic (non-hierarchical, horizontal), and multiple intercultures that respect difference while building solidarities. These types of collaboration involve resignifying as a process of negotiation across existing cultural formations and sign systems, a performative process of new, diasporic identity formation that forges meaning in studios, on stages, between stages and audiences, and within audiences. In practice these collaborations might employ tools such as: the tactical reappropriation of dominant culture texts (Djanet Sears's *Harlem Duet*, a prequel to Shakespeare's *Othello*, relocates the action to the heart of African-American culture); diasporic transnationalisms working across national borders and not (necessarily) centred in the west (Helen Gilbert and Jacqueline Lo cite productive "Aborasian" alliances in Australasia in their 2007 book, *Performance and Cosmopolitics* (209)); and dynamic and fluid urban *intra*culturalisms in the world's new global cities (groups such as Toronto's Cahoots Theatre Company with explicitly cross-cultural mandates are now bringing diverse marginalized groups within a city together in solidarity to create theatre).

I treat these cities, following Foucault, as "heterotopic spaces" ("Of Other Spaces"), defined by Kevin Hetherington as "spaces of alternate ordering" (viii), and it is such fluid and unstable spaces that a renewed semiotics occupies in the 21st century. Baz Kershaw refers to them as "ecologies of theatre" and "ecologies of performance" (*Theatre Ecology* 16), describing theatres and performances as "ecosystems" (15). Elsewhere he describes within these systems "the complicated and unavoidable inter-dependency between any element of a performance event and its environment," where "the smallest change of one element in some way, however minutely, effects change in all the rest" ("Oh" 136). He also notes that, as in all ecologies (and contra the totalizing tendencies of early versions of semiotics), the health of an ecosystem might best be judged by the diversity of its species – an insight with crucial relevance to intercultural work. Kershaw's ecosystem might be understood to be analogous to Juri Lotman's "semiosphere," in which "semiotic systems are in a constant state of flux" (*Universe* 151), a concept that both Meerzon and Jestrović use to broaden our understanding of diverse acts of "interpretation," including "reading into" (Jestrović 103) – and I would add misreading and translation – that might give rise to new, dynamic, and flexible semiotic possibilities, including what Jestrović calls the "experiential" (103).

One of the strongest arguments in Meerzon's issue of *Semiotica* is that of Michael Sidnell, advocating what he calls "semiotic arts of theatre": "there is no evading of the praxis of the signifying act," he urges; "there is no such thing as a non-pragmatic sign, no reference without a performance" (38). He concludes: "being arts, semiotic arts are (axiomatically) not only not identifiable with their productions and inseparable from qualities of their execution but are largely inaccessible without active involvement in their practices" (39–41). Pavis also ends *Analyzing Performance* with gestures toward "the field of practice" (303). He imagines an "ethnoscenologist who abandons the assurance of her critical and semiological positions, in order to immerse herself in a performance and in the universe that produced it" risking "being transformed into a dramaturge, a director, even an actor" (302). "In calling for new theories more appropriate to the task and continually updated," he argues, "performance practice also takes theory forward; and in return theory contributes to an improvement in the understanding we have of practice. In this way they feed (off) each other; out of this ongoing and generalized 'intercannibalism' arises a revolution that is nowhere near its end" (327).

Which takes us to Part 2: Practice.

Part Two
Practice

What use is all of this? Beyond using semiotics to develop a general, theoretical understanding of the modes and mechanisms whereby meaning is produced in theatre and performance, what might be the practical applications of seeing performance through a semiotic lens for the analysis of specific scripts, processes, and plays in production? Part II of this book attempts to answer these questions by focusing, in Chapter 4, on script analysis and devising, and in Chapter 5 on the analysis of actual performances. In each case I will keep in mind the problematics of representation, misrepresentation, recognition, and misrecognition that I discussed in the Introduction, focusing on some of the ways that an expanded semiotic analysis can help both scholarly and theatrical practitioners avoid some of the pitfalls inherent in the theatrical production of signs, particularly in productions that work across cultural and other forms of difference.

My focus here is on the production rather than simply the interpretation of signs; that is, I consider the act of analysis itself to be a generative one, an act of creation. A director, dramaturge or scholar selecting a project, or a scholar analysing a dramatic work, can usefully be understood to be engaging in an act of collaboration (with a script, with an idea, with a scenario) in the creation of a new work, whether it be a published essay, a performance, or simply a mental image. As we have seen in Chapters 2 and 3, something very similar can be said of a spectator.

From theory to practice

In shifting from theory to practice I find myself drawing up lists. First, there are a number of assumptions drawn from the history of semiotic theory as I have outlined it in Part I that inflect what follows in Part II, and productively contextualize the move from theory to practice. They are distilled here:

1. Everything on stage, and everything involved in "the entire theatre experience," is a sign.
2. Theatre stages representations, and all representations are misrepresentations, performing their cultural work in the gap between the "real" and the representation, selecting and "ostending" (foregrounding) certain things *as* signs and occluding other possible representations.
3. Each staging is performed before a "real" audience that brings certain competencies to the theatre but is nevertheless heterogeneous; at the same time each staging *constitutes* its audience as a specific, and specific kind of community, partly through the *interpellation* of audiences through technologies of recognition (and misrecognition): when audiences assent, either individually or collectively, to a given representation – "yes, that's true," "yes, I recognize in her what a Native American woman looks like," or "yes, that's an accurate representation of domestic life," – they are "hailed" into ideology, a set of "givens" that they are required to accept as "normal" if they wish to understand and enjoy the show.
4. Meaning in spoken language and other symbolic systems is arbitrary, the product of convention, coercion, or provisional agreement. In all cases meaning is relational, the product of a series of differentiations ("not…but").
5. The languages of the stage help to *constitute* rather than simply to reflect the so-called "real world"; that is, they are performative.
6. Finally, and perhaps completing the circle, while everything on stage is a sign, these signs are not "consumed in their sense"; that is, they do not lose their material reality: a

costume does not cease to be a piece of clothing when it is ostended as a sign.

A second list involves briefly reviewing some of concepts that I discussed in Chapter 2, shifting their focus from theory to "practice," and in particular the practices of making theatre. These include:

1. Estrangement (*ostranenie*), foregrounding (*aktualisace*), and showing (*ostension*) (see pp. 43–7): Each of these concepts, for the practitioner, has to do with finding ways of making the audience see what is staged clearly and from a fresh perspective, "as if for the first time." Directors often accomplish this by placing characters, events, or objects in new or unexpected contexts, removing them from their, and their audiences', comfort zones, or placing them in metaphorical quotation marks. Often this involves disrupting the taken-for-grantedness of the relationship between signifier and signified, sign and referent, denaturalizing expectations about cause and effect, or simply focusing on the materiality of something the audience has come to understand in metaphysical or symbolic registers, as when the sign of water onstage results in the actual soaking of audience members.
2. Actantial analysis (see pp. 50–3): Directors of a semiotic bent will productively focus in a rehearsal context, at least part of the time, on what human and non-human forces are being brought to bear on the action that may have nothing to do with the psychological probing of character and motivation, the naturalistic probing of cause and effect, or indeed representation of any kind. These forces can, of course, include the needs or wishes of naturalistically understood characters, but they can alternatively include the pressures put on texts and performances by certain kinds of delivery or juxtaposition or the undertaking of certain tasks. They can involve pressures having to do with story, with audience expectation, with aesthetic experimentation, with social convention, with ethics, politics, or economics. Productions can be usefully understood as the gathering or sequencing of "dramatic postulates,"

"what-if" propositions that explore through rehearsals and staging what might happen if certain pressures were brought to bear on one another in a way that might have to do with the represented action, but might equally be purely formalist, comparable to a painter's explorations of colour, pattern, and design; a sculptor's of weight, shape, and volume; or a musician's of rhythm, tempo, and pitch.

3. Performativity (see pp. 53–4): It is common for directors, dramaturges and actors in a rehearsal context to become exclusively caught up in issues of what a line or image, costume or cue, scene or sequence *says* or *means*, without sufficient consideration of what each of these *does*, what actions they perform, and upon whom. This can include considering performativity within a play world or naturalistic fiction, when anything a character says or does has a direct impact on the other characters and the world of the play; it can also include the ways in which any aspect of a production – ranging from the delivery of lines through various elements of design, movement, and blocking – impacts on the audience and the off-stage world. It is, after all, the "real-world" impact of a work that is usually understood to be the measure of its significance.
4. Structural analysis (see pp. 55–68): How a show is put together is not simply left either to the assumption that a script has already been structured and will automatically shape the show without further effort by the producers, or to post-show analysis. Any production in any style is the result of a process that has been consciously designed and that issues in work that is spatially and temporally organized to have specific effects and impacts. The creators of any theatrical work consciously attend to what a show is made of (its materials), its design (how those materials are put together), and its purpose (what the show is intended to do, its impact). This involves close attention to the relationships between elements of time and space that are both representational (within the fiction) and presentational (within the "real" world of the audience).
5. *Mise en scène* (see pp. 68–70): For practical purposes the *mise en scène* can best be understood to comprise the organizing

principles that determine relationships among the various elements of a production, the activities of foregrounding, blending, contrasting, harmonizing, and structuring that is the work of rehearsals.

6. Performance text (see pp. 70–2): For directors and dramaturges, the performance text is the idea or understanding of the show that begins to emerge in the mind late in the rehearsal process against which they test their initial goals and intentions in staging the *mise en scène*. At the point in rehearsals at which directors and dramaturges begin to function as surrogate audiences, they also begin to "read" the performance (to constitute the performance *as text*), and measure this reading against what they hope audiences will take away from the show.
7. Spectatorship (see pp. 72–80): I have introduced several concepts in Chapter 2 that are useful for practitioners. Chief among these are the "model spectator," interpretative "gaps," the "interpretative community," and the audience's "horizons of expectation."
   a. Theatre artists need to know both who their "model spectator" is and who is actually likely to be in the house. The model spectator is the one that the production wants to address. This means both the audience who will fully understand the show's semiotic codes and follow its intertextual references, *and* the audience who the creators have decided needs to hear what they have to say. This means knowing what audience the show is likely to attract and determining whether it is the one that it wants to talk to. But as audiences become increasingly heterogeneous, houses are unlikely to be filled with model spectators who know all the codes, get all the references, and are able or willing to respond to the show's imperatives. "Others," in most instances, need to be accommodated.
   b. Leaving interpretative "gaps" has to do with letting audiences in, resisting the urge to explain everything away, and engaging "emancipated spectators" on an imaginative level as active co-creators rather than simply considering them to be receivers of messages or consumers of a product.

c. Audiences can be understood to be single "interpretative communities" that are gathered together in a particular place and time, but they are also and increasingly made up of intersections of *different*, pluralistic interpretative communities with different competencies, reading strategies, and even languages (broadly understood). Theatre makers in the 21st century need to be cognizant of this likely heterogeneity in their audience, and many contemporary productions are consciously structured to take advantage of the drama that is constituted through tensions and struggles over meaning that occur offstage among audiences that can no longer be assumed to constitute a single homogeneous group.

d. Audiences' "horizons of expectations" are what they bring to the show with them, some of which can be shaped by the creators' conscious decisions, and some of which are determined by larger social and cultural conditions of which the creators of the show must be acutely aware. Horizons of expectation are created in part by the discourses of the producing theatre, including everything from its history and mandate, advertising, trailers, posters, and programs, to its audience amenities and neighbourhood. But it is also essential to be aware of the social, cultural, and political context within which the show is occurring. Audience response is as likely to be based on the daily news as on anything a producing company can consciously shape. One duty of the theatre is to respond to the shifting particulars of its place and time.

Style

Part I of *How Theatre Means*, focusing on theories of meaning production, was able to bracket off one of the first questions that is faced by anyone wishing to mount a production or undertake the analysis of a performance, and that is the key question of performance style and its relationship to function – or to what a production is setting out to accomplish.

So, in the move from theory to practice, another list. The following is not intended as a checklist of possible stylistic options, but as a guide to some of the vocabulary that is often used when discussing style in the theatre, with notes on why and how style matters.

In spite of modernist, postmodernist, postdramatic, and other developments, the predominant styles of theatrical production in the English-speaking world remain naturalism and realism.

Naturalism emerges from 19th-century science, and it has to do with understanding (or trying to understand) the laws of nature, including human nature. The basic drive of naturalism is cause and effect, so naturalistic theatre traces a logical, if manufactured, cause-and-effect throughline from a show's initiating action to its conclusion, each action clearly motivated by some prior action or condition (or character trait), and each leading with seeming inevitability to the next.

Naturalism relies for its effect on its iconicity, for the resemblance between what's on stage and what the audience would recognize as its "real-life" equivalent. In a naturalistic production all choices are made with a view to maintaining this resemblance and avoiding anything that shatters the illusion.

Naturalism can, however, and often is, heightened in various ways so that events that could happen in the real world (and therefore do not shatter the illusion) come to take on resonance, significance, or symbolism that exceeds in lyrical or poetic ways the demands of the form. This is often called "poetic naturalism."

Realism also relies on iconicity for its effects, but unlike naturalism its focus is not on cause and effect but on the unvarnished, unromantic representation of life and the world "as it is," with all its blemishes intact. It says a lot about realism to remember that the word is most often used in conjunction with adjectives such as "brutal," or "photographic."

Realism does not paint rosy pictures. A realist production will not only make every effort to avoid shattering the illusion, but will also keep its distance from anything decorative, sentimental, or merely allusive.

Realism also has it variations, most prominently *hyperrealism* and *magic realism*. Hyperrealism creates a false, more detailed and defined version of reality than realism itself, often de- or re-contextualized or placed in unusual circumstances, creating a simulation, or false reality. Magic realism uses an essentially realistic style or setting but incorporates events that are impossible in quotidian reality, usually without commenting on the fact.

Naturalism and realism are usually understood in opposition to stylization, and where naturalism and realism tend to normalize and naturalize their representations – the depiction of a racial stereotype is reified when audiences "recognize" what is depicted as being "true," accurate, or normal – stylization can draw attention to representation as a function of choice, selection, exaggeration, or critique. Stylized representations don't pretend to be "real;" rather they attempt to expose the selective and constructed nature of representation itself. They try to find or uncover things that naturalism and realism obscure.

There are an infinite number of ways beyond poetic naturalism, hyperrealism, or magic realism in which a production can be stylized. Most of them have to do with an attempt to delve more deeply than the "mere" reproduction of life and the world in all of their messy and quotidian detail, in search of an essence of some kind. Most aim for "truth" rather than settling for realism's facts and surfaces or naturalism's limiting causalities. Although types of stylization are potentially infinite, I list below some of those that are most familiar in western theatrical traditions and attempt to give a sense of what uses they might still serve, though many of them are often treated in scholarship as being bound by or limited to the historical moments at which they emerged.

Symbolism emerged in the late 19th century as an idealist reaction to naturalism. It tends to focus on the realm of the imagination, on dreams, and on spirituality, and it attempts to approach truths through a kind of indirection, endowing objects and images with larger-than-life symbolic meaning. Symbolist theatre often moves toward ritual in an attempt to approach what it considers to be the deep and hidden or intuitive truths of existence. It tends to operate in broad, primarily visual strokes rather than subtleties, and to employ a ritualistic acting style.

As its name implies, *expressionism* is generally concerned with the expression of emotion and the representation of deep psychic drives rather than the depiction of surface realities. It tends to be interested in individual psyches and mental states, often anguished ones. It relies for its effects on exaggeration and distortion, and is dominated by sharp angles, bold or brooding colours, and an acting style that relies on gesture, mask, lyrical movement and vocal expression – a style that naturalism would consider to be overwrought.

Impressionism has to do with perceptions, and with what mental impressions the world makes on individuals. It is less concerned with depths than with the play of surfaces, and less concerned with root causes than with relations. Its main concerns are the creation of atmosphere and mood rather than deeply felt emotions, and it requires a light directorial touch.

Surrealism is primarily interested in the unconscious and tends to work through the kinds of surprising juxtapositions and non-sequiturs that are most familiar from dreams. In theatre it often involves the mythological, archetypal, and allegorical; its methods tend toward collage and (filmic) montage; and its primary languages are image and movement rather than the spoken word.

Minimalism involves the distillation of everything to its essentials, avoiding anything that is decorative or merely theatrical and employing a minimum of props, furnishings, or set pieces. It tends to be interested in the unspoken or unspeakable and therefore in silences and indirections; even its use of spoken text is most often sparse and austere. For minimalism less is more.

The *theatre of the absurd* is associated with a body of modernist drama by an otherwise disparate group of playwrights including Beckett, Ionesco, Pinter, Albee and others, but it can also be thought of as a style of staging. It is often (though not always) associated with an existentialist vision of an existence that is understood to precede or be without meaning, or of a world that operates by inscrutable or illogical forces. As its name suggests, it employs situations and conventions that are fundamentally absurd. In terms of staging, the theatre of the absurd often uses confined spaces, parodic styles, clichés, and frequent repetition, and there is rarely any discernable connection between causes and their effects.

Epic theatre is the style invented and advocated by Bertolt Brecht. Epic theatre avoids immersion in the dramatic illusion and adopts a presentational format that operates by showing. This means that actors are required to "present" or quote rather than attempt to merge with their characters, and it involves, in acting and design, the selection of only those elements of people and the world that are relevant to understanding the social significance of the action. It is most useful for work that is explicitly political, because it attempts to portray action not as inevitable but as a function of human choices that it works to make visible.

Agit-prop (agitation-propaganda) is a theatre of political persuasion that attempts to arouse spectators to action. Its techniques are most often fundamentally allegorical, with characters, objects, and actions representing specific social and political positions. It is constructed to arouse rather than purge emotions, and it eschews satisfying conclusions within the frame of the action on the understanding that conclusions and catharsis will only result from the actions of its audiences after the show.

There are various types of *clowning*, but most involve an assumption of innocence on the part of sympathetic but naïve characters-as-clowns that reveals in the world and worldliness that they try to negotiate a certain illogical decadence or corruption – a *loss* of innocence. Clowning usually involves physical comedy and always involves actors with specialized clown training.

Postmodernist, *poststructuralist*, and *postdramatic performances* are related and overlapping styles (if indeed they are styles in the traditional sense) that can in practice be indistinguishable from one another.

Postmodern theatre emerged as a reaction to high modernist formalism with its enclosed structures of self-containment and self-referentiality. Most postmodern productions highlight uncertainty, employ structural openness, and tend toward interrogative rather than declarative modes.

Poststructuralist theatre has as its central feature scepticism about structuralist certainties and totalities, and a distrust of overarching or "master" narratives, but it is nevertheless deeply invested in form.

Postdramatic performance, a category introduced by Hans-Thies Lehmann, is a more precise term than the other "posts," and is distinguished by a number of specific features: it troubles, disrupts, or eschews the technologies of theatrical representation (including plot and character); it fractures temporal progression; it refuses to depict an enclosed fictional cosmos; it focuses on the materiality and autonomy of "text" (broadly understood); it employs digital and other media, mediation, and intermediality; it is fundamentally formalist; and it employs what Lehmann's English translator Karen Jürs-Munby calls "palimpsestic intertextuality" – the dense overlaying of citations (8). Lehmann lists the "palette of stylistic traits" of postdramatic theatre as: "parataxis [the juxtaposition of dissimilar images or fragments], simultaneity, play with the density of signs, musicalization, visual dramaturgy, physicality, irruption of the real, [and] situation/event" (86).

All three "posts" tend toward pastiche, paradox, irony, fragmentation, and the selective appropriation of other styles; all tend to employ metatheatricality; all presume a high level of audience sophistication; and all work to both denaturalize and defamiliarize everything they touch.

Performance style is closely related to form and genre, though style, form, and genre need not coincide or be mutually reinforcing. Some of the above styles are generally understood to be appropriate for tragedy, some for comedy, some for satire, some for farce – but productions that work against these commonsense pairings can be productive and powerful: expressionist farce can claim peculiar significance, for example, in mocking an overwrought world, and tragedy performed by clowns can be uniquely compelling and generate surprising new meanings while refusing to take itself too seriously.

Beyond the dominant western tradition there is a myriad of other styles, forms, and genres not considered above that range from Noh through Kabuki to Kutiyattam and Kathakali; from Japanese Bunraku through Islamic to Malaysian shadow and Vietnamese water puppetry; from Kunqu to Jingju Opera; and finally to innumerable ritual, ceremonial, and dance forms from Indigenous and other communities around the world. Many of these forms have been raided, distorted, appropriated, or treated *as* "mere styles" by western interculturalists, but many have their own rigidly coded communication systems, and few are available in any ethical way to theatre artists without membership in the specific cultures or communities and/or a lifetime of specialized training. And contemporary artists, especially those impacted by the historical and contemporary effects of dominant or colonizing representational technologies on their lives and bodies, are constantly forging new styles to serve new purposes. African American Ntozake Shange calls her movement-based *for colored girls who have considered suicide/ when the rainbow is enuf* a "choreopoem"; AfriCanadian Djanet Sears calls her *Harlem Duet* "rhapsodic blues tragedy" ("nOTES" 14), and Afro-Jamaican Canadian d'bi young anitafrika refers to all of her stage work, which she both writes and performs and which is grounded in the formal principles of Caribbean dub poetry, as "biomyth monodrama" (Email) (See Figure II.1).

The selection of a production's style is not a mechanical question of choosing from a shopping list of "isms," nor, indeed, are the styles I've listed (and the many others I haven't) entirely pure and distinct from one another. Nevertheless, an acute awareness of how style relates to function is essential, and for practitioners decisions about style precede all other decisions because they determine what skills are required of actors, designers, and others. It is important to recognize, however, that the style of a production may or may not follow that of any script on which it may be based, or any authorial intention, as is the case with *Mabou Mines DollHouse*, the object of one case study in Chapter 5, whose metatheatrical self-consciousness operates at a considerable remove from the naturalism of its dramatic inspiration.

Analysis: the semiotic arts of theatre

Every aspect of theatrical practice requires multiple layers of analysis before, during, and after the event, and each of these layers benefits from a systematic understanding of how meaning is produced in the theatre. Designers are experts at visual and spatial realms of representation, but an expanded

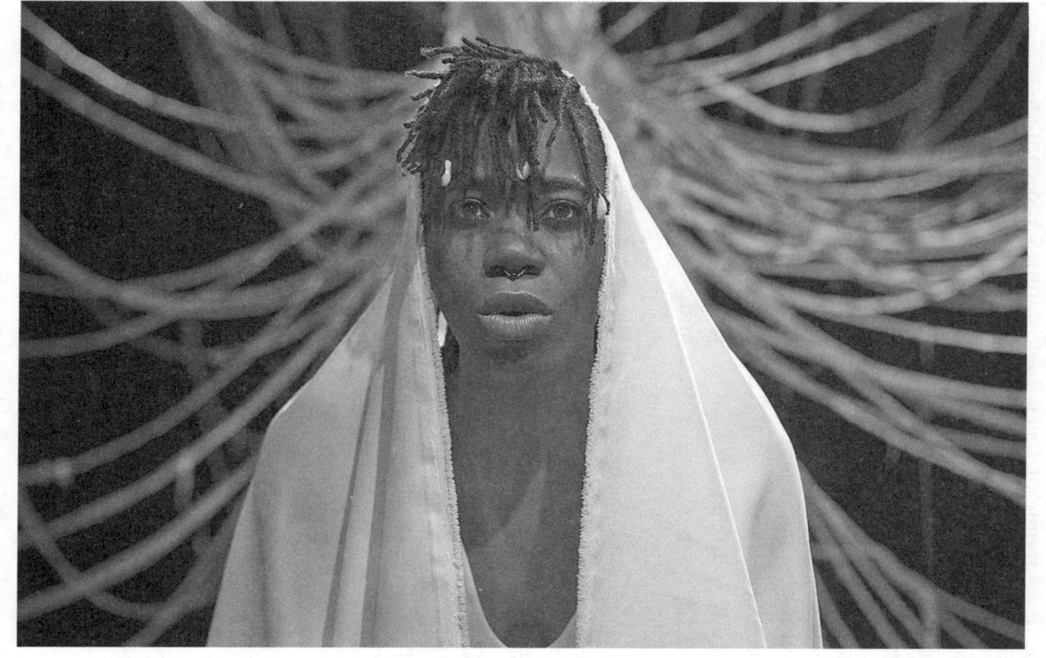

Figure II.1 **d'bi young anitafrika in benu, part two of her *sankofa trilogy* at Tarragon Theatre, Toronto, 2011**
Source: Photo by Cylla von Tiedemann courtesy Tarragon Theatre, Toronto.

semiotic analysis can help them talk to directors, production managers, carpenters, tailors, cutters, wigmakers, and technicians about how to realize their effects and communicate their meanings. Actors need all the help they can get in translating their often instinctive and often fragile inner impulses, emotions, and drives into meaningful and repeatable communicative speech, gesture, and action. Reviewers and critics require precise methodologies and vocabularies if they wish to move beyond consumer reporting and impressionistic description to precise analysis. I have neither the space nor the competence to model all of the analytical practices of all the contributors to the production of meaning in the theatre, particularly as they progress, morph, develop, and transform throughout a rehearsal process. Instead, Chapters 4 and 5 will focus on the book-end processes of script analysis and devising, on the one hand, and performance analysis on the other, treating both of these from the points of view – my own – of the practicing scholar, director, and dramaturge.

4 Script Analysis and Devising

Script analysis, whether in the service of staging or studying a work, and whether it is undertaken by directors, designers, actors, literary critics, or theatre historians, is fundamentally dramaturgical: it is concerned with how a work is put together. This chapter focuses first on scripts that have been written in advance of a production, and second on the various ingredients that come together in what is known as "devised" theatre – theatre in which all elements of a performance text evolve together in the course of a rehearsal/creation process. In both cases I am considering the dramaturgical analysis of "scripts" that either contribute to the shaping of the *mise en scène* and the making of the performance text, or function as a major part of its published or archived record after the fact: its remains.

I consider two different practices and purposes for undertaking such analysis: the scholarly consideration of plays as "dramatic literature," and the practical analysis of scripts and scenarios that is involved in preparing for a production. I will privilege the latter because the understanding of a script or scenario as one of many contributing factors in the making of a production benefits both approaches, and because scripts, apart from closet dramas ("plays" never intended for the stage), are not written, in the first instance at least, to be read and contemplated in the seclusion of a study, with the opportunity to reread, revisit, pause, or flip back to information that has previously been supplied. As has been established in Chapter 2, theatre, including the scripts or scenarios that feed into its construction, takes place in space and time in ways that do not apply to solitary reading. I consider any analysis of dramatic work to be dramaturgical and to be preparatory to staging, whether in an actual performance, in the pages of a scholarly paper, or simply in the mind. There are, however, different reasons for undertaking the analyses of scripts for the purposes of production, real or imagined. This chapter also privileges the positions of the dramaturge and director rather than those of designers, actors, technicians, or others, for whom the process is similar, but the focus and emphasis different. A set designer will be more narrowly focused on space and place, a sound designer on tempo and rhythm, an actor on language, action, gesture, and embodiment.

Preparation

Whether analysing a script for literary critical purposes or a script or scenario for the purposes of mounting a production, there are certain preliminary, reflexive questions that need to be asked before engaging with the specificities of analysis. These have to do with the initial selection of a script or proposal of a scenario or idea, and the reasons for undertaking the task in the first place: the *need* for this particular director or scholar to undertake this particular project at this a particular place and time for this particular audience or readership.

I find it useful, then, to consider the theatrical or scholarly staging of a production to be research, and to begin with what I think of as a research question, an attempt to understand or make sense of something that is urgent: "What do I want to know? Why do *I* want to know it? What key issues will the reading and production explore? Why does it matter? To whom?" How, in Ibsen's *A Doll House*, can a woman of independent spirit negotiate her identity in a patriarchal culture? How, in Monique Mojica's *Chocolate Woman Dreams the Milky Way*, can "a lost Dule Girl" (a woman of Guna ancestry) heal herself by connecting with those elements of her culture that are not broken after four hundred years of colonization? The greater the urgency of the question, as a rule, the more the project will matter. I find it useful to design a process under the assumption, to quote Algonquin playwright and director Yvette Nolan, that "maybe if we can work it out in this play, we can work it out in our lives too" ("Death").

Script analysis

The analysis of existing scripts ranging from classics to new work has a long history, and there have been many published guides and models for the aspiring director, dramaturge, or, critic concerning how to read scripts and how to analyse their plots, characters, language use, structures, and so on. What follows is intended to build on that work rather than replace it, and to inflect the work of script analysis with some of the lessons learned from semiotics. I will not undertake to provide a complete reading of any play as an example of or template for such an analysis; every script brings with it different imperatives, and every director, or every critic, must bring her own positioning to bear on each analysis she undertakes. Exemplary templates can be prescriptive, restrictive, or misguided. I will, however, thread throughout this section examples drawn from a single script, Rolfe Fjelde's English translation of Ibsen's *A Doll House*, which are intended to demonstrate method rather than fix meaning, while at the same time organizing a somewhat broader range of examples than might otherwise be possible around a single work that is familiar to many. Not all aspects of this analysis will apply equally to every script: some scripts don't have plots or characters, for example, and some involve little or no spoken language. But what follows is intended to cover most of the bases and to be applicable to a relatively broad range of scripts written in a relatively wide variety of styles.

There are many elements of a script analysis, and many languages through which a script speaks, and each of these requires careful and detailed consideration, both separately and in combination with one another. But first I find it helpful to engage with the script with as much phenomenological immediacy as possible, to first read it at a single sitting, without interruption, note-taking, or analysis. Only after completing the reading, and perhaps after an interval, do I take random and usually unsystematic note of first impressions and, most importantly, visceral responses. It is important throughout the process to be able return to these notes as a record of what first seemed powerful, compelling, significant, or intriguing about the script.

I find that a second reading, after an interval of perhaps a day or two, can productively test those reactions. Do they still hold up? What different aspects of the script drew attention the second time around? I tend to repeat this process as often as it continues to seem valuable, and until I feel I have a good generalist knowledge of the script and have notes about everything that it evokes for me: images, thoughts, ideas, colours, shapes, patterns, textures, sounds, associations, connections to other work or to the world and that of the audience. At this stage notes shouldn't involve specific ideas about staging, or even conscious or systematic interpretation. They are the invaluable record of an initial, raw response.

The next stage is to read for analysis, beginning with the overarching questions of what, for a culturally and historically situated reader, the script is about and how this is communicated. This is in part a process of selection: no script, and no production, can be about everything, and at least initially any analyst has to be concerned with primary meanings that she feels are *foregrounded* by the script. In the case of *A Doll House* these could have to do, for example, with gender, ethical behaviour, hypocrisy, integrity, the law, money, marriage, class, "the situation of women in the family and society" (Moi 225), or, more abstractly, as one popular "study guide" to the play suggests, with transformation and radical change (Unwin 17, drawing on Durbach). It is, of course, "about" all of these (related) things and more, but it is important to consider what the *central* concern of this analysis is, what (based on initial readings and subsequent analysis) the analyst wants to foreground as primary, to which the others play a contextualizing, supporting, or complicating role.

It is similarly the case that *how* the play's meanings are communicated involves a multiplicity of interrelated languages, styles, techniques, and sign systems, and part of the process of analysis is to decide what, in this particular instance, the play's *primary modes of communication* are: does it work chiefly through character? plot? action? imagery? dialogue? *gestus*? Again, most scripts use all of these and more, but decisions about which, in this moment, is (or are) primary allows for consideration of what *drives* the play and how each of the others relate to it. If a play's primary mode of communication is character, for example, does the plot put the characters in situations that reveal, challenge, modify, or undermine them? Is character revealed through the give-and-take of dialogue, through monologues (or soliloquys), through the way the character speaks (her choice of words and images, his syntax, their rhythms or silences). Or is it revealed through action, what the characters actually *do*, which may or may not reinforce or undermine what they say? If plot is foregrounded, is there an ideal hero or perhaps an unlikely central character or characters (or other forces) as primary "actants" driving the story? I tend to think semiotically of a play as an assemblage of "what ifs?": what I call "dramatic postulates" but actantial analysis would call "actants," that are thrown together in strategic combinations in order to see what happens as they interact. In *A Doll House*, for example, these would include, of course, the characters with their various drives, desires, and needs (for respectability, for freedom, for love, for someone to take care of, for money), but they also include societal pressures around respectability and social standing, the prescriptions of the legal and banking systems, and even the pressures exerted by letters, calling cards, occasions (such as Christmas), weather (the freezing black water that Nora contemplates), and social conventions.

A semiotic reading of a play script has to concern itself with the Saussurean dictum that a sign produces meaning only relationally within a sign system – a structure – that is agreed upon by members of an interpretative community and that is held together by convention. In the theatre, one aspect of this is the languages shared and the conventions agreed upon between the stage and the audience, and some of these have to do with "real-world" referents. At least until recently, most scripts, from monologues, to dialogue, to stage directions have been written in a single language that is intended to be spoken, is shared with its presumed audience, and helps to constitute that audience as a single interpretative – linguistic – community. And again until recently, most scripts, even if they put pressure on them, have assumed a set of theatrical conventions that serve a similar function. In recent years postdramatic writing for the stage has consciously challenged these assumptions, and intercultural scripts have increasingly used more than one spoken language and have drawn on theatrical conventions, styles, and cultural texts from a variety of cultures that are not necessarily "read" in the same way by all members of the audience, who are not assumed to share equal competency in each of the languages, styles, and conventions employed. Rather than assuming or constituting a single interpretative community, such scripts promote or provide a forum for negotiation across acknowledged differences.

But scripts, like the productions to which they contribute, do not simply draw upon existing linguistic and theatrical sign systems and structures. Scripts themselves constitute structures, sign systems in which, as in all sign systems, meaning is produced not in absolute but in relational terms, and part of the pleasure derived from reading a script or seeing a production involves learning those terms. What is often called "the world of the play" can be understood to be a literary or theatrical *structure* in which significance is determined, not by the referent of a sign in the "real world" outside of the play, but by the "not...but" of relationships within the play world, where "value" (vs "meaning") is determined by what everything is compared to and exchanged for, as discussed on pp. 21–3 above. Whether Nora, in *A Doll House*, is a "spendthrift" or is generous can only be understood in relation to a complex economic system of poverty, dependency, banking, and middle-class respectability that accumulates over the course of the play and is read within the cultures that receive it wherever the play is produced. Nora's initially inscrutable tipping of the Delivery Boy in the opening scene – she gives him twice his fee – accumulates meaning relationally as the play proceeds. Similarly, the "meaning" of the Christmas tree that enters the play in the first act, is dismantled in the second, and disappears in the third, can only be understood in relation to (among other things) the "trimming," dismantling, and departure of Nora with whom it is implicitly compared. In discussing the various elements that make up a script analysis, it must be kept in mind that these all function and acquire meaning relationally – in terms of comparisons and exchanges within *and* between each system.

The world of the play

Once the analyst has determined what, for her, the play is about and what its primary modes of communication are, it is useful to begin with an analysis of what is somewhat loosely called "the world of the play." This has often been understood to refer to a play's overall poetic and imagistic vocabulary and resonances, through which it can be understood whether the play participates in a society dominated by culture, nature, economics, sports, politics, and so on, and whether this can be realized in performance through design, staging, and stylistic choice. A startling example of such a literal realization, for example, is Punchdrunk Theatre's "immersive theatre" experience, *Sleep No More* (London 2003; Boston 2009; New York 2011), an adaptation of Shakespeare's *Macbeth* in which the audience walks through rooms and rifles through drawers that are literally stuffed with artefacts literalizing the imagistic mindscapes of that play's haunted central characters (see Worthen). Another is *Mabou Mines Doll House*, a postmodern production/adaptation of Ibsen's naturalist play that took its title and imagistic language literally and exaggerated its stylistic underpinnings, and from which I will draw for examples of performance analysis in Chapter 5.

But perhaps a more important object of analysis than a play's imagery is its logic. Naturalistic drama, because it sets out to investigate the cause-and-effect "laws of nature," including human nature, attempts to follow the logic of the "real world" and to make visible its workings. This, by and large, is the case with *A Doll House*, where the play is singularly concerned with causes and consequences that come to seem inevitable – at least until Nora surprises us at the conclusion. But much theatre operates by different rules entirely, often establishing its own conventions and following its own rules, and it is essential that any script analysis determine what these rules are, how and when they are established, and the relationship between the represented world they regulate and that of the audience. Sometimes this is as simple as agreeing that asides and soliloquies, heard by the audience, can't be heard by other characters occupying the space, or agreeing that walls exist that are manifestly not there, that other rooms exist in extra-diegetic space, or that "this cockpit [can] hold / The vasty fields of France" when a few armed extras rush across the stage representing two warring armies in Shakespeare's *Henry V* (Prologue 11–12). But sometimes a play world operates by different laws entirely, with (for example) space being compressed, stretched, or reconfigured according to the play's idiosyncratic physics, or with time being elongated, compacted, or reversed. Different performance styles, too, have their own internal logics and exert their own imperatives on the action. Finally, it is helpful to consider closely, in any type of theatre, what Elinor Fuchs calls "the social world of the play," asking such crucial questions as "who has power on this planet?" (Fuchs, "EF's Visit" 7).

In plays that invoke the supernatural it is necessary to determine how much power, say, the witches in *Macbeth* actually have, whether and when they can intervene in the quotidian world of the characters. When is a *deus ex machina* the logical and satisfying outcome of the action and when is it a monumental cop-out? In adaptations of Kafka, in Ionesco, or in Beckett, when is the play's twisted or absurd logic a productive commentary on the bureaucratic or absurd rules that seem to govern "real-world" experience, and when is it just silly (or Absurd)? What are the spiritual or cultural belief systems, epistemologies, and cosmologies that underscore the action, especially in culturally specific work such as *Chocolate Woman Dreams the Milky Way*? When the Rugaru (an ominous figure in Algonquin cosmology) appears in Algonquin playwright Yvette Nolan's *Annie Mae's Movement*, what is its ontological status? When a large half-naked Native man appears as the answer to Grace's prayers in Nolan's play, *Job's Wife*, who *is* he, and what relationship does he bear to the world of the audience?

Finally, in what Hans-Thies Lehmann calls "postdramatic" theatre (and in much theatre that is more loosely called "postmodern"), "the world of the play" is not a totalizable fictional reality, but a world of potential, not, as his English translator says, a whole, but "full of holes" (Jürs-Munby 12). In instances such as this, script analysis needs to address the nature and placement of those holes and the powerful work performed by potential that is strategically left to audiences to realize.

Intertextuality

A thorough script analysis needs to take into account a script's dialogism; that is, it needs to identify the various discursive fields in which the play participates and which it invokes. This involves, at a minimum, identifying intertextual references, intended or otherwise, that open the world of the play into the realm of the social, and this can be crucial for contemporary postmodern, poststructuralist, and postdramatic theatre, which can consist in large part of a pastiche of wide-ranging citations. But it is also important for the most naturalistic of plays.

When it was first produced, *A Doll House* participated intertextually not only in debates over women's rights, but more centrally in a debate within the theatre and philosophy of Ibsen's time between idealists and realists. Toril Moi reads the play as a critical engagement with post-romantic idealist aesthetics and thought in late 19th-century Norway, reading Torvald Helmer, with his inability to tolerate anything ugly (even knitting! (181)), as "a card-carrying idealist aesthete if ever there was one" (225). At the same time, the play employs a kind of intertextual, metatheatrical engagement with the theatrical melodrama of its time, at once borrowing from and critiquing what Errol Durbach calls its "crude division of people and ideas into the unequivocally 'right' and 'wrong'" (68), and its drive towards satisfyingly final, if often bathetic, resolutions. According to Durbach, Nora "succumbs too readily to the melodramatic frame of mind," and imagines a miraculous "scenario" involving her husband's heroic assumption of sole responsibility for her transgressions, followed by her own "fantasy of suicide" through which she hopes romantically and equally heroically to clear his name. In the end, of course, at a crucial moment of recognition, Nora comes to her senses and steps, as Durbach says, "out of Scribe [the French playwright who perfected the 19th-century "well-made play"] and into Ibsen" (69).

Much of this intertextuality would be inscrutable to readers of Ibsen in the Fjelde or other translations today, or to contemporary audiences, but it is important for scholarly or theatrical practitioners to research and to engage with it, if only to find other, contemporary resonances or references to help make Helmer's aestheticism or Nora's melodramatic fantasies comprehensible to a contemporary audience. Other intertextual resonances, on the other hand, accrue over time and would have been unavailable to original audiences. When Krogstad punctures Nora's suicide fantasy with the realist "one doesn't do these things" (170), it's difficult for contemporary Ibsen aficionados and modern drama followers more generally not to hear (pre)echoes of the final line of Ibsen's much later play, *Hedda Gabler* – "but good God! People don't *do* such things!" (778) – immediately after its titular heroine has shot herself.

Which introduces one of the prime functions of intertextuality: as discussed in Chapter 2, audiences adjust their horizons of expectations according to the discourses in which they recognize a play to be taking part. Recognizing the discourses and generic conventions of melodrama and anticipating idealist "uplift" (Moi 227), Ibsen's original audiences were more shocked than audiences today at the heroine's direct language and blunt departure at the play's close, much in the way that the original audiences for Shakespeare's *King Lear*, recognizing in it the structural conventions of comedy and anticipating the comic conclusion of its source and primary intertext (the earlier play *King Leir*), would have been devastated by the entrance of Lear with Cordelia dead in his arms. On the other hand, a contemporary audience's knowledge, after the fact, as it were, that Hedda had indeed "done such a thing," perhaps allows them to discredit Krogstad's dismissive brutalization of Nora's romantic fantasy.

Modes: narrative, lyric, and dramatic

Many approaches to the study of writing, including the typical course offerings at postsecondary institutions, divide the discipline into genres: poetry, fiction, non-fiction, and drama. This division has its uses. What this taxonomy often obscures, however, is the fact that each of these genres employs what I think of as different *modes*: the *narrative, lyric,* and *dramatic*, all of which can appear in a single work in any genre. The narrative mode, quite simply, has a story and a story teller. Much of the interest in most narratives is in the relationship between the two, and the degree to which the reader, listener, or audience trusts the narrator or shares her perspective. Narrative carries with it an element of pastness, of events already complete, always already told and retold. The lyric mode, on the other hand, while it also has a "story teller" – at least insofar as it has a presenting voice – has no story, traditionally understood: it is generally concerned with description, expression, and the evocation of an emotional response. It, too, can evoke the past – there is an element of reflection in much lyric writing – but it also conveys emotion that is "present-ed" (or made present). The third mode, the dramatic, in its purest form has a story but no story-teller: the story is *shown* (ostended) – the basic element of theatre. It has a sense of immediacy, and the audience is left to its own devices to determine its meaning.

Narrative is most frequently associated with novels, short stories, ballads, and historical non-fiction – each of which, nevertheless, can contain (dramatic) dialogue and moments of pure description or expression. The lyric mode is most frequently associated with lyrical poetry and song "lyrics" – which often, of course, emerge from an implicit or incipient situation or "story," and which can also include dialogue. And of course the dramatic mode, while it appears as dialogue in fiction, non-fiction, and verse, is most frequently associated with plays.

Most plays, while relying principally on the dramatic mode, employ all three, sometimes sequentially, sometimes at a single moment. In Shakespeare, soliloquies often lyrically and eloquently express the state of mind of Hamlet, Macbeth, Lear, or Othello, while direct address by messengers such as the Captain reporting on the battle in the second scene of

Macbeth, or by choric figures in *Pericles* or *The Winter's Tale* (where the play's title invokes the narrative form and the mustiness of its pastness), functions as pure narrative. The Chorus in *Henry V* might be understood as a narrator explicitly lamenting the limitations of the dramatic mode while stepping in between the acts to fill gaps in the story that dramatic presentation purportedly can't handle. Always, as here, the modes function and acquire meaning relationally, and it is important to identify as part of a script analysis what mode is at work, when and how these modes contribute to the play's functioning and shape its rhythms, how the shifts from one predominant mode to another occur, and how they vary the script's textures. Backstories, exposition, and gaps can be filled in through the use of narrative, for example, while varying the mode of address. Similarly, the immediacy and forward thrust of dramatic action can pause and be reflected upon in lyrical passages.

Not surprisingly, in *A Doll House*, which is often considered the first naturalistic play, the dominant mode is dramatic: the audience watches as events unfold before them over the three days of the action. But even here, Nora is left alone onstage on a number of occasions on which she waxes lyrical:

> NORA: (*with bewildered glances, groping about, seizing HELMER's domino* [a kind of caped coat], *throwing it around her, and speaking in short, hoarse, broken whispers.*) Never see him again. Never, never, (*Putting her shawl over her head.*) Never see the children either – them too. Never, never. Oh, the freezing black water! The depths – down – Oh, I wish it were over – He has it now; he's reading it – now. Oh no, no, not yet. Torvald, good-bye, you and the children – (*She starts for the hall; as she does, HELMER throws open his door and stands with an open letter in his hand.*) (186–7)

This moment is all the more affecting as lyricism after the earlier scene, which might be called lyrical *action,* in which

Nora plays with her children, with unscripted "*laughing and shouting*" permeating the playing space until Krogstad appears, ominous and silent in the doorway to the hall (143). Even the usually restrained Mrs Linde has a scene of pure lyrical expression when she looks forward with delight to having "someone to work for, to live for" just prior to leaving the play world and entering her new life with Krogstad (180).

This last example also, of course, has a dramatic function: it confirms that Mrs Linde is not simply sacrificing herself for Nora but is genuinely happy to renew her relationship with Krogstad. Narrative passages in naturalistic dramas are even more likely to serve such a dual function, often in the form of exposition. When the action is confined to only three days, as in *A Doll House*, backstory and necessary exposition can most easily be provided through narrative. Indeed, one suspects at her first appearance that Mrs Linde exists in *A Doll House* purely in order to give Nora an excuse to tell the story of her having saved Helmer by surreptitiously taking out a loan: "The whole amount?" Mrs Linde prompts. "But Nora, how is that possible?" "But where did you get it from then?" "Nora, I simply don't understand" (135). And of course Nora tells Mrs Linde what the audience needs to know.

When such a moment is well written, as it is here, the narrative is interesting in the ways that effective narrative always is, for what it reveals about the storyteller as well as for the story it tells. But it is at the same time as dramatic, even performative – Nora's story acts upon Mrs Linde and influences her subsequent actions – as it is lyrically expressive: we gain a window into Nora's pride at having saved her husband, her fear at his ever finding out. Nevertheless, lyrical and narrative moments within a naturalistic (or any) play need to be handled carefully, particularly by directors, because they can shatter the illusion or shift the terms of engagement in ways that require attention and awareness. This is why it is so difficult for many directors and actors to find ways to deal with the famous soliloquies in Shakespeare, when lyrical expression trumps action and the audience, in most productions, gets a window into the characters' souls.

Signs: iconic, indexical, and symbolic

Just as there are lyrical and narrative moments within the predominantly dramatic mode of most scripts, so there are indexical and symbolic signs within a type of writing that relies predominantly on the iconic. It is nevertheless important in undertaking script analysis to recognize when a sign evokes its referent iconically through resemblance and refers to meanings already assigned in the past, indexically through indications or pointings that establish their meaning in the here and now, or symbolically through arbitrary or unmotivated assignations of meaning that project into a future. Within a relatively broad interpretative community iconic signs – whether they be painted backdrops, real furnishings, or actors playing characters – can most often be easily read, but can also be least interesting for an audience familiar with the unchallenged theatrical conventions of the moment. Indexical signs can require more effort for a director, a dramaturge, a critic, or an audience member, working out where "here" and "there" are, who or what "you" and "she" or "this" and "that" refer to, and just what the dialogue or action is pointing to offstage or outside of the timeframe of the action. Most scripts require careful attention to such signs, some of which – such as Lear's famous last words, "Look there, look there!" (V.3.312) – are ultimately ambiguous or even enigmatic, and require directorial or scholarly decision-making: as an ungrounded indexical sign, Lear's "there" is up for directorial grabs. Symbolic signs, finally, require either insider knowledge (membership in the community that has assigned them meaning), translation (for non-members of that community), or participation in the script's own establishment of a henceforth shared (or shattered) convention: the scent of frangipani blossoms in Samoan playwright Makarite Urale's 2006 play

Frangipani Perfume may be unfamiliar to audiences beyond the tropics, but it becomes palpable and easily comes to represent home for the three Samoan women whose stories of drudgery as unskilled labourers in Aotearoa New Zealand constitute the evocative movement-based action of the play.

As I argued in Chapter 1, the iconic sign is particularly useful in naturalistic theatre, where resemblance between the sign and its referent is crucial to the interpellation of the audience into the world and myth (or ideology) of the play: "yes, that's a chair," "yes, I recognize that actor as an attractive young woman," or "yes, that's just what Black people are like." The indexical sign, however, can disrupt the naturalization of ideology, particularly in variations upon Epic theatre – "look, isn't *that* strange?", "how could something like *that* happen?", "how did *that* representation become an index of female attractiveness?", or "how has it come about that dominant culture thinks of Black people *that* way?" – as in the work of Brecht, or even, arguably, Ibsen. And the sign as symbol in expressionist, symbolist, and surrealist plays, particularly when it insists on its own arbitrariness, can create the possibility of new and emerging regimes of meaning, which may be a way of reading the ending of even so naturalistic a play as *A Doll House*. What, beyond the play, does Nora's exit point to? Finally, of course, icon, index, and symbol, like all signs, can occur not only in the same work, but in the same sign, and as always they do their work in relation to one another rather than independently. Mother Courage's silent scream is at once iconic (it mimics a recognizable expression of grief), indexical (it points to the causes of such grief), and symbolic (it stands for the devastation brought about by war), and this is how it gains its gestic force.

The naturalism of *A Doll House*, of course, relies on its iconic verisimilitude, and Ibsen accordingly describes sets, furnishings, and costumes in almost obsessive ways in his stage directions, locking them into iconic resemblances to identical items in the "real world." But the play also relies heavily on indices and symbols, sometimes when it matters most. *A Doll House* is structured around indexical signs of arrival – four prominent and progressively significant ringings of the doorbell signalling the arrivals of Nora (125), Mrs Linde (129), Krogstad (138), and the dying Dr Rank (162); numerous knocks on the play's multiply signifying doors; "*quiet footsteps* [...] *on the stairs*" (176); and various calling cards, useful because they do not necessarily or equally announce who has arrived to all the characters on the stage, or to the audience (see 167). And the play famously ends with an indexical sign of departure that was said to have shaken the western world: "*From below, the sound of a door slamming shut*" (196). Ibsen uses signs that are at once perfectly iconic, and yet at another level foreground by pointing indexically to social significance in a manner that is subtler than Brecht's sometimes is, but does similar work. In the wake of the supremely awkward scene in which Nora virtually seduces Dr Rank and then rebukes him for confessing his love for her, Nora calls for a lamp which, once provided, "sheds light" on the proceedings, for the characters and for the audience: "Aren't you a little bit ashamed, now that the lamp is here" she asks? (166). The lamp here serves as a kind of alienating and historicizing index that allows the audience – and perhaps the characters – to read the scene's social significance without ever shattering its iconic illusion.

A Doll House similarly makes use of signs as symbols to which it assigns specific and somewhat arbitrary meanings in addition to those summoned by their mere iconicity: the macaroons, the Christmas tree, the mailbox, the cross-marked calling cards announcing Dr Rank's terminal diagnosis. But the most notable and most complex of these is the tarantella dance that we see "rehearsed" in the second act and hear performed and discussed in the third. As a cultural text imported from southern Italy, the dance comes with certain symbolic encodings for those in the know: its name derives from that of the spider, the tarantula, the poison of which was thought to be purged from the body through frenetic, up-tempo dancing. For the cognoscenti it suggests, at least in Act 2, Nora's struggle for life through a delirious attempt to rid herself of the poison that has infected her. Torvald says, "you dance as if your life were at stake," and she confirms, "it is" (174). But the dance accrues other meanings as well, as a *danse macabre*, a dance of expiation, of "pure madness," of "fun," of hysteria, and of sexual titillation or humiliation. It is unclear what it signifies for Mrs Linde, who enters at its height and, "*standing dumbfounded at the door*" says, simply, "Ah–!" (174). But it *is* clear – and this may be the reason for her entry at this point – that it does not mean for her what it does for Nora, Helmer, or Dr Rank. Indeed, her entry seems to refocus the gaze of the audience and to insist on alternative significations based on positionality. Like the doubloon in Melville's *Moby-Dick* (for Ahab, "some certain significance lurks in all things" (427)), the dance seems to mean something different for everyone who encounters it, and like the doubloon, its interpretations perhaps say more about the interpreters – the characters in the play, its critics, its directors – than they do about the dance itself.

Structure: plot and character

Structure simply refers to how the script is put together. This involves analysing, as it would for the structural analysis of a bridge: its materials (what it's made of), its design (how those materials are arranged), and how these relate to its function. In the case of a bridge, it would be surprising if a footbridge over a stream were to have the same materials or design as a bridge for cars, trucks, and trains that also had to leave room for cargo ships beneath, and a similar logic applies to the structuring of plays. The materials for most scripts are all or some of: plot, characters (or roles), action, and language. Most are organized in time and space through the use of acts, scenes, exits, entrances, or other units. A structural analysis involves identifying the units, what is in them, how they relate to one another, and what those relationships serve to communicate.

i. Plot

As discussed in Chapter 2, plot consists of the organization and presentation of the story, if there is one. If there is no story (as in much postdramatic theatre) plot consists of the organization of the action(s). It is useful when analysing plot to distinguish it schematically – even mechanically – from purely chronological story. Indeed, it is often useful to go so far as to chart story chronologically from beginning to end, beginning with the earliest backstory, and mapping it against the plot. The *story* of *A Doll House*, surprisingly, begins with the dissolute life of Dr Rank's father, from whom he inherited the syphilis – "tuberculosis of the spine" (156) – from which he is dying and which literalizes the moral corruption that Torvald Helmer so dreads. The central story begins with Nora, a motherless child in the home of a father who treats her like a doll, cared for by Anne-Marie, a woman who has given up her own illegitimate child and has been hired to look after Nora.

These are not, of course, where the *plot* of the play begins; indeed, we don't hear of most of this until the beginning of the second act, and some of it, about Nora's father, we only hear fully in the play's final sequence. Indeed the plot begins *in medias res* (in the middle of things) on Christmas Eve many years later, after Nora has been married to a husband, Torvald Helmer, by whom she has had three children and who also treats her like a doll. After a brief entry and an opening scene between husband and wife that establishes the nature of their relationship, Mrs Linde arrives, a friend from Nora's schooldays, and through their exchanges – "tell me about yourself" (131) – the audience learns something of the contrasting stories of the women's lives in the ten years since they last met. This, though not completely filled in until later in the play, forms much of the play's important "backstory" and also briefly introduces what might be considered the play's major subplot: the story of Mrs Linde and Krogstad, which runs in contrasting parallel to that of Nora and Helmer. These two scenes – not labelled as such in the published script – can be considered the play's first two structural units, marked off, as are most units throughout the script, by entrances and exits. In subsequent units in the first act we are introduced to Dr Rank, to Nora's light-hearted relationship with her children, and, ominously, to Krogstad, whom we hear – with more backstory to be filled in later – has known Helmer from their student days (145). From Krogstad we also learn, a full 20 pages into the published script, about the key initiating action in the story: Nora's forgery of her father's signature, also ten years earlier, in order to borrow money from Krogstad, who is himself guilty of forgery.

Why is the story told in this way? And what is the purpose in charting the difference between the beginning of the story and the beginning of the plot, or more importantly the action or event that initiates it as significant dramatic action? How, in other words, does this relate to function? The initiating action in the play proper – in the plot – is Helmer's promotion to a position of power over Krogstad and his decision to fire Krogstad from his job at the bank for "moral" reasons, which of course turn out to be more petty and personal (and hypocritical) than genuinely ethical. It is this event that introduces the play's central conflict between idealism and realism, and puts into play the various actantial forces that are brought together in its first act, brought to a head in the second, and "resolved" in the third. These forces and their interaction constitute what the play is about.

It is the initiating action at which the structural analysis of any script begins. Such an analysis will then identify the various units, however defined, that together constitute the script, considering what these units consist of, how many of them there are, how they relate to one another, and what patterns and shapes they establish. It will consider such things as what new information is introduced to the audience in each unit, the points at which the action changes direction, and the shape of the script as it evolves. It is often useful to spatialize plot structure by plotting it on a chart or graph, with act, scene, and line numbers marking where significant events occur that change the course of the action. And it is useful within such a charting to consider such things as which and how many characters or other "actants" are present (physically or otherwise) in each scene, what forces they bring to bear on one another, and how these forces play themselves out. It is also useful to map the temporality of the represented action against the "real time" of the audience, and to chart the action's pace and rhythm.

In *A Doll House*, each act, while divided into units by the entrances and exits of characters, plays itself out consecutively in a way that coincides with the audience's temporal experience of it, without gaps, flashbacks, or flashforwards: the duration of each act is precisely the same in the represented action as in the "real time" of the audience, and this gives the play much of its naturalistic intensity. Between each act a day passes – perhaps while the audience is at intermission: Act 1 occurs on Christmas Eve, Act 2 on Christmas Day ending at 5:00 p.m., and Act 3 on Boxing Day at night. But the *shape* of the play is arguably more irregular, proceeding as it does through the fits and starts of Nora's increasing anxiety, achieving maximum tension in the frenetic rehearsal of the tarantella, and then moving inexorably towards the reversal that occurs when Nora's anticipated "miracle" fails to happen. And there is an identifiable music in all of this, moving (with identifiable rhythms) through various crescendos and diminuendos, through various keys, and from various atonalities and dissonances to varying degrees of harmony or (ir)resolution.

ii. Character

Character analysis, particularly for those trained in the Stanislavski System or American Method and their variants, or for the inheritors of an Aristotelian logic of mimesis (imitation) and catharsis (the vicarious purging of emotion through identification and empathy), is generally understood to consist of mining the script for clues about the characters' psychological depths, motivations, and objectives. In naturalistic plays this usefully consists of considering carefully not simply what a character says and does, what is said about them, and the tensions among these, but also how the character speaks. This last means analysing their word choice: What worlds do their words come from? Are they Latinate, sophisticated, and abstract, for example, or are they folksy, colloquial and earthy? A character who refers to "automobiles" can reasonably be understood to come from a different social and psychological realm than one who talks about "cars" and another who refers to his "wheels." Characters from different realms will talk about "excrement," "doo-doo," and "shit." Similarly a character might draw her imagery and figurative language from the corporate, legal, political, medical, sports, or natural worlds, and much is revealed when different characters talk in different metaphors about the bottom line, the finish line, or the line on the horizon. In *A Doll House* Torvald and Nora speak a nursery room language of little "larks and squirrels" with one another (128), but both shift to different registers when alone or speaking to others – and Nora reveals only to Mrs Linde and Dr Rank her secret longing to say "to hell and be dammed" (141).

Syntax can be similarly revealing. A character who speaks in long, convoluted sentences with multiple conditional clauses is easily distinguished from one who speaks in short, simple sentences. A prevalence of interrogatives reveals a different cast of mind than do declarative or even imperative moods. In their first scene together Torvald peppers Nora with what he takes to be rhetorical questions – "Is my little lark twittering out there?" (125); "Are your scatterbrains off again?" (126); "What are those little birds called that always fly through their fortunes?" (127). In their last scene Nora tellingly, and for the first time in the play, resorts to imperatives and direct statements, much to his surprise and dismay: "Sit down, Torvald; we have a lot to talk over" (190).

Similar analyses can be done of a character's rhythms (short and clipped, long and languid, regular or irregular) and even of their preference for voiced or unvoiced consonants, or for short or long, close or open, front or back vowels. Torvald's opening line in the play about his "little lark twittering" (125), with its clipped consonants and short, close vowels enacts his condescension and stands in stark contrast, in sound quality alone, for example, to Mrs Linde's "nine–ten long years" at her entrance (130), or Dr Rank's rancour-filled account of Krogstad at his: "a type of person who scuttles about breathlessly, sniffing out hints of moral corruption" (140). In their delivery, these phrases do specific and very different things to the mouths, faces, and bodies of the actors who speak them and therefore to the embodied receptors of audiences who hear them.

What a semiotic approach adds to this psychological and linguistic character analysis, and what leads me to consider character under the rubric of structural analysis, is consideration of the characters and other elements in the play (including abstractions, collectives, groups, and off-stage pressures) as *actants*, forces that are brought to bear on the action and on one another. "An actant," Anne Ubersfeld explains, "is not a substance or a being, it is an element in a relation" (45) – and semiotics, as always, is fundamentally concerned with (differential) relations. Actantial functions, when they *are* performed by characters, are usefully distinguished from Stanislavskian objectives and super-objectives because they operate on the level of plot rather than of character and motivation and because any one actant can simultaneously or sequentially bring different forces into play. Ubersfeld points, for example, to King Lear's eldest daughters, who begin the play in a supportive, what she calls "helper" role in relation to their father's intention to divide the kingdom, but who later become his opponents. "The change in their actantial role," Ubersfeld argues, "is not a function of a change in what they want [that is, their motivations or objectives] but rather a result of the complexity of Lear's situation" (40) and the relational play of actantial vectors that they and others bring to bear on the action.

The actantial forces at work in any script can be psychological, social, cultural, ethical, political, or ideological, and they can enter the force field of the action through character, collective, discourse, climate, fiat, directive, felt pressure, or belief system, among other things. In *A Doll House* Nora's desire for some kind of independence (from debt, from masculinist patronizing) shifts over the course of the action and comes into conflict with Torvald's desire for bourgeois respectability and male privilege, the mores of a middle-class culture, the strictures of a humanly indifferent legal system, her responsibilities to her children, and Krogstad's desire to renew his social and economic standing through blackmail. Nora is in part supported by the friendships of Dr Rank and Mrs Linde, partly subjected to Dr Rank's need for love and Mrs Linde's need to be needed, and partly mirrored by the parallel but opposite arc of Mrs Linde's story.

Actantial analysis is difficult, and it is in large part subjective, depending on the analysts' decisions about what the play is about, how it speaks to their audiences, and what force fields they wish to foreground as central. But its rewards are significant, perhaps even more so when the analysis is not of a pre-existing script but of the scenario for a devised performance.

Devising

"Scenario" analysis, which I have used to distinguish the process for devised as opposed to scripted work, is admittedly a misnomer. Most devised theatre starts "from scratch"

(Heddon and Milling 3) – or better, starts from a question, an idea, or, best, an urgency. Scenarios, if they exist at all (as in *commedia-del-arte* inspired shows), usually come later, posted on the walls of studios as maps of an exploration-in-progress. Devised projects are infinitely various, but they usually begin with a group of artists who share an interest in the initial question, idea, or urgency. They often also share "starting-point" resources of some sort: personnel, research, stories, interviews, news clips, books, poems, space, objects, artwork, interviews, personal reflection and memory, bodies, skills, training, consultants, or even writers "on" but not "of" the show. And perhaps most crucially they share a need for dramaturgical (structural) analysis of each of these things from the outset. Whether this comes in the form of an individual playing the role of development dramaturge or just a shared "dramaturgical sensibility" (Proehl), dramaturgy is crucial to devised work. Development dramaturgy is the script analysis of devising; it is the process of script analysis when there is no script.

There are not many accounts of the dramaturgy of script analysis in devised work, and devising processes are, as I've said, infinitely various. But most share some essential features that might illuminate what "script analysis" could mean, dramaturgically, for devising, and some of these are explicated clearly in two essays by Canadian scholar, director, and dramaturge Bruce Barton. Building on the foundational work of Alison Oddey, Barton outlines a general methodology for such work that includes: a refusal of primacy to text, a shift of priorities from product to process, a heightened engagement with space and place, an exploration of emergent technologies, and a fundamental interdisciplinarity (Barton, "Introduction" xviii). Barton argues that these principles underlie a distinctive approach to composition in devised work, which tends to rely on improvisation, multiple authorship, found and adapted text, physical gesture, and structural principles such as collage, montage, "con-fusion," weaving, or quilting (xvix).

In a second essay, writing about the role of director/dramaturge Ker Wells of Number Eleven Theatre in Halifax, Nova Scotia, working on show called *Icaria*, Barton provides an example of one such dramaturgical/compositional practice. Wells (together with the company he was leading) is part of what has become known as the "Grotowski diaspora," a loose affiliation of practitioners around the world who trained with the late Polish director and guru Jerzy Grotowski, his disciple Eugenio Barba, or members of Barba's own global network (in Wells' case, director Richard Fowler, Barba's English translator). Wells' process is representative of those of many in this diaspora, but it is also more broadly representative of the main features of theatrical devising as it has evolved elsewhere since the 1960s, including most of the otherwise diverse practices surveyed in Deirdre Heddon and Jane Milling's history of *Devising Performance* and described in more detail by the editors and contributors to Alex Mermikides and Jackie Smart's *Devising in Process*. Indeed, it is surprising, given the frequently acknowledged diversity of devising practices, how many features those practices can be understood to share, and how many of them can be productively understood to be semiological.

What Barton describes, though he is talking about the work of a director, is a dramaturgical process involving what I will here call "script" analysis. Having agreed on an initial loose inspiration – the story of Icarus from Greek mythology – the company begins with resources, in this case the bodies, training, and actions ("patterns of movement and voice") of each member working in isolation, together with their individual research, gathering "personal reflection and memory, works of visual art and music, and found or created text" ("Mining" 142). Building on this gathering phase, each of the actors shapes her material into one or more short movement/voice sequences:

> Then, under Wells' directorial eye and sensibility, and working from this already once digested raw material, the

company begins the long collaborative process of establishing connections and interpenetrations of meaning. Specifically, Wells assumes the lead role in the troupe's search for points of resonance (through similarity, contrast, and parallelism) among the individual preparatory sequences. At this stage, this resonance is primarily physical in nature (e.g. in terms of spatial dimensions, direction, size, tempo, rhythm, etc.). After carefully observing the performers individually, Wells begins to orchestrate multiple, simultaneous enactments of two or more sequences. Asking for bodily repositionings and modulations of scale, velocity, etc., the director initiates a process of sculpting in both space and time, seeking out the most evocative, striking and engaging points of physical correspondence [...]. Such sculpting is seldom an end in and of itself, however, and the most significant points of resonance are those that the director interprets as *thematic*. His early responses therefore assume a dominant authorial influence, as he attempts to identify the initial conjunctions, or sites of relational meaning, in the embryonic narrative structure. (143, emphasis in original)

Each of the elements Barton identifies in this work – similarity, contrast, parallelism, spatial dimensions, direction, size, tempo, rhythm, scale, velocity – is fundamental to any script analysis, and each is fundamentally dramaturgical. That he calls these "factors of signification" (143) acknowledges that they are also fundamentally semiotic. Wells' activities as Barton describes them – establishing connections and interpenetrations of meaning, searching for points of resonance, orchestrating, modulating, sculpting in space and time, identifying conjunctions and narrative structures – are also dramaturgical; insofar as the interpenetrations and conjunctions are "sites of relational meaning" and the points of resonance "*thematic*," they are also semiotic.

Geoffrey Proehl identifies dramaturgy as "the name given to that set of elements necessary to the working of a play at any moment in its passage from imagination to embodiment," and he identifies those elements as "its *repetitions and patterns*," "its unfolding *narratives*," "its unique *world*," "its *characters*," "its *spectacles*," its "*metatheatre*," and its literary (plot, character, theme, diction, music, and spectacle), organic ("stem-cell"), and spatial (architectural) "*structures*" (19–20, emphasis added). These elements generally characterize both scripted and devised work, but they are particularly apt as guideposts to structuring the dramaturgical analysis of devised work as it passes "from imagination to embodiment." It is not always necessary to address each of them separately or to address all of them, but they work well as a check list. Because devised work is so various and its discussion therefore so bound to descriptions of specific processes, I will draw for examples on a particularly rich intercultural work led by the Indigenous Guna and Rappahannock theatre artist Monique Mojica (Figure 4.1) on which I participated as dramaturge, *Chocolate Woman Dreams the Milky Way*. I will begin with the question, idea, and *urgency* that drive the project, and move through an account of *methodology*, the assembled *resources*, the *process* design, its *structures*, and its *languages*.

Urgency

The dramaturgical analysis that subtends all devising projects, as I have suggested, is driven by an idea that issues in a question that is urgent for the creators, and this question has to be foregrounded throughout. As Alison Oddey says, "Central to the devising process is problem solving" (22). There are many instances, particularly in postmodern and postdramatic productions, in which devisers claim that their inspirations are random, derived from arbitrarily or accidentally assembled resources; I would argue that while this may on the surface be true, the arbitrariness of the selection process usually masks an urgency that may not, at least in the

Figure 4.1 Monique Mojica in *Chocolate Woman Dreams the Milky Way*
Source: Photo by Ric Knowles

initial exploratory stages of the work, have risen to the level of consciousness. Where the initiating questions and organizing principles subtending a devised project are genuinely random, unmotivated, or opportunistic, in my experience the production that results tends to be hollow, self-obsessed, or uninteresting, however accomplished the participating artists.

Chocolate Woman Dreams the Milky Way began at an intersection of urgencies, but as with many major created works it began most urgently with crisis. Mojica initiated the project at a time of deep personal crisis (Carter, "Chocolate" 171), but also at a turning point in her professional life (she had left Turtle Gals Performance Ensemble), and in her sense of purpose around her art:

> I am very grateful to the process that Turtle Gals went through diving headlong into the dark places of victimization. The willingness to go there has allowed me to use those depths as a springboard – a trampoline that offers me the possibility of grounding myself in another place: a place where I cease to identify with my own victimization and no longer recognize my reflection as "the victim." (Mojica, "Chocolate" 164)

Mojica initiated the process, as she says, to save her life, but also to try to find a way both for herself *and for Native theatre more generally* to move beyond "rehashing a victim narrative" (Mojica, qtd in Bimm), a trap laid by colonization for Native artists. She began, then, by asking, "In the midst of dislocation and (oft-times) despair, how can the actions of the disaffected and spiritually embattled change the world? Or more to the point, how does the representation of action [...] reassemble the world and restore harmony?" (Carter, "Chocolate" 171). "What stories would I tell if I started from a place of connectedness instead of from a place of rupture?" (Mojica, qtd in Knowles, "Native" 74).

Methodology

In any devised production, the identification of an urgent research question must be followed by a methodology by which to go about answering that question: a sense of how to proceed. In semiotic terms this means discovering the means of producing meaning. *Chocolate Woman* builds on two pre-existing methodological pursuits: "Storyweaving," as developed by Mojica's Guna and Rappahannock mother and maternal aunts at New York's Spiderwoman Theater, and "Native Performance Culture" research, as developed by Plains Cree director Floyd Favel working with Mojica, her aunt Muriel Miguel, Tuscarora musician Pura Fé, and others in a number of workshops since 1991.

As described by Muriel Miguel, Storyweaving is a methodology derived from traditional forms of Indigenous storytelling and an Indigenous belief system rooted in the interconnectedness of all things. In the Spiderwoman methodology it is used in very specific ways "to entwine stories and fragments of stories with words, music, song, film, dance and movement, thereby creating a production that is multi-layered and complex; an emotional, cultural and political tapestry" (qtd in Mojica, "Chocolate" 176).

Native Performance Culture research is an exploratory project concerned with the relationship between contemporary performance and the traditional forms of Indigenous cultures, including "dances, songs, weaving, myths, and ceremonies" (Favel, "Poetry" 34). Native Performance Culture research had previously focused, in particular, on the Plains Cree Round Dance (Favel Starr, "Artificial" 70) and the Sioux winter count glyphs on which Favel drew for the rehearsal/creation of *The House of Sonja*, his Native adaptation of Chekov's *Uncle Vanya* (Appleford 253). The method attempts to "isolate the technical principles" of Indigenous cultural texts and use them as starting points for contemporary performance (Favel, "Waskawewin" 114). *Chocolate*

Woman was an extension of this research, neither imitating nor representing, but attempting to build upon "the DNA," as Favel says – the deep structure – of Guna textile and pictographic traditions in creating contemporary Native theatre (Favel Starr, "Artificial" 70).

A third evolving methodology for devising that was used in the development of *Chocolate Woman*, in addition to copious archival, library, and internet research, is a combination of what Mojica calls "embodied research" and "deep improvisation." Embodied research is deeply experiential; deep improvisation comes from embodied memory as activated though immersion in the culture. "I placed myself on the land, in the ocean, on a river, among [her Guna] relatives, and embodied them by assimilating and integrating myself with their vibrations," Mojica explains. "I listened to what [these experiences] had to tell me, and listened to how my body responded. I put it all in one big vat until I couldn't hold it any more" (qtd in Bimm). She then brings all of this information, stored in her body, into the studio, where she engages fully and deeply in an improvisatory process from which movement, gesture, and language emerge in a complex weave that constitutes a fully embodied "first draft" that is much more than simply text.

Resources

In addition to a methodology appropriate to the investigation, devisers need to assemble an archive of resources that are also appropriate and sufficient to addressing the central issues in the process-as-investigation. Each of these resources will have its own signifying value and potential, each will work together in tandem and in tension with the others throughout the process to generate new meanings, and all will be subject to on-going dramaturgical and semiotic analysis. To answer *her* particular questions, Mojica turned directly to the Guna part of her heritage – the people, stories, and material culture of the people of Guna Yala, an autonomous territory on the coast of Panama that has existed independently since the successful Guna revolution of 1925, and that retains uninterrupted many of its pre-colonial traditions and practices. These traditions and practices constitute, for her, "a place of connectedness" rather than one of rupture.

Mojica assembled a powerful constellation of resources, beginning with an almost entirely Indigenous but nevertheless broadly intercultural creative team. Oswaldo DeLeón Kantule, the show's set designer and cultural consultant, is the grandson of one of the leaders of the 1925 Guna revolution, the son of a *saila* (spiritual leader) on the island of Ustupu, and the brother of exquisite mola-makers there. He is an internationally known Guna visual artist whose work is grounded in the sacred stories and icons of Guna culture. Floyd Favel, who directed the early development stages of *Chocolate Woman*, is a Plains Cree director from the Poundmaker First Nation in Saskatchewan who was one of the last students of Polish director Jerzy Grotowski. Favel had worked with Mojica and others since the early 1990s in developing Native Performance Culture research. Jill Carter, who worked on the production as witness and scribe, is an Anishinabe scholar and theatre artist, Canada's first Native PhD graduate in Theatre Studies. Her expertise is in the Storyweaving work of Spiderwoman Theater and its progeny. These four constituted the initial creative team who entered the first workshop for the production in 2007.

After the initial workshop others were added to the team. Guna and Rappahannock performer Gloria Miguel, co-founder of Spiderwoman Theater and Mojica's mother, joined under contract as both actor and elder. Omushkego Cree designer Erika Iserhoff, with a specialized knowledge of Indigenous textile arts, joined as costume designer and co-designer of sets and props, while Mohawk and Anishinabe Michel Charbonneau designed lights and Mushkegowuk Cree designer Andy Moro served as technical director. After Favel had left the project, prominent Guna actor José Colman came from Panama City to take over its direction, and Guna musician Marden Paniza, also from Panama, joined as composer. In addition to these major Indigenous artists, anthropologist Brenda Farnell brought her expertise in the annotation of Indigenous movement and gesture to the project, working with Mojica on the recording and animation of its pictographic score, while I joined the team as a dramaturge with experience in Indigenous and intercultural performance. Venezuelan Gia Nahmens, of Basque heritage, served as stage manager.

Beyond the assembled personnel, resources for the project included, initially, an extensive gathering of the mola textile arts of Guna women, the deeply culturally coded paintings of DeLeón Kantule and his explications of their relationship to Guna belief systems, and Guna pictographic annotations of congress house chants. In addition to these primarily visual resources, the team collected cultural stories of major female figures in Guna cosmology, Haudenosaunee and Powhatan creation stories, and research on Guna culture, cultural texts, and practices, including archival, library, and online work and the "embodied research" of travel to Panama City and Guna Yala, involving meetings with contemporary artists, artists who work with traditional forms (including molas), cultural workers, sailas (spiritual leaders) and kantules (healers), and lived encounters with the land, river, and sea environments. A final and key resource was Mojica's own personal and cultural (auto)biography, (blood) memory, and lived experience, including apparently arbitrary memories of *Alice in Wonderland*, The Jefferson Airplane, and Perry Como.

This was an extraordinarily rich assemblage of personnel and other resources, but as I hope my discussion below reveals, as in all devising processes they required semiological analysis – "script" analysis – to unlock their potential in order to orchestrate them formally as the basis of an evolving process and performance.

Process

A key part of the dramaturgical and analytical work on any devised project is on the process itself: any work of art – and this is particularly true of performance – can perhaps best be understood as a record of its creation process, one that puts the audience through a distilled version of the creators' sequence of discoveries. Designing a devising process involves the orchestration of methodology against resources: *how* does the collective address the assembled materials; what patterns and relationships does it perceive among them; what stories, characters, actants, worlds, images, actions, and spectacles are incipient in them; and how can it work towards their organization into a performance that addresses the questions it has set out to ask?

Research and analysis, however, are never complete; most devising processes benefit from being structured as a series of creation workshops with enough time between each to conduct new research and undertake the analysis of what was accomplished in the previous one(s). And most devising processes consist of three overlapping phases: *analysis and embodiment* (of resources), *improvisation and annotation*, and *structuring*.

The first step is usually to address analytically what the members of the creative team bring to the project, both individually and as a collective: the initial question, quite literally, is "what are we all doing here?" For *Chocolate Woman* it was clear, for example, that DeLeón Kantule was there for his design sensibilities and his knowledge of Guna stories and culture, Favel for his central role in the evolution of Native Performance Culture Research, Carter for her knowledge of Storyweaving, Iserhoff for her specialization in Indigenous textile arts, Mojica for her personal and cultural autobiography, and so on. The second question is "what are these artefacts and other resources doing here, what do they consist of, and what pressures do they bring to bear on our central question(s)?" Two of the resources gathered for *Chocolate Woman* might serve as examples: molas and pictographs.

Molas are appliqué and reverse-appliqué panels hand-stitched and embroidered by Guna women in several layers of fabric and sewn together to form the fronts and backs of their blouses. The most traditional patterns, originally painted or tattooed on women's bodies, at once tell layered stories of Guna culture and conceal/protect those stories through abstraction. The layers of fabric and detailed stitching give the *molas* intricacy and depth of a very different kind – an interlaced layering of multiple surfaces – than the perspectival and characterological depth of most western dramaturgy, and their *ways* of meaning require careful and culturally sensitive kinds of semiological analysis.

Mojica relates the process of mola-making to the Story-weaving methodology that she inherited from Spiderwoman Theater. She compares the cutting away of layers of cloth in the creation of molas, revealing the colours and layers beneath, to the creation of her own performance as a process "of cutting away to reveal what is contained within our blood memory, between the cells" ("Project History"). Under DeLeón Kantule's guidance and in tandem with a detailed consideration of his paintings, the Chocolate Woman Collective pored over dozens and dozens of molas, analysing them for the stories they told, for their structural principles, for their designs, dualities, and abstractions, and for the windows they provided into Guna life and belief systems. The team ultimately distilled these semiological principles into dramaturgical codings for the production, to the extent that Jill Carter has called the show itself "a dense theatrical mola" in four layers, each encoded with its own palette of colours and specific detailing that stitch together a fragmented self ("Chocolate" 171–2).

Unlike molas, which in their traditional incarnations emphasize a semiotic geometry over iconicity, patterning over symbolism (Allen 118–19), Guna pictographs are abstracted *iconic* records of verbal (and verb- and action-based) healing chants, mnemonic devices that evoke text, movement, and, perhaps most importantly, cultural memory and recovery. "The pictographs are representations of the *kwage* [heart, essence]," Mojica explains, "of the vibrational frequency and energetical fields created through the language, chants, rattles, drums, flutes, and dancing during ritual and prayer. Therefore, embodying these could potentially create an energetic effect in the body" ("Excerpt" 61–2). The collective analysed not only the semioses of the pictographs themselves as they scrolled from right to left, then left to right, and so on down the page (originally wooden tablets) but also their use in the Guna congress houses by Guna apprentices to learn, memorize, and eventually embody the chants (Severi 252). As Jill Carter has said, "the investigative process for *Chocolate Woman Dreams the Milky Way* followed Guna protocol in that rehearsals began with tellings and retellings of traditional stories and chants by De León Kantule [...] to the 'apprentice' (Mojica), who began to more deeply explore these and her relationships therewith" ("Chocolate" 174). This exploration through deep improvisation following intense, embodied research on the culture and stories of the Guna people can be understood dramaturgically as the generation, playing out, and testing of the actantial forces at play in the process.

Eventually, even as the dramaturgy of *Chocolate Woman* constituted the show as a theatrical mola, the performance text evolved, through deep improvisations and the pictographic annotation of improvised movement, as an embodied, three-dimensional and animated pictograph that employed, in the constitution of its *mise en scène*, meaning-making technologies that are central to Guna culture. And astonishingly, when Mojica emerged from the improvisations and began to record them, her annotations unconsciously took the form of pictographs, drawn right to left, then left to right down the pages of her notebook (Mojica, "Chocolate" 166). The play's eventual script exists in its most fully realized form to date as pictographs on nine three-foot by nine-foot scrolls of newsprint.

Structures (literary, organic, architectural)

In most devising processes, although these stages inevitably overlap and loop, analysis and embodiment, improvisation and annotation are followed by some combination of conscious and organic structuring, the dramaturgy of the performance building on the patterns, designs, shapes, and worlds identified in the assembled resources and internalized by the performers.

In the case of *Chocolate Woman* it became apparent from our in-process semiotic analysis that both the molas and the pictographs embodied four central principles of Guna cosmology that would eventually inform the dramaturgy of our work:

1. *abstraction* (Guna art operates through several levels of abstraction, in part to protect the sacred);
2. *metaphor* (in Guna language and culture everything is protected by being evoked indirectly through figurative imagery and representation);
3. *duality and repetition* (deriving from the Baba/Nana, father/mother duality, which means that everything must be repeated. Even Guna households consist of two buildings, one for living, one for sleeping); and
4. *multidimensionality* (everything in Guna cosmology exists simultaneously on the four levels above and four below the earth plane, and Guna language also operates on four levels, from the quotidian to the sacred).

Through abstraction and metaphor Guna arts participate with other Indigenous semiotic systems that Chadwick Allen has called "deep patterning" (115), systems that he finds across the trans-Indigenous world, and that he analyses in the "dynamic symmetry" and "semiotic geometry" of Navajo weaving (117–19).

Structurally it became very clear that Guna art and the Guna world operate very differently from the taken-for-granteds of western dramaturgy, which tend to rely on tripartite organizational principles: beginning, middle, and end; rising action, climax, and falling action; thesis, antithesis, synthesis; and cherished scene structures in which a third character provides the complication that moves that action forward. These structures, perhaps emerging from a Christian understanding of a three-part God (Father, Son, and Holy Spirit), embody an understanding of time as linear and progressive, and an understanding of narrative as one of conflict, crisis, and resolution. The Guna world, the *Chocolate Woman* creative team discovered, deriving from a two-part (male and female) deity, is structured around multiples of two, with four and eight being particularly sacred. And of course two-part structures and their multiples embody different understandings of time, meaning, and story, in which contrast and balance replace conflict, past and future coexist in an eternal present, and stories renew themselves in ongoing re-creations and re-citations.

This understanding led to a conscious structuring of the show around two actors playing four characters each. Mojica played a fictionalized version of herself (the lost Dule Girl); Olonadili (the youngest of the Niz Bundor, the four Daughters from the Stars, who taught the people to nurture, mourn, and make poetry); Olowaili (the morning star); and Sky Woman. Gloria Miguel played the four *Muugana* (Grandmothers of Creation), women from Guna cosmology who are encountered by Dule Girl and who guide her: Nan Kapsus (Mother Night); Muu Osiskun (Grandmother Ocean); Ibedon (Napguana, or Earth Mother, a woman-shaped mountain "galu," or portal to the spirit world); and finally Buna Siagua (Chocolate Woman, who heals through her powerful smudge). These elemental Guna women are, in semiotic terms, the fundamental actantial forces in the play world. Their stories guide Dule Girl on her journey and they were interwoven in rehearsal with "personal," internalized versions (recreations, recitations, or re-citations) of them as they played out in Dule Girl's/Mojica's own life. All of this is framed and punctuated by the overarching and conflated journeys of Sky Woman Falling to earth (a retelling of the Haudenosaunee and Powhatan creation story), Alice falling down the rabbit hole (a formative story from Mojica's childhood), and the lost Dule Girl coming home to Guna Yala – not to mention Perry Como's "Catch a Falling Star" and the Jefferson Airplane's "White Rabbit." It is not a familiar structure, but it emerged from the company's dramaturgical analysis as the way the stories had to be told.

Languages

The languages of a devised process and production are perhaps the single most important and prominent elements likely to be taken for granted: it is easy to take as given that the devising team will use the languages – spoken, written and theatrical – of the dominant local (or national) culture. But semiotics, as we have seen in earlier chapters, is perhaps most valuable for making languages visible as ideologically coded technologies for meaning production. *Chocolate Woman Dreams the Milky Way* is a particularly resonant test case. Not only did the production draw on the languages of divergent non-dominant cultural texts, resulting in different ways of structuring and telling its stories, it also involved the use of two spoken languages in performance – English and Dule Gaya (the language of the Guna people), and of three different spoken languages in the rehearsal hall – English, Spanish, and Dule Gaya – with no one person being able to speak all of them.

English, like most western languages, tends to function primarily descriptively – that is, representationally – in its everyday use, and to use as its foundation a grammar of subjects doing things to objects, treating them as otherwise value-free raw material for its meanings. It tends, as a structure, both to objectify the world and immediately to relegate it to completeness, to history. The Guna language, particularly in congress house chants, works very differently. It is driven by verbs and dominated by present participles. Considering this difference, the devising team for *Chocolate Woman* tended to privilege story over narrative. The former in Dule Gaya is an embodied oral form taking place largely in the present, peppered with intransitive verbs and centrally concerned with keeping the ancestors alive; the latter, in English, often requires the violence of objectification and the relegation of the past, and the ancestors, to history (see De Certeau, *Writing* 86–102). One of the problems that "othered" cultures have with many Euro-American postdramatic attempts to move *away* from overarching narrative structures, however, is their tendency to throw the baby of story out with the narrative bathwater, and story is central to identity formation and cultural continuity in Indigenous and many other cultures.

Part of the *Chocolate Woman* process was to take any text that was generated in English and put it through a process of double translation into Dule Gaya and back again into a much-altered English, leaving syntactical traces. This practice means, for example, that in its English-language sections the show is replete with present participles – one central monologue begins "I rise rising," and other stories are of "twirl-twirling, whirl-whirling" and the like. The show also employs words, phrases, sentences, songs, and sections in Dule Gaya throughout, on the principle that, as Favel argues, "when a native language is not spoken, an understanding of the world-view of that nation is purely theoretical" ("The Theatre of Orphans" 32).

In addition to English, Dule Gaya, and Spanish, *Chocolate Woman*, as I have shown, employed the embodied pictographic language of movement and gesture. The use of the language of Guna pictographs for both script and performance was a further enrichment of the production and added another productive complication to the analytical process. Saussurean semiotics is grounded in western languages that are purely phonetic and, in Peirce's terms, overwhelmingly symbolic. As applied to languages that are ideographic or pictographic at root (and therefore at least partially indexical and iconic), significant slippages occur. Derrida argued that western Structuralism, including that of Saussure, is ethnocentric and logocentric: it privileges phonetic writing as the record of an originary speech, the language of civilization and intelligence, and the basis of metaphysics, while disregarding pictographic and other traditions of writing that have nothing to do with phonetics (*Of Grammatology* 3). The use of pictographic languages in *Chocolate Woman* forced the devising team analytically to treat movement, image, and symbol *as writing*, as expressive and performative "literature" imbued with meaning and productive of action.

Conclusion

To treat the dramaturgical analysis of a devising process as script analysis is perhaps perverse, but it is useful insofar as it reveals some of the limitations and blind spots caused by the focus of traditional script analysis on text (the record of and blueprint for speech), character, and linear narrative as the primary progenitors of theatrical (meaning) production. In my examples from Ibsen I have deliberately focused on a single late-20th-century English translation of *A Doll House*, but what would it mean to return to our script analysis of *A Doll House* with some of the dramaturgical questions raised here concerning such things as cultural difference, the instability of a text like that of *A Doll House* that was written in a language that is no longer in use, linguistic and cultural translation (see Durbach 27–39), historicity, and the visual and theatrical languages encoded in the script that are now largely inscrutable (see Moi 105–43). What would it mean to *devise A Doll House*?

5 Performance Analysis

This book has been about the semiotic analysis of performance; this final chapter deals with the practical analysis of specific performances. Much of what I have said about script analysis in Chapter 4 – particularly the sections on structure (plot, character), mode (narrative, lyric, dramatic) and language – applies equally to performance analysis; indeed, performance analysis encompasses script analysis if the latter is understood broadly as the dramaturgical formation of all elements of the performance text. But the sign systems of the theatre provide many and more ways of telling stories and revealing character than are apparent from a script: there are lyrical ways of moving and gesturing; the temporality of performance has its own semiosis that is independent of text; spaces, places, and spatial relationships directly shape meaning, as discussed in Chapter 2 – and this is particularly urgent in site-specific work that puts performances and audiences in conversation with specific, usually non-theatrical locations that co-generate the work; decisions about performance style have a direct impact on how representations are received; and the languages of communication extend well beyond those of the spoken word.

Costume, makeup, set design, sound cues, gesture, and movement tell their own stories and can function independently of one another and of any script. When Hamlet is first seen wearing black at his mother's wedding, costume says as much about his state of mind as does his opening soliloquy; in Flerida Peña's *Sister Mary's a Dyke?!*, a show on which I've recently worked with Toronto's intercultural Cahoots Theatre Company, the central character talks to Jesus, whose part of the conversation (and function as a key actant) is represented by shafts of light of varying angles, directions, and intensities; the application of "make-up" (though it is much more than that) towards the end of *Chocolate Woman Dreams the Milky Way* – the onstage painting of the face – completes the arc of Dule Girl's self-discovery; and it is a sound cue that provides the end of the story in most productions of *A Doll House*. Performance analysis takes into account all of the sign systems involved in a production, considering how they work in consort or in tension with one another to produce meaning.

This chapter will not repeat the structural aspect of performance analysis or revisit the categories of plot and character construction discussed in Chapter 4, but it *will* explore, in drawing for examples on the 2003–11 *Mabou Mines DollHouse*, the question with which I ended that chapter: What would it mean to devise *A Doll House*, or indeed what would it mean for performance analysis to consider any production as having been devised by a team of artists that may or may not include a playwright, rather than having been staged as an "interpretation" of an authoritative or originary script? What would it mean to consider a script, if there is one, as simply one of many resources that are gathered together in a theatrical collaboration across historical, linguistic, disciplinary, and other kinds of difference? And what would it mean to consider the production of performance analysis itself as a process of devising?

Performance analysis is undertaken for a wide variety of reasons, and no such analysis can be complete or exhaustive, in spite of the aspirations and excesses of theatre semioticians of the 1970s and 80s, nor can any such analysis rely exclusively on semiotics, narrowly defined. What the method or focus of any analysis is depends on its purpose; it begins, again, with "what do I want to know?" and "why do I want to know it?" It begins, that is, with a research question, which provides selection principles and drives the analysis. Some performance analyses are done by theatrical practitioners attempting to understand their own or others' work in order to expand their range or develop their practice; some are done by theatre artists and theatrical devisers in mid-process as part of the ongoing development of a project; some are reconstructions undertaken by theatre historians wishing to understand how performance is translated into and retrieved from the archival record; some are done by scholars wishing to recuperate the cultural work performed by a particular artist, production, theatre company, or body of work; some are done by literary critics who understand theatrical performances to constitute potentially illuminating interpretations of dramatic texts; and some are done as case studies by cultural theorists who want to illustrate arguments about representation, embodiment, performativity, spectatorship, or any of dozens of other issues.

Whatever the purpose, all performance analyses involve taking on board the ephemeral nature of work that won't sit still for analysis, disappears when it's over, and leaves only more or less arbitrary traces for archivists and theatre historians to pore over. Performance analyses therefore involve what I think of as analytical description, a process of translating performance into discourse in order to uncover what Marco de Marinis calls its "textual structure" (*Semiotics* 83). They involve working with raw materials, traces, notes, and memories in a way similar to the way theatrical devising works with its resources. And of course different kinds of performance analysis have access in different degrees to different kinds of resources. The theatre historian working on a show she didn't see is limited to what, for whatever ideological or accidental reasons, is in the archive. On the opposite extreme, the artist in mid-process has full access to all or almost all aspects of the production, but may have an angle of vision determined by her role as director, dramaturge, performer, designer, or technician, and may have limited access to or understanding of reception.

Resources

The two main resources that I will draw on for examples in this chapter are *Mabou Mines DollHouse*, and the Chocolate

Woman Collective's *Chocolate Woman Dreams the Milky Way*. I will not attempt to describe or analyse every aspect of these productions; rather I will draw on some of their most interesting signifying features in order to illustrate those issues that a performance analysis is concerned with from an expanded semiotic perspective.

Mabou Mines DollHouse opened in November 2003 at St Ann's Warehouse in Brooklyn, adapted by Lee Breuer, who also directed, and Maude Mitchell, who also dramaturged and played Nora. It toured internationally for eight years, its last performance (to date) occurring in November 2011 at the Cutler Majestic Theatre in Boston. Although the production treated Ibsen's text with anything but reverence and adopted an outrageously metatheatrical postmodern style, the cuts, rewrites, and rearrangements it made were no more than those made for almost any contemporary production of a classical script; the structure of Ibsen's text remained surprisingly intact. The show might nevertheless be considered to have been less a production "of" Ibsen's play than a kind of devised, collaborative collage to which his script served as one of many key resources.

Chocolate Woman Dreams the Milky Way premiered at the Helen Gardiner Phelan Playhouse in Toronto in June 2011 directed by José Colman, went to the Talking Stick Festival in Vancouver in February–March 2012, and was remounted in a coproduction with Toronto's Native Earth Performing Arts at the Aki Studio in Toronto in January–February 2013. Its first US performances were in November 2013 at the Krannert Center for the Performing Arts in Urbana, Illinois, and it has been invited to tour to Panama City. As we have seen in Chapter 4, its "text," movement, design, and all other elements were entirely generated as part of the devising process.

I saw *DollHouse* at Toronto's Harbourfront Centre as part of the New World Stage Festival in February 2007, have consulted reviews of performances in different cities and venues internationally, as well as interviews and articles from throughout the tour, and I have used the film that was made in 2008, based on the show, including a companion documentary featuring interviews with Breuer and the company (*Mabou Mines*). I worked as dramaturge on the research, development, and rehearsal processes for *Chocolate Woman Dreams the Milky Way* and had access to the personnel and various resource materials through all but the first stage of its development. I also consulted reviews, interviews, and writings about the show, and I served as remount director for the Talking Stick Festival.

Theory and method

Performance analyses are most often performed by scholars or artists as part of a larger project, the interests of which will determine the kinds of questions they ask of the production, the selection principles, and the theoretical approach used beyond or supplementary to the semiotic. A project interested in the representation of gender and sexuality will probably involve a feminist, queer, or gender studies approach; one interested in the representation of race might use critical race studies, whiteness studies, diaspora studies, or postcolonial studies; one interested in motivations, drives, identifications, and transferences will draw upon psychoanalysis; one interested in the performative constitution of social identities will draw on speech act theory and the performativity side of performance studies; and one interested in politics and economics will draw upon materialist theory.

Any single production can be approached through innumerable or multiple theoretical lenses. *Mabou Mines DollHouse*, for example, would clearly reward a feminist reading, but might equally be illuminated by a reading grounded in psychoanalytical theory. Crucially, projects that focus on Indigenous or other marginalized or colonized cultures need to derive their methodologies and theoretical approaches from sources grounded in and under the control of the cultures being represented. Analyses of a production such as *Chocolate Woman Dreams the Milky Way* need to be approached through culturally specific Guna sources and need to draw upon Indigenous research methodologies and ethics (see Denzin, Lincoln, and Smith; Kovach; Smith; and Shawn Wilson).

Representation and recognition

Early in the Introduction to this book I discussed representation – one thing standing for another – as being at the heart of meaning production in the theatre as elsewhere. I also talked about how the process of recognizing and accepting a representation as standing in for something else is ideological, risks stereotyping, and "legitimates and privileges certain kinds of knowledge" (Hutcheon 53). Partly for this reason, not all theatre aspires to be representational. Indeed, some, such as Michael Kirby, have set out deliberately to create and theorize what he has called "nonsemiotic performance" (Kirby). But as I suggested earlier, a regime of non-semiotic performance emerging in the west at the precise moment when "othered" cultures are gaining access to the technologies of representation and (re)gaining control of their own is troublesome. And in any case, as Silvija Jestrović demonstrates in an essay entitled "Semiotics of Nonsemiotic Performance," purportedly "non-semiotic" work tends to be "grounded in a suppressed semiotic approach" (93). Besides, whatever the artists' intentions, most performance tends to be read by audiences as representational. For better or worse, the 21st century is a society of signs.

If the recognition in a performance of, for example, certain types of dress and behaviour as male or female, has the capacity to interpellate audiences into a dominant sex-gender system, as I've argued, a production also has the capacity at once to draw upon and disrupt such a system by interpellating audiences differently. In *DollHouse* the primary mode of communication was scale; indeed, Breuer calls the show a "comedy of scale" (Moritz). It began with the question:

> What if Nora [in Ibsen's play] were literally the bigger of the two spouses, if her larger spirit and yearning were made concrete in the person of a large woman? And if Torvald's stunted vision, compassion, and maturity were similarly made manifest by casting an actor of short stature in the part? What if all the women and men were big and small, respectively? What if the house in which the action unfolds were built to his scale rather than hers? (Green 257)

To address these questions, Breuer cast all the men in the production with actors of small stature (between three-foot-six and four-foot-six in height), while the women, some of them over six feet tall, towered over them. The action took place on a set and with props and furnishings scaled for the men and children (Figure 5.1): the doll-house set consisted of frilly pastel walls, windows, doorways, and sugar-candy arches, purchased by Nora as a Christmas gift for her children and assembled by her with the help of omnipresent stage hands at the outset of the performance. The outsized women bent to enter through doorframes half their height and perched on toy chairs at a miniature table sipping vodka out of tiny teacups – or, in the case of the towering and very pregnant maid, straight from the bottle. The rearranged text allowed the play's three men, their entrance delayed, to swagger in together, upright, through the same doors as the women, smoking cigars and slapping one another on the back in evident comfort and control.

However surprising and seemingly distorted an image of gender relations this *mise-en-scène* presented, the *recognition* it elicited – "yes, that's just how puffed-up men can be, that's just how women must uncomfortably confine themselves to roles that diminish them" – interpellated the audience into ideological critique rather than assent. The relational semiotics of

Figure 5.1 Honora Fergusson (Mrs Linde), Mark Povinelli (Torvald), Kristopher Medina (Krogstad), Ricardo Gil (Dr. Rank), and Maude Mitchell (Nora), in ***Mabou Mines DollHouse***, dir. Lee Breuer

Source: Photo by Richard Termine

the production insisted on a literalization and exaggeration of size and scale: the women *were* huge, but only in relation to a shrunken patriarchal world. The size difference also played itself out as gender critique in the play's graphic sexuality, as the women stooped to "service" the men in various explicit ways, Nora crawling subserviently across the floor to Helmer (Figure 5.2) or dancing a tarantella that devolved into a nightmarish sado-masochistic fantasy, and Mrs Linde convincing Krogstad of her sincerity by fellating him at their reunion.

Other theatrical languages and representational economies supported the same critique. The production foregrounded the fact that, as feminist scholar Amy S. Green observes, even in Ibsen's script, "Nora plays her part consciously" (Green 251). In her scenes with Helmer Nora spoke in an openly faux, generically Scandinavian accent ("it's yust a yob"), using, particularly when she wanted something from him, ingratiating squeaks, baby talk, and a childishly high-pitched voice variously compared by reviewers to Marilyn Monroe, "Betty Boop of the fiords" (Spencer), Shirley Temple, Mickey Mouse, Lily Tomlin's Edith Ann, and "the nasal strains of a New Joisy housewife" (Hatherell). All of this open presentation of gender as a performance (and one fuelled by the men's more than willing suspension of disbelief) was supported by costumes and props. Nora, her daughter, and the oversized dolls that each carried were all dressed in identical cerulean, lace-trimmed and bustled silk Victorian dresses, and they sported identical rouged cheeks and blonde ringlets. Taken together, the four figures in their different sizes and scales resembled nothing so much as a deconstructed Russian nesting doll. Nora disconcertingly ripped open the hinged skull of her doll early on to retrieve a stash of forbidden macaroons (others were hidden in the top of the set's miniature piano and behind the tail of its rocking horse), again making physical the image of women as dolls whose heads are stuffed with sweets.

The overall effect of this literalization of the play's title and central metaphor – the audience collectively held its breath for

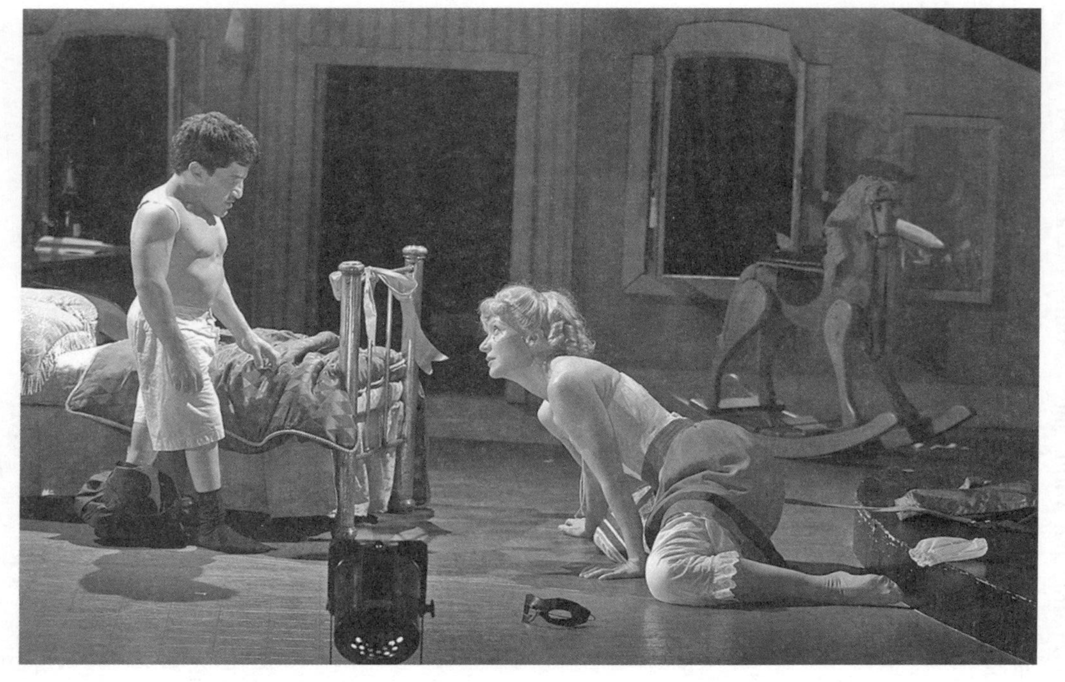

Figure 5.2 **Mark Povinelli (Torvald) and Maude Mitchell (Nora) in *Mabou Mines DollHouse***

Source: Photo by Richard Termine.

a moment when Helmer, responding to Nora's accusation of pettiness, said "you think I'm *small?*" – worked "to call attention to the power relationships in every scene," to "how arbitrary were the power dynamics of gender in society" (Carlson, "Ibsen" 48). Or as Singaporean reviewer, poet, playwright, and gay performer Ng Yi-Sheng observed, they worked to highlight "the absurdity of patriarchy, literalizing the dynamics of the 19th century realist play in which prideful, small-minded men attempt to control and dominate strong, great-spirited women" (Yi-Sheng). As Breuer himself said,

> The patriarchy is really three feet tall, but has a voice that will dominate six-foot women. Male power isn't dependent on physical size. At the same time we're exploiting the metaphor from the woman's point of view, the way maternal love is lavished on these child-sized men, which only infantilizes them further. (qtd in McNulty)

As critic Charles McNulty sums up the concept in his review in New York's alternative weekly *The Village Voice*, "Gender roles in bourgeois society…stunt the growth of both sexes."

What most of these readings leave unexamined, however, is the question of the representation of short-statured people in the production; at issue, and worthy of analysis, is whether the production helped to retrieve performers of short stature from centuries of degrading representations by providing them serious acting roles in a western classic, or whether the moral degradation and pettiness of the characters they portrayed participated in and prolonged that history. This is a question about visibility, about what is or is not worthy of representation, as well as one about *how* minoritized populations appear, when they do, in western representations.

The representational economy of *Chocolate Woman Dreams the Milky Way* functioned very differently from that of *Doll-House*. At issue here was the representation of Indigenous people, and more specifically Native women, who since first contact have either been left unrepresented (considered unworthy of representation) or have been plagued with grotesque, demeaning, or exoticizing representations of "squaws" or "Indian Princesses" disseminated by the colonizers. In Monique Mojica and Gloria Miguel, *Chocolate Woman* cast two strong Indigenous women in control of their own representation performing their own stories. It also brought into representation something largely omitted in western theatre: elders and the elderly, particularly women. Gloria Miguel, playing the *Muugana* (Grandmothers of Creation), major female figures from Guna cosmology, is in her mid-80s and suffers from arthritis that severely limits her mobility. Although she is a senior artist and founding member of New York's Spiderwoman Theater, she is now largely overlooked by casting agents. For *Chocolate Woman*, however, she was contracted as both actor and elder, and she made visible (brought into representation) elderly Native women as powerful and respected members of the community (see Carter, "Shaking"). The play's representations, moreover, of a universe in which the grandmothers are present, supportive, and alive to the needs of their daughters and granddaughters offered a corrective to the grotesqueries of non-Native representations while establishing for the production an economy of sign relations in which life-giving and life-framing elements – the night, the ocean, the earth – were signified by and embodied in elemental female figures who were more than simply "characters."

The lesson provided for performance analysis by these two very different examples of relational representational economies is that, whatever a production is thematically "about," and whatever its style of presentation, much of its meaning is produced by its technologies of representation. *DollHouse* was arguably "about" making visible unequal power relations between men and women, while what the audience recognized as representations of women, at least in the first instance, were outsized dolls. *Chocolate Woman* was "about" a lost Dule Girl finding herself by reconnecting with the figures, stories, and land of her ancestors, but what the production also made available for the audience's affirmative recognition were Native women as figures of strength, beauty, and power.

The world of the play

Performance analysis also needs centrally to concern itself with what in Chapter 4 I called "the world of the play" – its rules, its logic, its characteristic imagery and rhythms – but might also usefully be considered the play's *representation* of the world, even in work that is non-representational. (A chaotic, fragmented, non-representational postmodern performance will nevertheless "represent," in some fashion, a chaotic, fragmented world that is shared by the performers with an audience that on some level, at least, grants it recognition.) Performance analysis involves considering how the entire technology of performance, including all elements of design, acting, and the use of space and time, come together to create a play from which the audience somehow derives meaning. In the words of the UK-based Third Angel theatre company's co-founder Alex Kelly, "you take your audience into a world, where they put things together" (qtd in Mermikides and Smart 117).

The world of *Chocolate Woman* is the Guna cosmos, and the play takes place, according to the unpublished production script, in "the present, between the eight layers of reality" (Mojica, *Chocolate*). I have outlined the logical, spatial, and temporal dimensions governing this world in Chapter 4. On stage it is represented in a variety of ways (Figure 5.3). The star world itself is painted (reflected) in a swirling milky way on the stage floor, onto which images of molas (see Chapter 4) are projected late in the show. Located centrally, as it is in the Guna congress house, is a hammock, "the heart of [G]una culture," according to the show's designer and cultural consultant Oswaldo DeLeón Kantule: "one is born in a

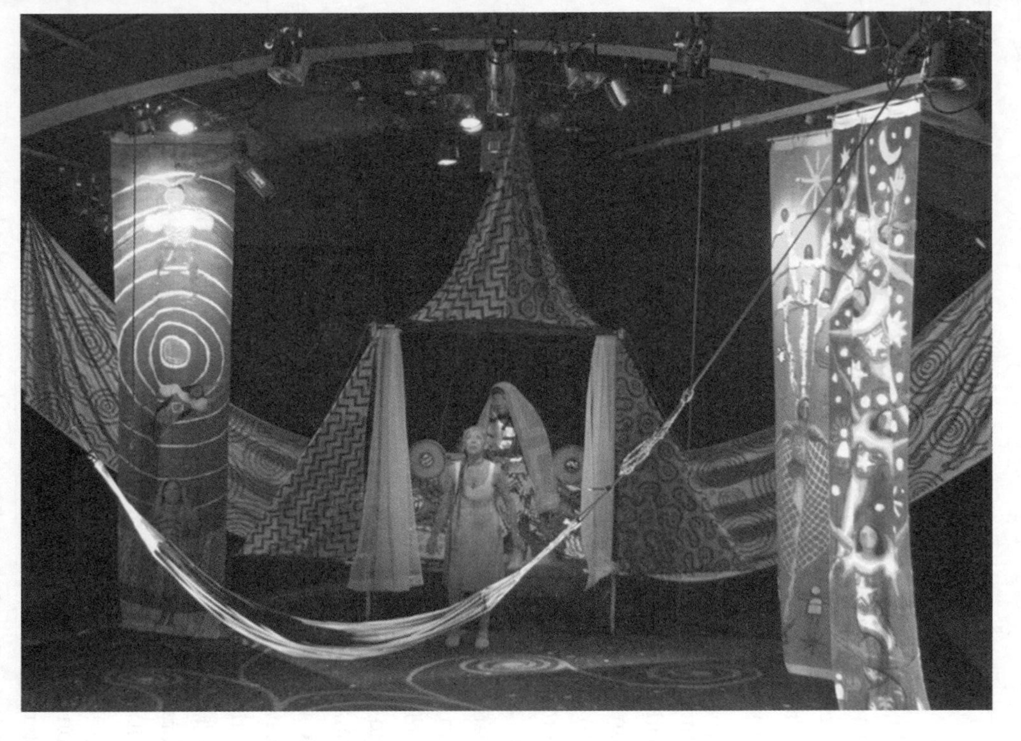

Figure 5.3 **Gloria Miguel and Monique Mojica in Mojica's *Chocolate Woman Dreams the Milky Way***

Source: Photo by Ric Knowles.

hammock; leaders sit in hammocks at the Gathering House to tell stories; and after death the [G]una body is wrapped in a hammock to be buried" (qtd in Carter, "Chocolate" 174). Mojica performs athletically in, around, above, and beneath the hammock throughout, and many of Dule Girl's crises and revelations occur there. Upstage of the hammock is a brightly coloured *galu*, or spirit house. *Galus* for the Guna are portals that provide access to different layers of the cosmos, and this construction serves as the main set piece for the production, housing all of the characters played by Gloria Miguel. This set piece grounds the production, and serves as a site and symbol of connectivity around which the action swirls and circles. Rigged above and in a semicircle upstage are three 15′ × 3′ silk panels painted by De León Kantule, which Mojica releases sequentially throughout. These panels serve as actants putting different kinds of pressure on the action. Dule Girl interacts with them and derives specific energies associated with the figures that are painted on each of them.

The three breathtakingly beautiful panels represent different elemental female figures in Guna cosmology and different aspects of Mojica herself. The stage right panel represents *Muu Osiskun,* Grandmother Ocean, but also, below her, Mojica/Dule Girl as mermaid (a complex and not entirely positive figure in Guna culture). At the bottom is a representation of her dream, recounted near the end of the production, of arriving at the beach on Guna Yala to be greeted by Kikadiriyai, the prophet Ibeorgun's sister who introduced mola making to the Guna people. The central panel, stage left of the galu, is *Buna Siagua,* Chocolate Woman, rising in the purifying smoke of smudged (smouldering) cacao beans. Her net is extended to capture the spirits of illness and to rescue the spirit of the sick person. The beads on her necklace are portals to the spirit realm, to which Guna healers travel on the smoke of her smudge. At the top of the panel is the pictographic symbol for cacao, which is a staple in the Kuna diet, the only plant in the culture that can heal on its own. Finally, the stage left panel shows *Nis Bundor,* the four Daughters of the Stars after whom every Guna woman is named, including Mojica, who was given the name of the youngest, Olonadili, when she was a child. This last identification forms a central layer of *Chocolate Woman*'s theatrical weave: the key narratives of the show tell the stories of the Daughters of the Stars (traditional Olonadili narratives), and Mojica's own "personal Olonadili stories" of her own recent life and of her life "once in a time of war" – the American Indian Movement (AIM) struggles of the 1970s. It is this interweaving of traditional with personal stories that constitutes Guna (and much Indigenous) pedagogy: the passing on through the generations of wisdom that heals through the repetition, recitation/re-citation, and renewal of the stories that give events their meaning.

DeLeón Kantule's silk panels, together with the painted floor, galu and hammock, constitute the "set" of the production and make manifest its world, but they are not mere set decoration, nor, as Carter argues, are they "emblems or static mnemonic devices, but [...] living texts" with which Mojica, herself a living text, interacts ("Chocolate" 175). They also body forth the principles and rules by which the world of the production operates, a world overseen by the male/female deity (or deities) Baba/Nana (Father/Mother), in which the ancestors are very much alive and active in an (eternal) present, in which under certain conditions traffic is possible between the earth plane and the eight levels of the cosmos, and in which cultural values are communicated intergenerationally through rich, patterned textiles, stories, songs, and chants.

It is crucial when undertaking performance analysis across cultural difference to do the hard work of research, coming to understand and respect the epistemologies (ways of knowing), principles, and world views embedded in the languages, bodies, and cultural texts on which the performances are based or which are embedded in them. This requires bringing a certain humility to the exercise when operating from outside of the culture, avoiding the kinds of objectifying, controlling, and totalizing ways of knowing associated with the colonizing project itself. A performance analysis, especially when working across cultural difference, needs to establish a collaborative relationship with the performance rather than treating it as the analyst's "object of study" and thereby, quite literally, objectifying it and the culture from which it emerges.

The world of *DollHouse* was self-consciously that of 19th-century theatre, one of its primary modes of communication was style – an exaggerated, almost expressionist metatheatricality that reinforced its central metaphors of size and scale: everything was over the top. As the show opened on a bare stage, a woman in a formal evening gown entered carrying a musical score, bowed, and took her place at a piano whose surreally extended lid formed the surface of a slightly raised stage surface downstage left. Back to the audience like the pianist at a silent film, she began to play the melodramatic score – mostly Grieg – whose trills and swelling crescendos supported the show throughout. Red plush drapes with gold tassels dropped from the grid to situate the set and action within the frame of "a cozy baroque opera house" (Fuchs, "Mabou" 498). The acting style was also parodically melodramatic. Actors burst into song at particularly wrought moments, wrists were held to foreheads, hands to beating hearts, and entire speeches – including Torvald's "no more melodrama!" – were delivered "out" to the audience. The melodrama was heightened by the use of Mary Louise Geiger's steeply angled and deeply shadowed lighting plot and by expressionist dreamscapes accompanied by strobe lights between Ibsen's Acts. The metadrama was made more self-conscious by interpolated moments, as when actors cued the piano player or the lights, or when Torvald's dismissive comments on knitting as ugly, with "something very Chinese about it," prompted Chinese-American pianist Ning Yu to stand, slam the piano keys in protest, and stop playing. She was cajoled back through Nora's apologetic "Ning, please, it's in the text."

The "rules" of such a parodic world blending metatheatricality, surrealism, expressionism, and melodrama are no more "natural" than those of *Chocolate Woman*, and they similarly require research to uncover and articulate – in the case of *DollHouse* research into the conventions, practices, and venues of 19th-century theatrical melodrama, among other things. Metatheatricality is most often playful, but games are uniquely framed by rules, which are nothing if not serious. The rules by which *DollHouse* operated were what Breuer calls "a marriage of Brecht and Stanislavski, distance and interiority" that was strangely moving. The interviews with the actors in the documentary made about the production, in fact, are surprisingly familiar: the actors' main focus is on psychological motivation to the point that they could be discussing any naturalist production of Ibsen's play (Moritz). Combined with the neo-expressionist, melodramatic style of presentation, however, this psychological approach to characterization evoked a kind of Freudian uncanny: at once strange, familiar, and disquieting. And this uncanniness was enhanced by the use of real and figurative dolls and puppets, archetypical examples of the uncanny, which Breuer says offer "a deconstruction of human behaviour" (qtd in Moritz).

Transformation

Theatrical representations, from the classical through the naturalistic to the symbolist, expressionist, and postdramatic, are not, of course, static, most productions representing some kind of change, growth, collapse, metamorphosis, or transformation, and this is a central part of the cultural work they perform and the meanings they produce. Performance analysis has to chart such transformations, which means paying attention to overt or subtle, abrupt or gradual changes in lighting, sound, costume, set, rhythm, tempo, and performance style – even, as in the case of *DollHouse*, in vocal register. It can also often involve paying close attention to patterning and repetition where similar motifs recur with significant differences or shifts, or to (re)framing devices that can work to resignify elements of the performance that are otherwise constant.

The final sequence of *DollHouse* involved not only Nora's transformation but that of the entire play world. It began with the arrival of Krogstad's second letter, delivered by the huge (and very pregnant) maid wearing a screamingly symbolist death's head. When Nora responded to Torvald's joyous "Nora, I'm saved…(you too, of course)," she dropped her "soprano twitter…from the top of her [vocal] range to the bottom" (Weckwerth 139), saying gruffly, "I have fought a hard fight, these three days." But the anticipated break from the hypertheatricality of the rest of the play to any "real" in the final confrontation between Nora and Torvald never came; rather, the production ramped up its theatricality yet another notch. When Nora exited "to take off my costume," Torvald lay on the small bed stage centre and engaged in a masturbatory fantasy prompted by his own imagined generosity in "forgiving" Nora and her anticipated complete dependence upon him in the future. Rather than return either in something more comfortable, as in Torvald's fantasy, or in travelling clothes, as in Ibsen's script, Nora reappeared in a classical white tunic and white opera-length evening gloves, standing in a theatrical side box above and beyond the frame stage left. While stage hands carried off the doll-house set, the red velour curtains that had framed the space lifted and the upstage filled with three walls of half-scale opera boxes, each box occupied by Torvald and Nora puppets, quarrelling. (Breuer says that the inspiration for these replicated quarrelling puppets came at an early preview of the show, in which a disgruntled man headed for the exit and asked his partner if she was coming: "'No, I think I'll stay and see a little more,' she replied. Angrily, he asked when she wanted to be picked up. 'Don't bother,' was her terse reply" (Fisher)).

Nora confronted Torvald from her stage box. As he moved toward her, a supplicant pleading that no man could surrender his honour, even for love, she switched to lip-synched grand operatic contralto for her famous response: "hundreds of thousands of women have done just that." What ensued one New York reviewer in 2009 called "a lover's quarrel of oversized, Wagnerian proportions" (Patterson), though the music played (composed by Eve Beglarian) was closer to Sibelius and was underscored by military snare drums. In an interview Breuer explained, "if you have an anthem, you've got to sing it. It was just like La Marseillaise" (Del Signore). As Nora and Torvald sang, the puppet men in the boxes echoed Torvald's "monstrous" and the puppet women, echoing Nora's "hundreds of thousands," collapsed one by one. When Nora sang "I am leaving you" she stripped off her clothes, corset, gloves, and wig to reveal herself, naked and hairless in an image that the actor herself said felt "like a moment of transcendence, a moment of purity" (Moritz), and was variously interpreted by reviewers as: "at once Amazonian and desperately vulnerable, like a newborn babe about to stride out into the world" (Gardner); "a rebirth of physical and mythological dimensions" (Al-Solaylee); and "both the death and rebirth of Nora" (Baldwin).

Her transformation complete, Nora sang the return of the wedding rings – "Here's your ring back. Give me yours" – and faded out of sight in a haze of smoke (Figure 5.4):

> Torvald is left alone onstage, his pants stuck on one shoe and dragging behind him. He descends from the stage, mewling "Nora! Nora!" as he climbs up through the aisle of the auditorium, while their daughter lurches back and forth on a rocking horse center stage, waving a toy sword and echoing one of her mother's final lines. (Weckwerth 141)

The famous door slam here, with appropriate theatricality, was the banging shut of the piano lid.

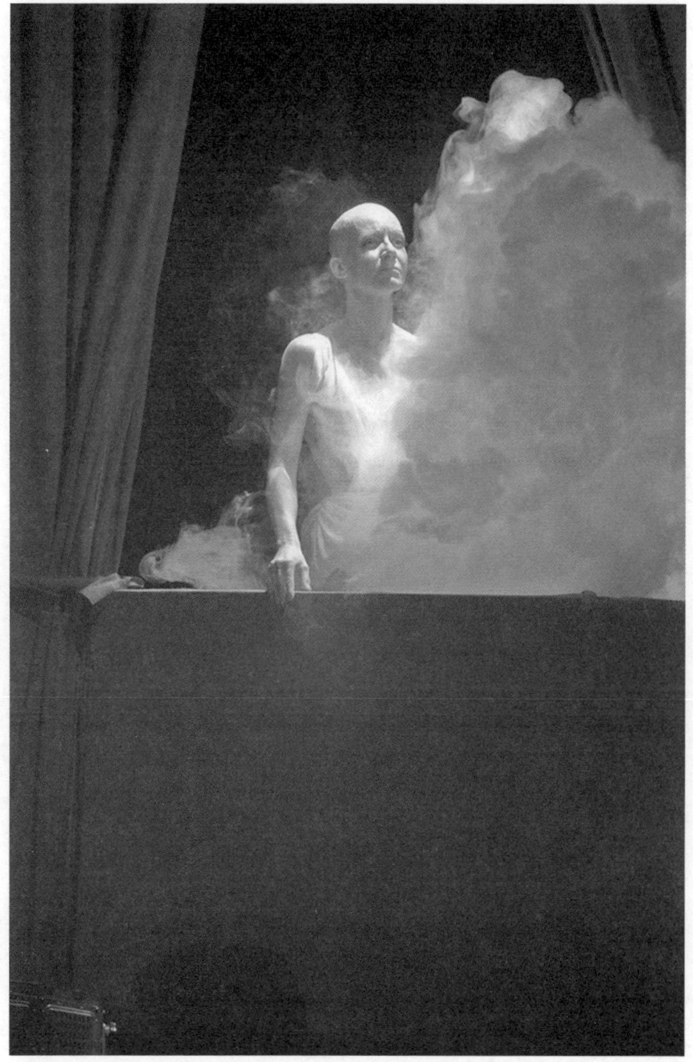

Figure 5.4 Maude Mitchell (Nora) in *Mabou Mines* DollHouse
Source: Photo by Richard Termine.

Again, reviewers interpreted variously the final image of the Helmers' daughter riding into her future, holding aloft the sword she had appropriated from her brother and echoing her mother's "here's your ring back. Give me yours." For Alisa Solomon in *The Village Voice* the image suggested "that there is no ground left for women between warbler and warrior." For Lyn Gardner, reviewing the show at the Edinburgh Festival for the socially liberal British daily, *The Guardian*,

> it is an ambivalent representation that suggests this tot might indeed carve out a new role for herself in the world, but also hints at how, a century after Nora slammed the door, many men and women are content to remain in the doll's house, where they will always be vulnerable. (Gardner)

Scholar and critic Martin Puchner, who has edited Ibsen, was left "with the sense that the next generation of Noras will not be content with abandoning their dollhouses. They will return as avenging angels, breaking toys, husbands, and opera houses apart."

This concluding sequence brought together a complex set of signifiers, each of them producing meanings in relation to sign systems having to do with casting, costume, movement, gesture, set design, vocal register, style, music, and various theatrical genres and conventions that had been established throughout the course of the production, and at the same time producing meaning in relation to one another and the tensions between them. The show's closing moments also, of course, were powerfully affective, bringing together the uncanny (de)familiarity of puppets, dolls, and mimicking children; the emotional impact of opera and anthemic music; the phenomenological *frisson* of nudity; and the metatheatrical blurring of representation provided by the production's generally self-conscious theatricality and Torvald's final exit through the audience. Whatever its purpose, a performance analysis needs to take all of this into account if it wishes to do any kind of justice to the complexity of theatrical signification, particularly in a postmodern age where slippage between signifier and signified, sign and referent, is the rule rather than the exception.

Chocolate Woman's very different transformations are about healing, and are framed by a story *about* a transformation that issued in the creation of the world. In a synopsis of the play prefacing the unpublished manuscript Monique Mojica writes:

> The play begins with Sky Woman, First Woman from the Powhatan (southern Algonquin) and Haudenosaunee creation stories as She is falling from Her home in the Sky World. Her trajectory [...] as She falls (like Alice down the rabbit hole) is the overarching structure within which other stories are told. We always return to Sky Woman because when She landed on Turtle's back (the earth) there was transformation. (Mojica, *Chocolate*)

This story is directly parallel to and overlapping with the return of the lost Dule Girl to Guna Yala, and it is intercut with traditional Guṇa narratives and the personal stories from Mojica's life that are illuminated and culturally contextualized by them. They are told through a complex of signifying systems drawn from movement, gesture, music, song, voice, and spoken language(s), all grounded in Guna cultural textile and pictographic "texts" (as outlined in Chapter 4), but ranging outward from there to multiple Indigenous story systems (including movement and dance) as well as the meaning-producing technologies of western theatre.

Key moments marking Dule Girl's transformation, moments that require explication in any performance analysis, include the powerful wordless moment toward the end of *Chocolate Woman* when Sky Woman has landed and Dule Girl has arrived "on sacred land...where the grandmothers walked"

(Figure 5.5). Dule Girl shares a bowl of water with Ibedon, the mountain galu and earth mother who proceeds to rouge her cheeks with bright red dye made from achiote seeds, and to draw a black line down the centreline of her nose. To the Guna, as is typical of Guna cultural texts, the face paint has many meanings, some of them practical (it protects from the sun), and some of them too sacred to divulge. In the context of the show, however, as the culmination of Dule Girl's journey and the beginning of the transformation and healing that conclude the show – it is not until her face is painted that she is able to encounter Buna Siagua (Chocolate Woman) – the primary meaning of the moment has to do with the completion of a search for self. As Mojica put it in a personal email,

> For me it has always been one of those Guna things that I was missing. I knew I was supposed to have it on when fully dressed in mola, but using conventional make up to do it always felt hollow. When I went to a chichi ceremony for the first time [chichi is fermented sugar cane juice used for ritual purposes; a chichi ceremony marks a girl's coming of age], the women made it very clear that I had to be painted. For me (and in the play) it's about being endowed with the marks that signify identity. (Mojica, email)

This moment seems to "read," in a general way, to most audience members, even as most audience members seem to be able to understand the metatheatrical references drawn from European cultural texts in *DollHouse*. But in both cases it is the responsibility of a performance analysis as precisely as possible to explicate exactly how a transformational moment such as Nora's removal of her clothing and wig, or Dule Girl's acquiring the markings of Guna identity, produces its meanings. Both moments have key significance within the larger structure of their respective shows, neither rely on spoken language, and both draw on complex signifying systems to transform the worlds of their respective plays.

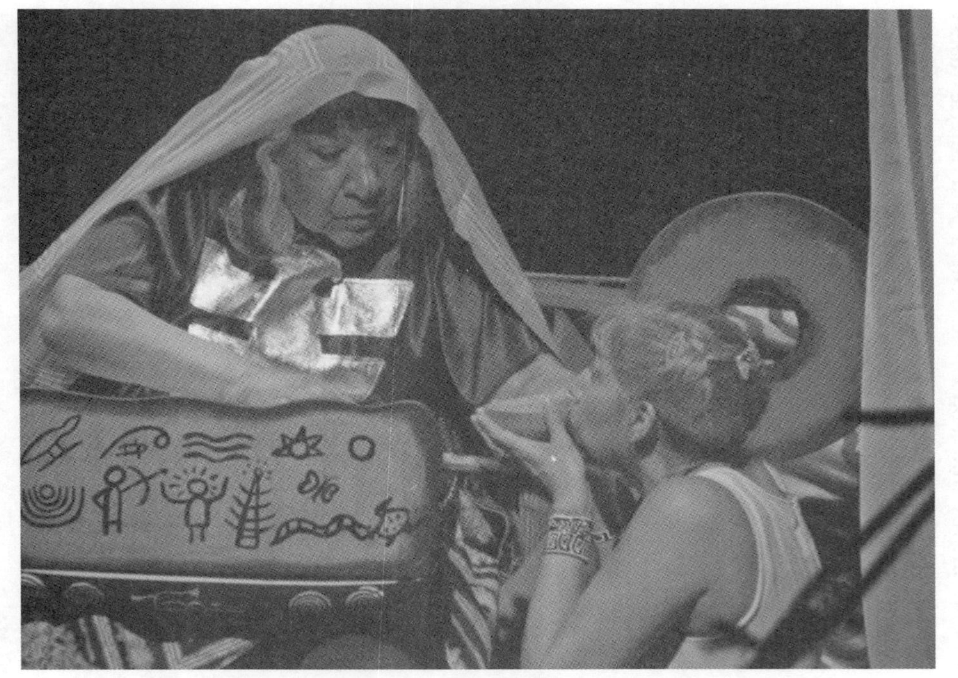

Figure 5.5 Gloria Miguel and Monique Mojica in Mojica's ***Chocolate Woman Dreams the Milky Way***
Source: Photo by Ric Knowles.

Intertextuality

Part of any performance analysis is the identification of the work done by intertextual references and intertextuality more generally, as each element in a production participates in multiple discursive systems, each differently coded. This can involve paying attention to language use and reference. When Dr Rank, in *Dollhouse,* renders a line that in the Fjelde translation reads "one never gets something for nothing in life" as "nothing will come of nothing," he invokes through direct quotation the world of Shakespeare's *King Lear* (I.1.90) and with it the discourses of Renaissance tragedy as another self-consciously theatrical frame for the production. When the children first enter in the production, they are wearing troll masks that conjured for some theatregoers Ibsen's earlier *Peer Gynt* and the world of Norwegian folkloric drama. Both *DollHouse* and *Chocolate Woman* employ intertexts with *Alice in Wonderland,* the former through the disorienting image of grotesquely large women in an unfamiliar world (Hatherell), the latter by way of sung snatches of the Jefferson Airplane's song "White Rabbit," to similar effect. Martin Puchner even found the dream sequence in the second act of *DollHouse* to be riffing on Stanley Kubrick's film, *The Shining,* and most audience members of a certain age in the west would presumably be pleasantly interpellated across cultures when Mojica as Sky Woman sings snatches of Perry Como's "Catch a Falling Star."

But merely pointing out intertextual references isn't enough. Performance analysis also involves the hard intellectual labour of considering exactly what is invoked by those references, and for whom. What does it *mean* in the context of *DollHouse* to momentarily see Dr Rank as a presumably diminished Lear, self-centredly demanding love from his youngest daughter? What does it mean to invoke the vast landscape of late Shakespearean tragedy in the middle of a self-consciously melodramatic performance of Ibsen's domestic drama? Marvin

Carlson offers a perceptive intertextual reading of the final exit of Dr Rank in *Mabou Mines DollHouse* that is evocative but falls short of such analysis. He notes that Rank was carried off to his death by the maid, played by the tallest of the production's women, who was also eight months pregnant:

> Breuer [...] converted the Maid into a kind of Valkyrie figure, bearing off the dying Rank to some sort of Valhalla. Indeed, the Valkyrie associations were stressed to the point of parody. The actress entered with a Valkyrie helmet, announced herself with lines from Ibsen's most notably actual Viking female, Hjordis in *The Vikings of Helgeland*, hoisted up the diminutive Rank like a disobedient child and bore him off to strains of Wagner from the accompanying piano. ("Ibsen's" 49)

Given the production's concern with power relations and gender, one might expect Carlson to engage with the disturbing discourses conjured by Wagner and the Valkyrie. Not only do the Valkyrie as outsized warrior maidens have a particular resonance for this production and its outsized women, but Wagner's famous "Ride of the Valkyries," from the third act of his Ring Cycle opera, *Die Walküre* was, after all, famously used in Nazi newsreel propaganda, as well as by D.W. Griffiths for the soundtrack of his racist 1915 film *The Birth of a Nation*. Wagner himself is often linked to Nazism and anti-Semitism. Carlson, however, dismisses the choice as one made merely "to create comic or theatrical effect" (48). Whatever it was created for, I suggest, a responsible performance analysis needs to take into account its disturbing resonances.

Audience response

Audience response is at once crucial and notoriously difficult to gauge in performance analysis. My own practice is, first, to limit the range, not only of productions, but of actual located performances that I study almost exclusively to ones I have seen myself as a culturally positioned (white, male, Canadian, professional) spectator, where possible moving from site to site to see and analyse different performances within their local contexts of production as well as various contexts of reception. Second, I draw heavily on local reviews of the same productions, where possible in different places, contextualizing and locating the reviewers themselves within their cultural and journalistic settings. (A review in *The Guardian* means differently than one in *The Times* (London) or *The Sun (*London); one in the *New York Times* may be a world away from one in the *New York Daily News* or *The Village Voice*; and all of these have a different resonance than an independent or variously sponsored online reviewing site or blog.) But I consider these reviews as neither consumer reports nor aesthetic assessments; rather, I treat them as providers of evidence of readings that were enabled by particular local stagings for specific audiences. Third, I try to cite my own, reviewers,' bloggers,' and others' interpretations and responses, not as evidence of what audiences-in-general felt and understood – and therefore what the performance "really meant" – but as evidence of meanings and responses that specific performances in particular locations made available. And finally, I consider audiences themselves to be constructed and "performed," particularly in terms of class, race, gender, sexuality, ability, and other social and cultural positions, by the mutually constitutive technologies of production, performance, and reception, rather than situating them, as most social-science-based methodologies do, as independent agents operating somehow outside of the loop.

I and others have been criticized by scholar Helen Freshwater for relying on reviewers and scholars rather than on "'ordinary' audience members who have no professional links to the theatre" (33), and apart from the privileging of some hypothetical "ordinariness" I agree with her – except that I have never seen a satisfactory example of the kind of empirical methodology she calls for that might provide such information in ways that would be analytically useful. Every version I have seen both predetermines and undermines its results through the kinds of focus groups and surveys it marshals and through the kinds of questions it asks and the times at which it asks them. Most such surveys, moreover, seem to issue in evidence that is so general as to be unhelpful for readings that aim for any degree of analytical specificity. And it is increasingly the case that theatregoers, "ordinary" or not, are responding to productions through easily accessed, more or less formal online "reviewing," commentating, and blogging – not to mention the potentially endless recursive loop of leaving comments on what has been posted by others.

Audience response, I suggest, is best understood as the meanings produced by specific audiences in particular places and times, and these are determined in large part by the local conditions of production and reception. *DollHouse* was produced by the Manhattan-based Mabou Mines theatre company in November 2003 at St Ann's Warehouse, a performing arts venue in Brooklyn, New York's "DUMBO" district (**D**irectly **U**nder the **M**anhattan **B**ridge **O**verpass), dedicated to innovation, multi-disciplinary theatrical collaborations, concerts, and new works for puppet theatre. Mabou Mines is a long-running experimental company founded in 1970 by such luminaries of the American avant-garde as JoAnne Akalaitis, Lee Breuer, Philip Glass, Ruth Maleczech, and David Warrilow to explore new ideas in language, literature, music, performance, and the visual arts, and run on collective, non-hierarchical principles. This history shapes the horizon of expectations of audiences for any of their shows, audiences who come prepared to see formal experimentation across disciplines and the use of music, puppets, and strong visual elements.

According to the company's mission statement, Mabou Mines is "an artist-driven experimental theatre collective generating original works and re-imagined adaptations of classic plays through multi-disciplinary, technologically inventive collaborations among its members and a wide world of contemporary composers, writers, musicians, puppeteers and visual artists":

> Mabou Mines is dedicated to the development of a new theatrical language by exploring the latest concepts in music, visual arts, technology and animation with traditional forms of creative expression: puppetry, text, movement, theater design. Mabou Mines works in multiple languages, re-casts classical works with non-traditional performers, collaborates with disabled performers, artists and otherwise marginalized populations, connecting with the best artists it can find and reaching audiences from the art world to the street. (Mabou Mines Homepage)

Many viewers and reviewers of the St Ann's Warehouse premiere located *Dollhouse* within this context, and more specifically within the context of the company's early stagings of Beckett and their adaptations of classic theatrical texts, including Breuer's 1981 production of *The Tempest* in Central Park, their 1985 production, *Gospel at Colonus* (an adaptation of Sophocles' *Oedipus at Colonus*), and especially their gender-bending 1990 production of *Lear* with Ruth Maleczech in the title role. Margo Jefferson in *The New York Times* cited the company's earlier work to frame Breuer as "a wizard director, an alchemist who blends ideas, genres, styles, texts, and technologies to make new kinds of theater." Elinor Fuchs in the academic *Theatre Journal* situated *DollHouse* as one of Mabou Mines' "metaphysical cartoons" in the tradition of their early productions of Beckett "shorts" and of their *Tempest* in High Park ("Mabou" 498). Scholar of the New York avant-garde Gerald Rabkin cited a similar but more extended genealogy of "Lee Breuer's classic comics" in an essay half of which is about *DollHouse* and half about its predecessors in Breuer's previous "dialectical" treatments of classic texts. In these productions, for Rabkin, Breuer forges a "new dialectic...between the classic text, overlayed by the sedimentations of history, and contemporary performance styles," including the deconstructive (41). Writer, critic, publisher and poet Douglas Messerli similarly reviewed *DollHouse* in the context of four earlier, if different, Breuer productions, but argued that the show re-, rather than deconstructs Ibsen's play: "rather than eviscerating Ibsen's dramatic achievement, Breuer simply revisits the text, investing its metaphors and Victorian structures with startling new meaning."

For many seeing the first performances of the show, then, it was very much about the New York avant-garde and its relationship to classical texts, but it was also about Mabou Mines' unique position within the New York scene as an experimental company linking "formalist" with Method-based psychological approaches to acting and character. Breuer himself spoke in interviews with Simon Houpt and John Del Signore of the ways in which his approach differentiates Mabou Mines' work from that of its Manhattan-based avant-garde contemporaries, particularly the Ontological-Hysteric Theater of Richard Foreman and the Wooster Group, led by Elizabeth LeCompte:

> We really differ from both Richard and Liz LeCompte. [...] [W]e have a certain approach to acting that is a mixture of the motivational and the formal. [...] I'm a member of the Actor's Studio. I love old-style motivational acting. Brando and Dean and all that stuff. And at the same time I love formalism. Richard is a total formalist; he's not interested in knowing much about acting...in the psychology of acting. We're a little bit more complex, and, in a way, old-fashioned, in that we try to mix up the formalism with motivational acting....
>
> Liz has a very modernistic, formalistic approach to acting.[...] I actually feel we're on to something new, this

> combination of motivational and formalism, going back and forth where the formalism makes jokes about the motivational and the motivational takes the formalism and deeply embeds it in psychology. (qtd in Del Signore)

It is this mixed approach to the production of meaning in the theatre that explains many viewers' and reviewers' accounts of the roller-coaster ride that the production was for them, the combination of an over-the-top formalist exploration with a nevertheless powerful and affective exploration of characters pushed to emotional (and highly theatrical) extremes.

Further shaping both production and reception and requiring the attention of the performance analyst is a show's particular *moment* of production. *Dollhouse* was created and first seen in New York, only two years after the attacks on the World Trade Centre in Manhattan on 11 September 2001, and only eight months after the US and UK launched a politically divisive war on Iraq, without UN approval or support, on what proved to be the false justification of the existence there of weapons of mass destruction. In this social context it was difficult not to be conscious, as producers or patrons, of the production's concerns with the capricious exercise of power, be it patriarchal, political, or economic. "Everyone lies; everyone keeps secrets," as one New York reviewer said of the show (Jefferson). Perhaps more directly significantly, the show premiered in 2003 at the apex of a "postfeminist" moment, when young women, the beneficiaries of the feminist movement of earlier decades, were nevertheless seen to be ambivalent about the term – the year that Sociologist Pamela Aronson published her influential essay, "Feminists or 'Postfeminists'?" At some conscious or unconscious level this context must surely have influenced the rehearsal process for *DollHouse* and the reception of the show by audiences in New York. It is not surprising that most reviews there focused their interpretations on the status of women: "who hasn't seen a woman make a fool of herself to get something she needs from a powerful man?" (Jefferson).

Beyond the New York premiere the show was read differently and variously by local and festival audiences over the next nine years. In fact, the production was particularly malleable in that its use of deliberately faux Scandinavian accents and its location within a world of theatrical simulacra seemed to replace any consciousness of an originary social context for the action. This, combined with the fact that many of its performances were at international festivals, meant that the show gained attention more for its formal qualities as theatre than for its perceived social relevance. One reviewer of the show at Toronto's New World Stage Festival in 2007 characteristically began by "speaking purely from a theatrical perspective," and addressed "any true lover of theatre" (Colbourn). A reviewer at the Brisbane Festival, calling the show "world theatre of the highest standard," found it to be "just the sort of thing that festivals should bring to us, an opportunity to look outside the familiar terrain of the local theatre scene" (Hatherell). Lyn Gardner, reviewing the Edinburgh Festival performances in *The Guardian* wrote of "the shock of the new," and noted the ways in which the show "is always commenting upon performance itself." Indeed the only local resonance noted by festival reviewers, ironically, was the observation that the production's "mix of vaudeville, grand opera, backed by lavish expanses of red plush, has [never] looked better than in the Edwardian splendour of [Edinburgh's] King's Theatre" (Dawson).

Other performances took place in academic contexts, where the show tended to be read against either theatre history or Ibsen's text. One New York reviewer of a 2009 remount began with her credentials as a former graduate student at Columbia and read the production against the play's history as "a fundamental breakthrough for realistic drama" by the "infuriatingly predictable [...] Father of Modern Theater" (Sandman). The conservative reviewer for the Harvard *Crimson*, focusing explicitly on theatrical productions as interpretations, enhancements, or reinterpretations of texts, felt that *Mabou Mines DollHouse* at the end of its eight-year tour "leaves Ibsen's work sullied like a once beautiful field mercilessly trampled by a garish carnival" (Smurro).

What one takes away from a production depends on what one brings to it, and this applies to performance analyses as well as to reviews. Some coverage of the production focused on the controversial representation of short-statured people (see Fisher). Amy S. Green, reading the production through the lens of "a century of feminisms," found it to be "a graphic critique of Gender" (257). Wendy Weckwerth, reading it against a hypothetical "'standard' production of the play," saw it as "at once parody and homage" that served to "recreate the disorientation that Ibsen's earliest audiences experienced" (142). And Marvin Carlson, reading the production in the context of a survey of *A Doll House* in America, found that it "remains distinctly in the American tradition of reviving *A Doll's House* primarily in order to make some sort of social statement about the relationship between men and women" ("Ibsen's" 51).

Chocolate Woman Dreams the Milky Way was produced and received in a quite different material context. It was produced over four years in a largely academic and art gallery context, and first performed in June 2011 by the Chocolate Woman Collective at the Helen Gardiner Phelan Playhouse on the campus of the University of Toronto. The premiere was accompanied by an exhibition of contemporary paintings by its designer, Oswaldo DeLeón Kantule. Deeply grounded in Guna culture and featuring female figures from Guna cosmology, these paintings had been among the key resources in the play's devising. DeLeón Kantule's work was also featured on the show's poster and program cover, and it helped to frame the production within the context of contemporary Indigenous visual arts.

The Chocolate Woman Collective is an ad-hoc group of senior, mainly Indigenous artists formed in 2007 for the purpose of researching, creating, and producing *Chocolate Woman*. According to its mandate,

> Chocolate Woman Collective is dedicated to the rigorous application of a creative process that privileges Indigenous Knowledges, cultural aesthetics and performance principles. Our artistic practice integrates theory, research (both archival and field) and embodied studio work in the creation of new work that dislodges colonialism from the body. Our mandate is to create collaborative, interdisciplinary, cross-cultural and intergenerational Indigenous theatrical performances and to tour them hemispherically and throughout the world. The performances created from this practice serve, for our audiences, as interventions that shift cultural paradigms and contribute to a larger project of cultural/historical reclamation. (Chocolate Woman Collective Homepage)

Audiences attending the premiere and later productions could have read this mandate in their programs, and further could have read program notes concerning the specific origins and goals of *Chocolate Woman Dreams the Milky Way* itself, including a brief synopsis, an explication of the show's use of molas as a structural/processual principle (see Chapter 4), and an explicit statement of the intention of "dislodging colonialism from the body [...] through performance as intervention that gives agency to our identities through artistic practices."

> The collaborators of Chocolate Woman Collective are deconstructing the "house of colonization" [...] through practice-based research that *deliberately* privileges Indigenous aesthetic and performance principles, to create art that returns to the site of cultural origin and restores us to wholeness, much as our healers deconstruct illness through ceremony. (Mojica, "Playwright's," emphasis in original)

Chocolate Woman was also first produced and received in the immediate social context of the repression of the Indigenous people of Panama, of ongoing treaty rights negotiations between the Canadian government and the original occupants of the land, and of Canada's troubled Truth and Reconciliation Commission concerning the residential school abuse of Indigenous children, established in 2008 with a mandate to complete its work within five years. As Jenn Stephenson notes, "Autobiographical storytelling in this context is intended to serve a healing purpose, and yet the structure of speaking and witnessing testimony in this context can itself be problematic" (157) – partly because it focuses on individuals rather than collectives, cultures, or histories, partly because its focus on personal experiences of abuse, trauma, and grief can be consumed by the larger public as spectacle (see Regan 9–10), partly because it neglects ongoing practices of discrimination and abuse, and partly because it positions Indigenous peoples as perpetual victims.

Within this context audiences were often surprised and delighted by *Chocolate Woman*'s refusal of the victim narrative. Reviewers stressed the show's beauty and recognized its carving out of a performative space of healing (Art and Culture, Fabiano, Weerdenberg, Cole). But once again, reviews of and blogs about the production were conditioned and shaped by their material circumstances and by reviewers' horizons of expectation. Feminist reviewer Susan G. Cole, writing for Toronto's alternative weekly *Now*, focused on the show's strong women, the women's art forms that subtended the show, and the show's "magical" capacity to "disrupt the audience's expectation of theatre": "there is no one in the world like [Monique Mojica] and you've never seen anything like Chocolate Woman Dreams the Milky Way." A similarly positive review came from the Centre for Women's Studies in Education at the University of Toronto, where Andrea Weerdenberg saw the show as part of a course on Aboriginal world views and education. Weerdenberg stressed the "moral authority" held by the women in the show, something she "had rarely experienced as a white woman growing up in Anglo-Canadian culture." She acknowledged some difficulty following the show, but was prepared to read this as a purposeful defamiliarization, concluding that "'Chocolate Woman Dreams the Milky Way' not only teaches the content of Indigenous stories, but it is an act of resistance and a celebrated reclamation of Indigenous language, healing, art, and ways of being."

After its premiere, *Chocolate Woman*'s participation in the Indigenous Talking Stick Festival in Vancouver, British Columbia drew much less sympathetic responses from some reviewers. British Columbia was and remains in the midst of ongoing treaty negotiations over large portions of the province that have been appropriated from Indigenous Nations without negotiation or compensation, and reviews of the production there may have reflected some of the tensions this process causes. Whatever the reason, reviewers of the Talking Stick remount were less willing to surrender spectatorial control over the production's meanings than Weerdenberg had been. Colin Thomas, of the alternative weekly *Georgia Straight*, while praising the performances, the design, and the "inventive" direction, complained, "where the hell is the way into this material? ... Spit it out, for God's sake":

> I'm sure there will be some who will argue that I just don't get *Chocolate Woman* because I'm white and male, but I'm more than willing to engage. And to be clear, I like nothing more than a piece that challenges my narrative expectations – as long as it does so in a satisfying way.

Allyson McGrane's response was similar, if at once more restrained, more generous, and more revealing. Lamenting that she couldn't, "as an outsider to [...] [G]una culture," "follow the stories completely," McGrane wrote perceptively that "at times, I felt like I was watching a creation story of another culture and thought to myself, 'Is this what it's like for a non-Christian to hear the Nativity story for the first time?'" She also wondered about whether her lack of "complete" understanding was a function of her and her culture's having lost the capacity to listen to stories: "at one moment in the performance, I closed my eyes and just listened [...] [I]n the stillness, what had seemed to be nonsense slowly began to make sense to me."

Indigenous reviewers of the Native Earth Performing Arts performances in 2013 (Native Earth is the largest Indigenous performing arts organization in Canada) had little difficulty following the show. In an article entitled "Chocolate Woman a creation of the transformational spirit," Anishinabe journalist Barb Nahwegahbow wrote: "The story has no plot but Mojica seems to take us by the hand and we feel privileged to accompany her on her journey, trusting she will not lead us astray and that all will be right in the end." It will be fascinating to see responses to the show outside Canada, particularly if and when it tours to Panama, where it will attract audiences with a detailed knowledge of Guna culture and history, including knowledge of the success of the Dule revolution in 1925 that won autonomy for Guna Yala. When a delegation of Guna elders attended the premiere in Toronto, their receptive and welcoming understanding was palpable and infectious.

Conclusion

There is no template for performance analysis, and in spite of documents such as the various versions and applications of Patrice Pavis's famous questionnaire (Pavis, "Theatre Analysis"), there is no uniform checklist that applies to all productions, or indeed any standard procedure that responds to all reasons for undertaking an analysis. And no performance analysis is or could be complete and totalizing, answering all questions that might be asked about how a given work produces its meanings and effects. If it is possible, however, to abstract one general principle from the expanded semiotic approach to performance analysis that I have articulated, it is the one pointed to by Saussure himself when he argued that all meaning is relational and is culturally determined. Any good performance analysis, I suggest, must be interested in articulation, differentiation, and power. Whether it is asking questions on the large scales of culture and form or on the smallest of scales concerning the individual sign and its constituent parts, performance analysis can always usefully inquire about the ever productive "not…but," and can always fruitfully inquire into who, in each specific instance, controls the semiosis. Finally, any good performance analysis in the 21st century must pay primary attention, not to building huge and universal edifices of meaning, but to the shifting grounds of difference.

Works Cited

Ahmed, Sarah. *The Cultural Politics of Emotion*. London: Routledge, 2004. Print.

Allen, Chadwick. *Trans-Indigenous: Methodologies for Global Native Literary Studies*. Minneapolis: U of Minnesota P, 2012. Print.

Al-Solaylee, Kamal. "Resized Ibsen Is a Must-see." *The Globe and Mail* [Toronto] (27 January 2007): R8. Print.

Althusser, Louis. *For Marx*. Trans. Ben Brewster. New York: Pantheon, 1969. Print.

Althusser, Louis. "Ideology and Ideological State Apparatuses (Notes Towards an Investigation)." *Lenin and Philosophy and Other Essays*. Trans. Ben Brewster. New York: Monthly Review, 1971. 127–86. Print.

Ambros, Veronika. "Prague's Experimental Stage: Laboratory of Theatre and Semiotics." *Semiotica* 168.1–4 (2008): 45–65. Print.

"Annie Sprinkle's Cervix." YouTube. 15 April 2013. Web. 14 May 2013.

Appleford, Rob. "'No, the Centre Should Be Invisible': Radical Revisioning of Chekhov in Floyd Favel Starr's *The House of Sonja*." *Modern Drama* 45.2 (2002): 246–58. Print.

Aristotle. *The Poetics*. Trans. John Warrington. London: Dent, 1963. Print.

Aronson, Pamela. "Feminists or 'Postfeminists'?: Young Women's Attitudes toward Feminism and Gender Relations." *Gender and Society* 17.6 (2003): 903–22. Print.

Aston, Elaine and George Savona. *Theatre As Sign-System: A Semiotics of Text and Performance*. London: Routledge, 1991. Print.

Austin, J. L. *How to Do Things with Words* [1962]. 2nd edn. Ed. J. O. Urmson and Marina Sbisà. Oxford: Clarendon, 1975. Print.

Bakhtin, M. M. *Art and Answerability: Early Philosophical Essays*. Ed. Michael Holquist and Vadim Liapunov. Trans. Vadim Liapunov. Austin: U of Texas P, 1990. Print.

Bakhtin, M. M. *The Dialogic Imagination*. Trans. Caryl Emerson and Michael Holquist. Austin: U of Texas P, 1981. Print.

Bakhtin, M. M. *Problems of Dostoevsky's Poetics*. Ed. and Trans. Caryl Emerson. Minneapolis: U of Minnesota P, 1984. Print.

Bakhtin, M. M. *Rabelais and His World*. Trans. Helen Iswolsky. Bloomington: Indiana UP, 1984. Print.

Bakhtin, M. M. *Speech Genres and Other Late Essays*. Ed. Caryl Emerson and Michael Holquist. Trans. Vern W. McGee. Austin: U of Texas P, 1986. Print.

Baldwin, Jane. "Mabou Mines' DollHouse: At the Cutler Majestic in Boston, MA." Capital Critics' Circle. 21 November 2011. Web. 18 May 2013.

Balme, Christopher. *Decolonizing the Stage: Theatrical Syncretism and Post-Colonial Drama*. Oxford: Clarendon, 1999. Print.

Bannerji, Himani, ed. *Returning the Gaze: Essays on Racism, Feminism, and Politics*. Toronto: Sister Vision, 1993. Print.

Barba, Eugenio. *The Paper Canoe: A Guide to Theatre Anthropology*. Trans. Richard Fowler. London: Routledge, 1995. Print.

Barber, C. L. *Shakespeare's Festive Comedy: A Study of Dramatic Form and Its Relation to Social Custom*. Princeton, NJ: Princeton UP, 1959. Print.

Barthes, Roland. "Literature and Signification." *Critical Essays* [1964]. Trans. Richard Howard. Evanston: Northwestern UP, 1972. 261–79. Print.

Barthes, Roland. *Mythologies* [1957]. Trans. Annette Lavers. London: Granada, 1972. Print.

Barton, Bruce, ed. *Collective Creation, Collaboration and Devising*. Toronto: Playwrights Canada, 2008. Print.

Barton, Bruce. "Introduction: Devising the Creative Body." Barton, *Collective* vii–xxvii. Print.

Barton, Bruce. "Mining 'Turbulence': Authorship Through Direction in Physically-Based Devised Theatre." Barton, *Collective* 136–51. Print.

Baudrillard, Jean. *Simulacra and Simulation*. Trans. Shelia Faria Glaser. Ann Arbor: U of Michigan P, 1994. Print.

Bennett, Susan. *Theatre Audiences: A Theory of Production and Reception*. 2nd edn. London: Routledge, 1997. Print.

Berger, Harry. *Imaginary Audition: Shakespeare on Stage and Page*. Berkeley: U of California P, 1989. Print.

Bhabha, Homi. *The Location of Culture*. London: Routledge, 1994. Print.

Bharucha, Rustom. *The Politics of Cultural Practice: Thinking Through Theatre in an Age of Globalization*. Hanover, NH: Wesleyan UP, 2000. Print.

Bharucha, Rustom. "Somebody's Other: Disorientations in the Cultural Politics of Our Times." Pavis, *Intercultural* 196–212. Print.

Bharucha, Rustom. *Theatre and the World: Performance and the Politics of Culture*. London: Routledge, 1991. Print.

Bimm, Jordan. "A Taste of Chocolate." *Now Magazine* [Toronto] 2–9 July 2011. Web. 16 April 2013.

Bogatyrev, Petr. "Costume as a Sign (The Functional and Structural Concept of Costume in Ethnography)" [1936]. Trans. Y. Lockwood. Matejka and Titunik 2–19. Print.

Bogatyrev, Petr. "Forms and Functions of Folk Theater." Matejka and Titunik 51–56. Print.

Bogatyrev, Petr. "Semiotics in the Folk Theater." Matejka and Titunik 33–50. Print.

Brannigan, John. *New Historicism and Cultural Materialism*. New York: St. Martin's, 1998. Print.

Brecht, Bertolt. *Brecht on Theatre: The Development of an Aesthetic*. Trans. John Willett. London: Methuen, 1964. Print.

Breuer, Lee. "Director Lee Breuer, *Mabou Mines DollHouse*." Interview with Lee Breuer by John Del Signore. *Gothamist*. 27 February 2009. Web. 18 January 2011.

Brušák, Karel. "Signs in Chinese Theater." Matejka and Titunik 59–73. Print.

Bruss, Neal. "The Birth of Psychoanalysis in Semiotics, or of Semiotics in Psychoanalysis." *The Sign: Semiotics Around the World*. Ed. Richard W. Bailey, Ladislav Matejka, and Peter Steiner. Ann Arbor: U of Michigan P, 1978. 119–31. Print.

Burián, Emil František. "Příspěvek k problému jesvištní mluvy" [A Contribution to the Problem of Stage Language]. *Slovo a Slovesnost* 5 (1939): 24–32. Print.

Carlson, Marvin. "Ibsen's *A Doll's House* in America." *Global Ibsen: Performing Multiple Modernities*. Ed. Erika Fischer-Lichte, Barbara Gronau, and Christel Weiler. London: Routledge, 2011. 39–52.

Carlson, Marvin. "Intercultural Theory, Postcolonial Theory, and Semiotics: The Road Not (Yet) Taken." *Semiotica* 168.1–4 (2008): 129–42. Print.

Carlson, Marvin. *Places of Performance: The Semiotics of Theatre Architecture*. Ithaca: Cornell UP, 1989. Print.

Carlson, Marvin. "Semiotics and its Heritage," Reinelt and Roach. Rev. and enlarged edn. 13–25. Print.

Carlson, Marvin. *Theatre Semiotics: Signs of Life*. Bloomington: Indiana UP, 1990. Print.

Carter, Jill. "Chocolate Woman Visions and Organic Dramaturgy: Blocking-Notation for the Indigenous Soul." *Canadian Women Studies* 26.3–4 (2008): 169–76. Print.

Carter, Jill. "Shaking the Palu Wala Tree: Fashioning Internal Gathering Houses and Re-Fashioning the Space of Popular Entertainment Through Contemporary Investigations into Native Performance Culture (NPC)." *alt.theatre: Cultural Diversity and the Stage* 6.4 (2009): 8–13. Print.

Case, Sue-Ellen. *Feminism and Theatre*. London: Methuen, 1988, Print.

Chaudhuri, Una. "The Future of the Hyphen: Interculturalism, Textuality, and the Difference Within." Marranca and Dasgupta 192–207. Print.

Chaudhuri, Una. *Staging Place: The Geography of Modern Drama*. Ann Arbor: U of Michigan P, 1995. Print.

Chocolate Woman Collective Homepage. 2011. Web. 9 June 2013.

Clough, Patricia Ticineto, ed., with Jean Healey. *The Affective Turn: Theorizing the Social*. Durham, NC: Duke UP, 2007. Print.

Colbourn, John, "'DollHouse' Larger than Life." *Toronto Sun*. 26 January 2007. Web. 18 January 2011.

Cole, Susan G. "Chocolate Woman Dreams the Milky Way." *Now Magazine* [Toronto]. 9–16 June 2011. Web. 18 June 2013.

Dasgupta, Gautam. "*The Mahabharata*: Peter Brook's Orientalism." Marranca and Dasgupta 75–82. Print.

Dawson, Robert. "Mabou Mines Dollhouse." *Times Online*. 28 August 2007. Web. 18 January 2011.

Debord, Guy. *The Society of the Spectacle*. New York: Zone, 1994. Print.

De Certeau, Michel. *The Practice of Everyday Life*. Trans. Stephen Rendall. Berkeley: U of California P, 1984. Print.

De Certeau, Michel. *The Writing of History*. Trans. Tom Conley. New York: Columbia UP, 1988. Print.

Del Signore, John. "Director Lee Breuer, Mabou Mines DollHouse." *Gothamist*. 27 February 2009. Web. 18 January 2011.

De Marinis, Marco. "Dramaturgy of the Spectator." Trans. Paul Dwyer. *TDR (The Drama Review)* 31.2 (1987): 100–14. Print.

De Marinis, Marco. *The Semiotics of Performance* [1982]. Trans. Áine O'Healy. Bloomington: Indiana UP, 1993. Print.

Denzin, Norman K., Yvonna S. Lincoln, and Linda Tuhiwai Smith, eds. *Handbook of Critical and Indigenous Methodologies*. Los Angeles: Sage, 2008. Print.

Derrida, Jacques. "Différance." *Margins of Philosophy*. Trans. Alan Bass. Chicago: U of Chicago P, 1982. 1–27. Print.

Derrida, Jacques. *Of Grammatology* [1967]. Trans. Gayatri Chakravorty Spivak. Baltimore: John's Hopkins UP, 1975. Print.

De Toro, Fernando. "The End of Theatre Semiotics? A Symptom of an Epistemological Shift." *Semiotica* 168.1–4 (2008): 109–28. Print.

Diamond, Elin. *Unmaking Mimesis: Essays on Feminism and Theater*. New York: Routledge, 1997. Print.

Dolan, Jill. *The Feminist Spectator as Critic*. Ann Arbor: U of Michigan P, 1988.

Durbach, Errol. *A Doll's House: Ibsen's Myth of Transformation*. Boston: Twayne, 1991. Print.

During, Simon. "Michel de Certeau, Walking in the City, Editor's Introduction." *The Cultural Studies Reader*. Ed. Simon During. London: Routledge, 1993. 151. Print.

Eco, Umberto. "The Role of the Reader." Bloomington: Indiana UP, 1979. Print.

Eco, Umberto. "Semiotics of Theatrical Performance." *TDR (The Drama Review)* 22 (1977): 107–17. Print.

Edelman, Gerald and Giulio Tononi. *A Universe of Consciousness: How Matter Becomes Imagination*. New York: Basic Books, 2000. Print.

Elam, Keir. "Much Ado About Doing Things with Words (and Other Means): Some Problems in the Pragmatics of Theatre and Drama." *Performing Texts*. Ed. Michael Issacharoff and Robin F. Jones. Philadelphia: U of Pennsylvania P, 1988. Print.

Elam, Keir. *The Semiotics of Theatre and Drama*. 2nd edn. London: Routledge, 2002. Print.

Eliade, Mircea. *Myth and Reality*. Trans. Willard R. Trask. New York: Harper & Row, 1963. Print.

Eliade, Mircea. *The Myth of the Eternal Return: Cosmos and History*. Princeton: Princeton UP, 1971. Print.

Emmeche, Claus, and Kalevi Kull, eds. *Towards a Semiotic Biology: Life Is the Action of Signs*. London: Imperial College Press, 2011. Print.

Esslin, Martin. *The Field of Drama: How the Signs of Drama Create Meaning on Stage and Screen*. London: Methuen, 1987. Print.

Evans, Dylan. *Emotion: The Science of Sentiment*. Oxford: Oxford UP, 2001. Print.

Favel, Floyd. "Poetry, Remnants, and Ruins: Aboriginal Theatre in Canada." *Canadian Theatre Review* 139 (2009): 31–5. Print.

Favel, Floyd. "The Theatre of Orphans/Native Languages on Stage." *Aboriginal Drama and Theatre*. Ed. Rob Appleford. Toronto: Playwrights Canada, 2005. 32–6. Print.

Favel, Floyd. "Waskawewin." *Topoi* 24.1 (2005): 113–15.Print.

Favel Starr, Floyd. "The Artificial Tree: Native Performance Culture Research 1991–1996." *Aboriginal Drama and Theatre*. Ed. Rob Applford. Toronto: Playwrights Canada, 2005. 69–73. Print.

Figgis, Mike, dir. *Miss Julie*. Beverley Hills, CA: MGM, 1999. Film.

Fischer, Iris Smith. "C.S. Peirce and the Habit of Theatre." *Changing the Subject: Marvin Carlson and Theatre Studies, 1959–2009*. Ann Arbor: U of Michigan P, 2009. 118–48.

Fischer-Lichte, Erika. "Staging the Foreign as Cultural Transformation." Fischer-Lichte, Roy, and Gissenwehrer 277–87. Print.

Fischer-Lichte, Erika. "Theatre, Own and Foreign: The Intercultural Trend in Contemporary Theatre." Fischer-Lichte, Roy, and Gissenwehrer 11–19. Print.

Fischer-Lichte, Erika, Josephine Roy, and Michael Gissenwehrer, eds. *The Dramatic Touch of Difference: Theatre, Own and Foreign*. Tübingen: Gunter Narr, 1990. Print.

Fish, Stanley. *Is There a Text in This Class?* Cambridge: Harvard UP, 1980. Print.

Fisher, Mark. "'We've Really Upset Some Men'." *The Guardian* 7 August 2007. Web. 18 January 2011.

Foster, Susan Leigh. *Choreographing Empathy: Kinesthesia in Performance*. London: Routledge, 2011. Print.

Foucault, Michel. *The Archaeology of Knowledge* [1969]. Trans. A. M. Sheridan Smith. London: Routledge, 1989. Print.

Foucault, Michel. *Discipline and Punish: The Birth of the Prison* [1975]. Trans. Alan Sheridan. New York: Vintage, 1995. Print.

Foucault, Michel. "Of Other Spaces." *Diacritics* 16.1 (1986): 22–7. Print.

Foucault, Michel. *The Order of Things: An Archeology of the Human Sciences* [1966]. New York: Random House/Vintage, 1973. Print.

Foucault, Michel. *Power/Knowledge: Selected Interviews and Other Writings, 1972–1977*. Ed. and Trans. Colin Gordon. New York: Pantheon, 1980. Print.

Freedman, Barbara. *Staging the Gaze: Postmodernism, Psychoanalysis, and Shakespearean Comedy*. Ithaca, NY: Cornell UP, 1991. Print.

Freshwater, Helen. *Theatre & Audience*. Basingstoke: Palgrave Macmillan, 2009. Print.

Frye, Northrop. *Anatomy of Criticism: Four Essays*. Princeton, NJ: Princeton UP, 1957. Print.

Fuchs, Elinor. "EF's Visit to a Small Planet: Some Questions to Ask a Play." *Theater* 34.2 (2005): 4–9. Print.

Fuchs, Elinor. "Mabou Mines DollHouse." *Theatre Journal* 56.3 (2004): 498–500.

Fuchs, Elinor and Una Chaudhuri. "Introduction: Land/Scape/Theatre and the New Spatial Paradigm." Fuchs and Chaudhuri, *Land/Scape/Theater*. Ann Arbor: U of Michigan P, 2002. 1–7. Print.

Fuchs, Elinor. ed. *Land/Scape/Theater*. Ann Arbor: U of Michigan P, 2002. Print.

Gallese, Vittorio. "Empathy, Embodied Simulation and the Brain: Commentary on Aragno and Zepf/Hartmann." *Journal of the American Psychoanalytic Association* 56 (2009): 769–81. Print.

Gallese, Vittorio, Luciano Fadiga, Leonardo Fogassi, and Giacomo Rizzolatti, "Action Recognition in the Premotor Cortex." *Brain* 119 (1996): 593–609. Print.

Gardner, Lyn. "Mabou Mines DollHouse." *The Guardian* 27 August 2007. Web. 18 January 2011.

Garner, Stanton B., Jr. *Bodied Spaces: Phenomenology and Performance in Contemporary Drama*. Ithaca, NY: Cornell UP, 1994. Print.

Garner, Stanton B. "Urban Landscapes, Theatrical Encounters: Staging the City." Fuchs and Chaudhuri, *Land/Scape/Theater*. Ann Arbor: U of Michigan P, 2002. 94–118. Print.

Garvin, Paul L., ed. and trans. *A Prague School Reader on Esthetics, Literary Structure, and Style*. Washington, DC: Georgetown UP, 1964. Print.

Gilbert, Helen. "Black and White and Re(a)d All Over Again: Indigenous Minstrelsy in Contemporary Canadian and Australian Theatre." *Theatre Journal* 55.4 (2003): 679–98. Print.

Gilbert, Helen and Jacqueline Lo. *Performance and Cosmopolitics: Cross-Cultural Transactions in Australasia*. Basingstoke: Palgrave Macmillan, 2007. Print.

Green, Amy S. "Nora's Journey Through a Century of Feminisms to the Postmodern Stage of *Mabou Mines DollHouse*." *Feminist Theatrical Revisions of Classic Works: Critical Essays*. Ed. Sharon Friedman. Jefferson, NC: McFarland, 2009. 247–66.

Greimas, A. J. *Structural Semantics: An Attempt at a Method* [1966]. Trans. Daniele McDowell, Ronald Schleifer, and Alan Velie. Lincoln, Nebraska: U of Nebraska P, 1983. Print.

Hall, Edward T. *The Hidden Dimension*. Garden City, NY: Doubleday, 1966. Print.

Hatherell, William. "Small Wonders: *Mabou Mines DollHouse*." *M/C Reviews* 23 July 2006. Web. 18 January 2011.

Havránek, Bohuslav. "The Functional Differentiation of the Standard Language." (1932) Garvin 3–16. Print.

Heddon, Deirdre and Jane Milling. *Devising Performance: A Critical History*. Basingstoke: Palgrave Macmillan, 2006. Print.

Heritage, Barbara Salvadori. "Of Structure and Scene: Visual Intertextuality between Commedia dell-Arte and Boal's Theatre of the Oppressed." Paper delivered at Performance: Visual Aspects of

Performance Practice conference, Prague, 11–13 November 2010. Paper.

Hetherington, Kevin. *The Badlands of Modernity: Heterotopia and Social Ordering*. London: Routledge, 1997. Print.

Holledge, Julie and Joanne Tompkins. *Women's Intercultural Performance*. London: Routledge, 2000. Print.

Honzl, Jindřich. "The Dynamics of the Sign in the Theater." Matejka and Titunik 74–93. Print.

Honzl, Jindřich. "Herecká postava" [The Figure of the Actor]. *Slovo a Slovesnost* 5 (1939): 145–50. Print.

Honzl, Jindřich. "The Hierarchy of Dramatic Devices." (1943). Trans. S. Larson. Matejka and Titunik 118–27. Print.

Honzl, Jindřich. "Pohyb divadelniho znaku" [The Movement of the Sign in the Theatre]. *Slovo a Slovesnost* 6 (1940): 177–88. Print.

Hopkins, D. J. *City/Stage/Globe: Performance and Space in Shakespeare's London*. New York: Routledge, 2008. Print.

Hopkins, D. J., Shelley Orr, and Kim Solga, ed. *Performance and the City*. Basingstoke: Palgrave MacMillan, 2011. Print.

Houpt, Simon. "A Giant of the Avant-Garde Stoops to Conquer." *The Globe and Mail* [Toronto] 25 January 2007: R1, R2. Print

Houser, Nathan. Introduction. Peirce, *Essential Peirce*, Vol. 2 xvii–xxxviii. Print.

Hurley, Erin. *Theatre & Feeling*. Basingstoke: Palgrave Macmillan, 2010. Print.

Hutcheon, Linda. *The Politics of Postmodernism*. London: Routledge, 1989. Print.

Ibsen, Henrick. *The Complete Major Prose Plays*. Trans. Rolf Fjelde. New York: Farrar Straus Giroux, 1978. Print.

Ibsen, Henrick. *A Doll House*. Ibsen, *Complete* 119–96.

Ibsen, Henrick. *Hedda Gabler*, Ibsen, *Complete* 689–778.

Iser, Wolfgang. *The Act of Reading: A Theory of Aesthetic Response*. Baltimore: Johns Hopkins UP, 1978. Print.

Iser, Wolfgang. *The Implied Reader: Patterns of Communication in Prose Fiction from Bunyan to Beckett*. Baltimore: Johns Hopkins UP, 1874. Print.

Jakobson, Roman. "A Glance at the Development of Semiotics." Trans. Patricia Baudoin. *Language in Literature*. Ed. Krystyna Pomorska and Stephen Rudy. Cambridge, Mass.: Belknap Press, Harvard UP, 1987. 436–54. Print.

Jauss, Hans Robert. *Towards and Aesthetics of Reception*. Trans. Timothy Bahti. Minneapolis: U of Minnesota P, 1982. Print.

Jefferson, Margo. "Fun-House Proportions Turn Dominance Upside-Down." *New York Times* 24 November 2003. Web. 9 June 2013.

Jestrović, Silvija. "Semiotics of Nonsemiotic Performance." *Semiotica* 168.1–4 (2008): 93–107. Print.

Jeyifo, Biodan. "The Reinvention of Theatrical Tradition: Critical Discourses on Interculturalism in the African Theatre." Fischer-Lichte, Roy, and Gissenwehrer, *Dramatic* 239–51. Print.

Johnson, Mark. *The Meaning of the Body: Aesthetics of Human Understanding*. Chicago: U of Chicago P, 2007. Print.

Johnstone, Keith. *Impro for Storytellers*. New York: Routledge, 1999. Print.

Jürs-Munby, Karen. "Preface to the English Edition." *Postdramatic Theatre*. By Hans-Thies Lehmann. Trans. Karen Jürs-Munby. London: Routledge, 2006. 1–15.

Kennedy, Dennis. *The Spectator and the Spectacle: Audiences in Modernity and Postmodernity*. Cambridge: Cambridge UP, 2009. Print.

Kershaw, Baz. "Oh for Unruly Audiences! Patterns of Participation in Twentieth-Century Theatre." *Modern Drama* 44 (2001): 133–54. Print.

Kershaw, Baz. *Theatre Ecology: Environments and Performance Events*. Cambridge: Cambridge UP, 2007. Print.

Keyssar, Helene. "Drama and the Dialogic Imagination: *The Heidi Chronicles* and *Fefu and Her Friends*." *Modern Drama* 34.1 (1991): 88–106. Print.

Kim, Christine. "Performing Asian Canadian Intimacy: Theatre Replacement's *Bioboxes* and Awkward Multiculturalisms." *Asian Canadian Theatre*. Ed. Nina Lee Aquino and Ric Knowles. Toronto: Playwrights Canada, 2011. 183–94. Print.

Kirby, Michael. "Nonsemiotic Performance." *Modern Drama* 25 (1982): 105–11. Print.

Knowles, Ric. "Native Performance Culture, Monique Mojica, and the *Chocolate Woman* Workshops." *"Crosstalk": Canadian and Global Imaginaries in Dialogue*. Ed. Diana Brydon and Marta Dvorak. Waterloo, ON: Wilfrid Laurier UP, 2012. 73–93. Print.

Knowles, Ric. *Reading the Material Theatre*. Cambridge: Cambridge UP, 2004. Print.

Knowles, Ric. *Theatre & Interculturalism*. Basingstoke: Palgrave Macmillan, 2010. Print.

Knowles, Ric and Jen Harvie. "Dialogic Monologue: A Dialogue." *The Theatre of Form and the Production of Meaning: Contemporary Canadian Dramaturgies*. By Ric Knowles. Toronto: ECW Press, 1999. 193–210. Print.

Kobialka. Michal. "Theatre and Space: A Historiographic Preamble." *Modern Drama* 46.4 (2003): 558–79. Print.

Kovach, Margaret. *Indigenous Methodologies: Characteristics, Conversations, and Contexts*. Toronto: U of Toronto P, 2009. Print.

Kowzan, Tadeuz. "The Sign in the Theater." *Diogenes* 61 (1968): 52–80. Print.

Kristeva, Julia. *Revolution in Poetic Language*. Trans. Margaret Waller. New York: Columbia UP, 1984. Print.

Kristeva, Julia. "Word, Dialogue, and Novel." *Desire in Language: A Semiotic Approach to Literature and Art*. Ed. Leon S. Roudiez. Trans. Thomas Gora, Alice Jardine, and Leon S. Roudiez. New York: Columbia UP, 1980. 64–91. Print.

Kull, Kalevi, Claus Emmeche, and Jesper Hoffmeyer. "Why Biosemiotics? An Introduction to Our View on the Biology of Life Itself." Emmeche and Kull 1–21.

Lacan, Jacques. "The Mirror Stage as Formative of the Function of the I as Revealed in Psychoanalytic Experience" [1949]. *Écrits: A Selection*. Trans. Alan Sheridan. New York: Norton, 1977. 1–7. Print.

LaCapra, Dominick. *Writing History, Writing Trauma*. Baltimore: Johns Hopkins UP, 2001. Print.

Lee, Esther Kim. "Interruption, Intervention, Interculturalism: Robert Wilson's HIT Productions in Taiwan." *Theatre Journal* 63.4 (2011): 571–86. Print.

Lefebvre, Henri. *The Production of Space* [1976]. Trans. Donald Nicholson-Smith. Oxford: Blackwell, 1991. Print.

Lehmann, Hans-Thies. *Postdramatic Theatre*. Trans. Karen Jürs-Munby. London: Routledge, 2006.

Lévi-Strauss, Claude. *Structural Anthropology* [Vol. 1]. Trans. Claire Jacobson and Brooke Grundfest Schoepf. New York: Basic Books, 1963. Print.

Lo, Jacqueline and Helen Gilbert. "Toward a Topography of Cross-Cultural Theatre Praxis." *TDR* (*The Drama Review*) 46.3 (2002): 31–53. Print.

Lotman, Juri. "Theses on the Semiotic Study of Cultures (as Applied to Slavic Texts)." *Structure of Texts and Semiotics of Culture*. Ed. Jan van der Eng and Mojmir Gyrgar. The Hague: Mouton, 1–28. Print.

Lotman, Juri. *Universe of the Mind: A Semiotic Theory of Culture*. Trans. Ann Shukman. Bloomington: Indiana UP, 1990. Print.

Mabou Mines Homepage. 14 February 2011. Web. 8 May 2013.

Mabou Mines Dollhouse. Adapt. Lee Breuer and Maude Mitchell. Dir. Lee Breuer. Prod. Mabou Mines. Pour Voir 2008. DVD.

Marranca, Bonnie. "Thinking About Interculturalism." Preface to Marranca and Dasgupta 9–23. Print.

Marranca, Bonnie, and Gautam Dasgupta, ed. *Interculturalism and Performance: Writings from PAJ*. New York: PAJ Publications, 1991. Print.

Matejka, Ladislav and Irwin R. Titunik, eds. *Semiotics of Art: Prague School Contributions*. Cambridge, Mass.: MIT Press, 1976. Print.

Maufort, Marc and Dorothy Figueira, eds. *Theatres in the Round: Multi-ethnic, Indigenous, and Intertextual Dialogues in Drama*. Brussels: Lang, 2011. Print.

McAuley, Gay. *Space in Performance: Making Meaning in the Theatre*. Ann Arbor: U of Michigan P, 1999. Print.

McConachie, Bruce. *Engaging Audiences: A Cognitive Approach to Spectating in the Theatre*. New York: Palgrave Macmillan, 2008. Print.

McConachie, Bruce. "Falsifiable Theories for Theatre and Performance Studies" *Theatre Journal* 59.4 (2007): 553–77. Print.

McConachie, Bruce. *Theatre & Mind*. Basingstoke: Palgrave Macmillan, 2013.

McConachie, Bruce and F. Elizabeth Hart, eds. *Performance and Cognition: Theatre Studies and the Cognitive Turn*. London: Routledge, 2006. Print.

McConachie, Bruce and F. Elizabeth Hart. "Introduction." McConachie and Hart, *Performance and Cognition* 1–25. Print.

McGrane, Allyson. "Chocolate Woman – Not What I'd Call Mind Candy." *Plank* 29 February 2013. Web. 18 June 2013.

McKinnie, Michael. *City Stages: Theatre and Urban Space in a Global City*. Toronto: U of Toronto P, 2007. Print.

McNulty, Charles. "Welcome to Lee Breuer's Dollhouse: Lee Breuer Goes Little – and Literal – With His Production of Ibsen's Classic." *Village Voice* 11 November 2003. Web. 21 May 2013.

Meerzon, Yana. "Introduction: Theatrical Semiosphere: Toward the Semiotics of Theatre Today." *Semiotica* 168.1–4 (2008): 1–10. Print.

Melville, Herman. *Moby-Dick or, The Whale*. Ed. Luther S. Mansfield and Howard P. Vincent. New York: Hendricks House, 1962. Print.

Mermikides, Alex and Jackie Smart, eds. *Devising in Process*. Basingstoke: Palgrave Macmillan, 2010. Print.

Messerli, Douglas. "You Great Big Beautiful Doll." UStheater.blogspot. 6 August 2010. Web. 18 January 2011.

Moi, Toril. "'First and Foremost a Human Being': Idealism, Theater, and Gender in *A Doll's House*." *Henrik Ibsen and the Birth of Modernism: Art, Theater, Philosophy*. Oxford: Oxford UP, 2006. 225–47. Print.

Mojica, Monique. *Chocolate Woman Dreams the Milky Way*. 22 May 2011 Unpublished production draft. Play manuscript.

Mojica, Monique. "Chocolate Woman Dreams the Milky Way." *Canadian Woman Studies* 26.3–4 (2008): 160–8. Print.

Mojica, Monique. Email to the author. 30 May 2013.

Mojica, Monique. "An Excerpt from 'Scoring the Body Through Kuna Aesthetic Principles: Indigenous Dramatic Arts in Theory, Process, and Practice'." *Canadian Theatre Review* 146 (2011): 61–2. Print.

Mojica, Monique. "Playwright's Notes." *Chocolate Woman Dreams the Milky Way*. Program. Toronto, 29 January–3 February 2013. Print.

Mojica, Monique. "Project History." Undated manuscript prepared for a grant application for *Chocolate Woman Dreams the Milky Way*. Personal files.

Moritz, Reiner E. "Looking for a Miracle: Reflections on Ibsen's *A Doll's House*." On *Mabou Mines DollHouse*. 2008. Film.

Mukařovský, Jan. "Intentionality and Unintentionality in Art" [1943]. *Structure, Sign, and Function: Selected Essays by Jan Mukařovský*. Ed. and Trans. John Burbank and Peter Steiner. New Haven: Yale UP, 1978. 89–128. Print.

Mukařovský, Jan. "Tentativo di analisi del fenomeno delll'attore." *Ill significato dell'estetica*. Turin: Einaudi, 1973. 324–9. Print.

Mulvey, Laura. "Visual Pleasure and Narrative Cinema." *Screen* 16.3 (1975): 6–18. Print.

Muñoz, José Esteban. *Disidentifications: Queers of Color and the Performance of Politics*. Minneapolis: U of Minnesota P, 1999. Print.

Murphy, Colleen. *The December Man (l'homme de décembre)*. Toronto: Playwrights Canada, 2007. Print.

Nahwegahbow, Barb. "Chocolate Woman a Creation of the Transformational Spirit." *Windspeaker* 30.12 (2013). Web. 18 June 2013.

Nolan, Yvette. *Annie Mae's Movement*. *Staging Coyote's Dream: An Anthology of First Nations Drama in English* [Vol. 2]. Ed. Monique Mojica and Ric Knowles. Toronto: Playwrights Canada, 2008. 133–70. Print.

Nolan, Yvette. "The Death of a Chief: An Interview with Yvette Nolan." Interview with Sorouja Moll. Native Earth Performing Arts Office, Distillery District, Toronto. 12 March 2006. *Canadian Adaptations of Shakespeare Project*. 7 July 2006. Web. 18 June 2013.

Nolan, Yvette. *Job's Wife, or the Delivery of Grace*. *Staging Coyote's Dream: An Anthology of First Nations Drama in English* [Vol. 1]. Ed. Monique Mojica and Ric Knowles. Toronto: Playwrights Canada, 2003. 237–63. Print.

Oddey, Alison. *Devising Theatre: A Practical and Theoretical Handbook*. London: Routledge, 1994. Print.

Patterson, Richard. "Mabou Mines DollHouse." MusicOMH. 1 February 2009. Web. 17 May 2013.

Pavis, Patrice. *Analyzing Performance: Theater, Dance, and Film*. Trans. David Williams. Ann Arbor: U of Michigan P, 2003. Print.

Pavis, Patrice. *Dictionary of the Theatre: Terms, Concepts, and Analysis* [1996]. Trans. Christine Shantz. Toronto: U of Toronto P, 1998. Print.

Pavis, Patrice. "From Text to Performance." *Performing Texts*. Ed. Michael Issacharoff and Robin F. Jones. Philadelphia: U of Pennsylvania P, 1988. 86–100. Print.

Pavis, Patrice. ed. *The Intercultural Performance Reader*. London: Routledge, 1996. Print.

Pavis, Patrice. *Languages of the Stage: Essays in the Semiology of the Theatre*. New York: PAJ Publications, 1982. Print.

Pavis, Patrice. "Theatre Analysis: Some Questions and a Questionnaire." *New Theatre Quarterly* 1.2 (1985): 208–12. Print.

Pavis, Patrice. *Theatre at the Crossroads of Culture*. Trans. Loren Kruger. London: Routledge, 1992. Print.

Peirce, Charles Sanders. *Collected Papers*. 8 Vols. Cambridge: Harvard UP, 1931–58. Print.

Peirce, Charles Sanders. *The Essential Peirce*. 2 Vols. Ed. Nathan Houser, Christian Kloesel, and the Peirce Edition Project. Bloomington Indiana UP, 1992, 1998. Print.

Peirce, Charles Sanders. "Excerpts from Letters to Lady Welby." *Essential Peirce*. Vol.1 477–91. Print.

Peirce, Charles Sanders. "The Fixation of Belief." *Essential Peirce*. Vol. 1 109–23. Print.

Peirce, Charles Sanders. "On the Nature of Signs." *Peirce on Signs* 141–3. Print.

Peirce, Charles Sanders. "One, Two, Three: Fundamental Categories of Thought and of Nature." *Peirce on Signs* 180–5. Print.

Peirce, Charles Sanders. *Peirce on Signs: Writings on Semiotic by Charles Sanders Peirce*. Ed. James Hoopes. Chapel Hill: U of North Carolina P, 1991. Print.

Peirce, Charles Sanders. "Pragmatism." *Essential Peirce*, Vol. 2 398–433. Print.

Peirce, Charles Sanders. *Semiotic and Significs: The Correspondence of Charles S. Peirce and Victoria Lady Welby*. Ed. Charles S. Hardwick. Bloomington: Indiana UP, 1977.

Peirce, Charles Sanders. "Sign." *Peirce on Signs* 239–40. Print.

Peirce, Charles Sanders. "What is a Sign?" *Essential Peirce*, Vol. 2 4–10. Print.

Pirandello, Luigi. "Spoken Action" [1908]. *The Theory of the Modern Stage*. Ed. Eric Bentley. Harmondsworth: Penguin, 1968. 153–7. Print.

Proehl, Geoffrey S., with D. D. Kugler, Mark Lamos, and Michael Lupu. *Toward a Dramaturgical Sensibility: Landscape and Journey*. Cranbury, NJ: Associated UP, 2008. Print.

Propp, Vladimir. *Morphology of the Folk Tale* [1928]. Trans. Laurence Scott. Rev. and ed. Louis A. Wagner. Austin: U of Texas P, 1968. Print.

Puchner, Martin. "Toying with Ibsen." *Hotreview*. Web. 18 January 2011.

Rabkin, Gerald. "Lee Breuer's Classic Comics." *PAJ: A Journal of Performance and Art* 26.2 (2004): 40–6. Print.

Rancière, Jacques. *The Emancipated Spectator*. Trans. Gregory Elliott. London: Verso, 2009. Print.

Regan, Paulette. *Unsettling the Settler Within: Indian Residential Schools, Truth Telling and Reconciliation in Canada*. Vancouver: U of British Columbia P, 2010. Print.

Reinelt, Janelle G. "Introduction [to Semiotics and Deconstruction]." Reinelt and Roach. 1st edn. 109–16. Print.

Reinelt, Janelle G.. "Performance Analysis." Reinelt and Roach. Rev. and enlarged edn. 7–12. Print.

Reinelt, Janelle G., and Joseph R. Roach, ed. *Critical Theory and Performance*. 1st edn. Ann Arbor: U of Michigan P, 1992.

Reinelt, Janelle G., and Joseph R. Roach. *Critical Theory and Performance*. Rev. and enlarged edn. Ann Arbor: U of Michigan P, 2007. Print.

Rekdal, Anne Marie. "The Female *Jouissance*: An Analysis of Ibsen's *Et dukkehjem*." *Scandinavian Studies* 74.2 (2002): 149–80. Print.

Revermann, Martin. "The Semiotics of Curtain Calls." *Semiotica* 168.1–4 (2008): 190–202. Print.

Ridout, Nicholas. *Stage Fright, Animals, and Other Theatrical Problems*. Cambridge: Cambridge UP, 2006. Print.

Roach, Joseph R. "Introduction [to Hermeneutics and Phenomenology]." Reinelt and Roach. 1st edn. 353–5.

Rozik, Eli. "The Homogeneous Nature of the Sign." *Semiotica* 168.1–4 (2008): 169–90. Print.

Rozik, Eli. *Metaphoric Thinking: A Study of Nonverbal Metaphor in the Arts and Its Archaic Roots*. Tel Aviv: The Yolanda and David Katz Faculty of the Arts, Tel Aviv University, 2008. Print

Rubin, Gayle. "The Traffic in Women: Notes on the Political Economy of Sex." *Deviations: A Gayle Rubin Reader*. Durham, NC: Duke UP, 2011. 33–65. Print.

Ryan, Kiernan, ed. *New Historicism and Cultural Materialism: A Reader*. London: Arnold, 1996. Print.

Sandman, Jenny. "*Mabou Mines' DollHouse*." *CurtainUp* 16 February 2009. Web. 18 January 2011.

Sassen, Saskia. *The Global City: New York, London, Tokyo*. Princeton: Princeton UP, 1991. Print.

Saussure, Ferdinand de. *Course in General Linguistics*. Ed. Charles Bally and Albert Sechehaye with Albert Reidlinger. Trans. Roy Harris. Chicago: Open Court, 1986. Print.

Schmid, Herta. "A Historical Outlook on Theatrical Ostension and Its Links with Other Terms of the Semiotics of Drama and Theatre." *Semiotica* 168.1–4 (2008): 67–91. Print.

Searle, John R. *Speech Acts*. Cambridge: Cambridge UP, 1969. Print.

Sears, Djanet. *Harlem Duet*. Winnipeg: Scirocco, 1997. Print.

Sears, Djanet. "nOTES oF a cOLOURED gIRL: 32 sHORT rEASONS wHY I wRITE fOR tHE tHEATRE." Sears, *Harlem Duet* 11–15. Print.

Severi, Carlo. "Kuna Picture-Writing: A Study in Iconography and Memory." *The Art of Being Kuna: Layers of Meaning Among the Kuna of Panama*. Ed. M. L. Salvador. Los Angeles: UCLA Fowler Museum of Cultural History, 1997. 245–72. Print.

Shakespeare, William. *The Riverside Shakespeare*. Ed. G. Blakemore Evans. Boston: Houghton Mifflin, 1974. Print.

Shange, Ntozake. *for colored girls who have considered suicide/when the rainbow is enuf: a choreopoem* and *spell #7*. London: Methuen, 1990.

Shklovsky, Viktor. *Theory of Prose*. Trans. Benjamin Sher. Elmwood Park, IL: Dalkey Archive, 1991. Print.

Sidnell, Michael. "Semiotic Arts of Theatre." *Semiotica* 168.1–4 (2008): 11–43. Print.

Smith, Linda Tuhiwai. *Decolonizing Methodologies: Research and Indigenous Peoples*. London: Zed, 1999. Print.

Smurro, Clio C. "'Mabou Mines DollHouse' Oversimplifies." Harvard *Crimson* 8 November 2011. Web. 3 May 2013.

Sofer, Andrew. *The Stage Life of Props*. Ann Arbor: U of Michigan P, 2003. Print.

Solomon. Alisa. "Growing Pains: Lee Breuer's 'Little Woman' Takes Revenge in Her Dollhouse." *Village Voice* 25 November 2003. Web. 21 May 2013.

Souriau, Étienne. *Les Deux Cent Mille Situations Dramatiques*. Paris: Flammarion, 1950. Print.

Spencer, Charles. "Edinburgh Festival Review: Mabou Mines Dollhouse." *The Telegraph* 27 August 2007. Web. 17 January 2011.

Staniškytė, Jurgita, "Rewriting the Canon: The Nature of the Political in Contemporary Lithuanian Theater." *Lituanus: Lithuanian Quarterly Journal of Arts and Sciences* 52.3 (2006). Web.

States, Bert O. *Great Reckonings in Little Rooms: On the Phenomenology of Theater*. Berkeley: U of California P, 1985. Print.

States, Bert O. "The Phenomenological Attitude." Reinelt and Roach. Rev. and enlarged 26–36. Print.

States, Bert O. *The Pleasure of the Play*. Ithaca, NY: Cornell UP, 1994. Print.

Stephenson, Jenn. *Performing Autobiography: Contemporary Canadian Drama*. Toronto: U of Toronto P, 2013. Print.

Styan, J. L. *Max Reinhardt*. Cambridge: Cambridge UP, 1982. Print.

Tam, Kwok-Kan. "The Dialogic Self in *A Doll's House* and *The Wild Duck*." *Ibsen and the Modern Self*. Ed. Kwok-Kan Tam, Terry Siu-han Yip, and Frode Helland. Hong Kong: Open U of Hong Kong P, 2010. 78–90. Print.

Thomas, Colin. "Chocolate Woman Dreams the Milky Way May Not Engage All Audiences." *Georgia Straight* 1 March 2012. Web. 18 June 2013.

Tompkins, Joanne. *Unsettling Space: Contestations in Contemporary Australian Theatre*. Basingstoke: Palgrave Macmillan, 2006. Print.

Trezise, Bryoni. "Spectatorship that Hurts: Socìetas Rafaello Sanzio as Meta-affective Theatre of Memory." *Theatre Research International* 37.3 (2012): 205–20. Print.

Turner, Jane. "Dreams and Phantasms: Towards an Ethnoscenological Reading of the Intercultural Theatrical Event." *Semiotica* 168.1–4 (2008): 143–67. Print.

Turner, Victor. "Liminal to Liminoid in Play, Flow, and Ritual: An Essay in Comparative Symbology." *From Ritual to Theatre: The Human Seriousness of Play*. New York: PAJ Publications, 1982. 20–60. Print.

Ubersfeld, Anne. *Reading Theatre* [1996]. Trans. Frank Collins. Ed. Paul Perron and Patrick Debbèche. Toronto: U of Toronto P, 1999. Print.

Uexküll, Jakob von. *A Foray into the Worlds of Animals and Humans: with A Theory of Meaning*. Trans. Joseph D. O'Neil. Minneapolis: U of Minnesota P, 2010. Print.

Unwin, Stephen. *Ibsen's A Doll's House*. London: Nick Hern, 2007. Print.

Veltruský, Jiři. "Basic Features of Dramatic Dialogue." Matejka and Titunik 128–33. Print.

Veltruský, Jiři. *Drama as Literature*. Semiotics of Literature 2. Lisse: Peter De Ridder, 1977. Print.

Veltruský, Jiři. "Dramatic Text as a Component of Theater." Matejka and Titunik 94–117. Print.

Veltruský, Jiři. "Man and the Object in Theatre." (1940) Garvin 83–91. Print.

Verdecchia, Guillermo. *Fronteras Americanas (American Borders)* [1993]. Vancouver: Talonbooks, 1997. Print.

Voloshinov, V. N. *Marxism and the Philosophy of Language*. Trans. Ladislav Matejka and I. R. Titunik. Cambridge, MA: Harvard UP, 1986. Print.

Weckwerth, Wendy. "Playing with Dolls and Houses." *Theater* 34.3 (2004): 134–42. Print.

Weerdenberg, Andrea. "Chocolate Woman Dreams the Milky Way." Centre for Women's Studies in Education, OISE, University of Toronto. Web. 18 June 2013.

Weimann, Robert. *Author's Pen, Actor's Voice: Playing and Writing in Shakespeare's Theatre*. Ed. Helen Higbee and William West. Cambridge: Cambridge UP, 2000. Print.

Weimann, Robert. *Shakespeare and the Popular Tradition in Theatre: Studies in the Social Dimension of Dramatic Form and Function*. Ed. Robert Schwartz. Baltimore: Johns Hopkins UP, 1978. Print.

Wilcox, Dean. "Ambient Space in Twentieth Century Theatre: The Space of Silence." *Modern Drama* 46.4 (2004): 542–57. Print.

Wiles, David. *A Short History of Western Performance Space*. Cambridge: Cambridge UP, 2003. Print.

Williams, Tennessee. *The Glass Menagerie*. New York: New Directions, 1966. Print.

Williams, Tennessee. *A Streetcar Named Desire*. New York: New Directions, 1947. Print.

Wilson, Scott. *Cultural Materialism: Theory and Practice*. Oxford: Blackwell, 1995. Print.

Wilson, Shawn. *Research Is Ceremony: Indigenous Research Methods*. Halifax: Fernwood, 2008.

Wirth, Andrzej. "Interculturalism and Iconophilia in the New Theatre." Marranca and Dasgupta 281–90. Print.

Worthen, W. B. "'The Written Troubles of the Brain': *Sleep No More* and the Space of Character." *Theatre Journal* 64.1 (2012): 79–97.

Yi-Sheng, Ng. "The Valley of the Dolls." *Flying Inkpot Theatre Reviews* 21 June 2007. Web. 4 May 2013.

Young anitafrika, d'bi. Email to the author. 12 April 2011. Email.

Zich, Otakar. *Estetika dramatického umění: teoretická dramaturgie*. Würzburg: Jal-reprint, 1977. Print.

Index